The Circuit

**The true story of a policewoman's journey
from the streets of London into the dangerous world
of covert operations.**

Jacquieline Davis

Lucky Press

For Michael, Elizabeth and Rebecca . . .
thank you for letting me be a part of your lives.
And for children everywhere who are not where they want to be.

Note: While the stories in *The Circuit* are all true, in consideration of privacy, character and place names and identifying characteristics have, at times, been changed.

ISBN: 0-9713318-9-8

Lucky Press, LLC
126 S. Maple St.
Lancaster, Ohio 43130
Phone: 740-689-2950
www.luckypress.com/thecircuit
E-mail: books@luckypress.com

Book Design: Janice Phelps
PRINTED IN THE UNITED STATES OF AMERICA

Library of Congress Cataloging-in-Publication Data
Davis, Jacquieline.
  The circuit : the true story of a policewoman's journey from the streets of London into the dangerous world of covert operations / Jacquieline Davis.
      p. cm.
First published in London by Penguin, 1998.
  ISBN 0-9713318-9-8 (pbk. : alk. paper)
  1. Policewomen--Great Britain--Biography. 2. Bodyguards--Great Britain--Biography. 3. Undercover operations--Great Britain. 4. Crime prevention--Great Britain. I. Title: Policewoman's journey from the streets of London into the dangerous world of covert operations. II. Title.
  HV7911.A2D39 2003
  363.2'092--dc21

                                                          2003007626

Foreword

UK Care Of Police Survivors was formed to help those left behind by UK police officers who lose their lives in the line of duty. It aims to help them rebuild lives shattered by the trauma of a line of duty death. This peer based support service will ensure that they remain for all time members of the police family.

Jacquie Davis has been a supporter of the UK C.O.P.S. since its formation. Her work in promoting the safety of women and children in various areas of the world is well known. Jacquie's offer of a donation for each sale of her new book is greatly appreciated, and will further our ability to ensure that these officers and their families are never forgotten. It also means that you, as readers of her exploits, will be helping to maintain these efforts.

–Jim McNulty
Executive Director
UK C.O.P.S.

Acknowledgments

This book has taken some time to reach the USA and for this I am indebted to several people, Chris and Liz Davey for all their help and patience, my executive editor at Lucky Press Janice Phelps, and all Lucky press staff.

Apart from these I have to thank the following people for their help and friendship when I sometimes could not see the light at the end of the tunnel: Helen and Michael Cliffe, Barbra, Simon, Lizzie and Becky Prentice, Michael for his friendship and support over the years, all on the Police Roll of Honour Trust, Don and Judy Feeney for allowing me to use their house like a hotel on my many visits to the USA, David and Helene Schifter for their help and lastly Jo Rowling for saving my sanity and restoring my belief in human kindness on more than one occasion.

I WAS NINETEEN — ALL SHINY AND NEW WITH GLOSSY HAIR NEATLY CUT
and my uniform pressed by my mum — and talking to the sergeant
in the police canteen, when the chair opposite me scraped away
from the table and a man with a leather jacket and a smirk sat down. He
spoke across me to the sarge as if I wasn't there.

"All right, mate?"

"All right."

The sergeant went on munching his beans and fries. I glared at this
bloke, finished what I had been saying and went on eating. He leaned
back in his chair with his thumbs in his jeans pockets and stared. He
really fancied himself. God, I hate that.

Mr. Wonderful glanced at my plate of spaghetti Bolognese, the
finest that the canteen ladies could produce. "That looks nice," he said.

"It's OK."

"Who are you, then?"

"Who are you?" I retorted.

He didn't answer, but rose halfway out of his chair and reached
over to the steel cans where the clean forks were and took one. Sitting
down again, he hunched over the table, began picking with his fork at
my food, and started talking to the sergeant.

"You want my dinner?" I asked, giving it a shove that sent the plate spinning. "You can have it." It landed splat on his lap as I stood up and left.

He was cursing and people were turning round and sniggering, as well they might, because he had a steaming pile of pasta in his crotch.

"Jacquie!" The uniformed sergeant caught up with me down the corridor. "You know that's the new detective sergeant, don't you? You'd better go back and apologize."

"Apologize nothing," I said. "He can apologize to me. Big-mouthed creep, he is."

I had always had attitude. I probably got it from my dad, who was a senior nurse at Friern Barnet, a vast red-brick crenellated Victorian institution for the mentally ill. For years he was in charge of a closed ward that held the overflow from Broadmoor, a hospital for the criminally insane. Dad had learned defensive living. You react first and ponder the ethics later. Having picked up on that, I was well suited for the police force. I was quick-minded, fit, assertive, and stood no messing.

It was 1977, and I was going to be the first woman police commissioner. Not that my ambition knew no bounds; I prided myself on being realistic. I'd set my sights on chief superintendent first. At that time, no woman had ever been a chief super.

I had been born and brought up in Barnet, a town on the northwest fringes of London, within a few miles of Hendon Police College. I had done all the right things and, in theory, give or take a plate of spaghetti tipped over a detective sergeant, there was nothing to stop me from climbing the ladder the way it said in the recruitment literature.

But after eighteen months on the job I was beginning to suspect that there was a lot more to this than they told you at Police College. First there was the whole issue of who you had to get to know to be noticed. You needed to be in a squad — Flying Squad, Serious Crime Squad, Drug Squad, C11 (dealing with active criminal networks). There were others, too. I was just dimly aware of MI5 and MI6, Special Branch and the Special Patrol Group.

None of them operated out of our "nick" — the affectionate name for a precinct station.

The other thing was that, as a woman, most of the officers who could get you promoted ranked females somewhere between wimpy kid at the back of the class and sex symbol. This major disadvantage had not yet struck me as forcibly as it should have.

I was on patrol duty in Barnet High Street at two in the morning. This meant strolling along past the grocer's and the liquor store, downhill past the magistrate's court, and walking round the bend in the road where it swooped down off the high ridge that Barnet stood on and rolled, thick with traffic, eleven miles to Charing Cross in the heart of London. The city came up this far, crowded, baying and needy. Behind me was the county of Hertfordshire, detached houses set in woods interspersed with riding academies. Here at the top of the hill stood Barnet, all neat three-floor, red-brick homes upright as a banner, advertising a way of life for the common herd down there in the "smoke," as we called the city, to aspire to.

We were all Conservatives, in Barnet. We did not have a problem with crime. What we had was a "criminal element." This consisted of a couple of dim, violent and persistently offending families on what we called the Alcatraz Estate, a rundown housing project, and the "diddicoys" — gypsies who came every year to the Horse Fair and stole ponies from the riding schools. If it rained on fair day, the dye used to disguise the stolen animals came off on your hands when you stroked them.

So the High Street was looking as sedately pleased with itself as usual, on this particular morning, when the station called over my radio to tell me CID, the Criminal Investigation Department, wanted to speak with me. I was pretty sure it wasn't about crime. Fidgeting from foot to foot in the cold, I scanned my recent past for some gaffe and could think of only one.

An unmarked car rolled up: a GPV (general purpose vehicle). The detective sergeant told me to get in, so I left the High Street unattended, and we drove about a bit, talking. When we had exhausted the topic of crime in Barnet, it got more personal.

Then we parked, so the detective sergeant could enlighten me as to the full potential of a GPV.

His name was Steve, he was thirty and divorced and living in what was called a section house (single cops accommodation) near his old posting on the other side of London. He was an attentive boyfriend. I mean, he was interested in spending time with me personally, not socializing with me and a bunch of other officers. Until now I had spent a lot of my free time at the Police Club in the nearby town of Bushey, but once I met Steve I never went there. He always wanted to be alone with me, or if not alone then at my mum's house.

This was already known as the sub-station, because we all used to drop in for cups of tea when we were on duty, and my mum and dad thought the world of Steve. He was respectful, never swaggered or seemed less than a dutiful copper when he was around them, and was obviously devoted to me. I had just broken off an engagement to a rich young man who cringed when I told his friends I was in the police force. Now along came Steve, who was friendly, understood the work I did, and was obviously in love with me. My parents were much relieved.

We dated for months. There was an exciting unpredictability to the affair because of the job we were both doing. We were on different shifts, and if you arrest somebody just before you go off shift you have to stay late, so there was no knowing when we would finish. And in his case, because he was a detective, he never even knew which part of London he might be in; he might have to cancel a date at the last minute or he might suddenly find himself free to take me somewhere interesting. It all added spice and I was happy. Also, he was giving me ideas about getting into the CID and making my way toward promotion.

One day I climbed the stairs to his office to see him, and we talked for a while before he went to the washroom. I hoisted myself idly onto his desk and peered down through the office window at a police van maneuvering its way into the yard below, and then the phone rang.

"Hello. DS Adams' phone."

"Is Detective Sergeant Adams there?" a woman asked.

"Sorry, he's away from his desk at the moment. Can I take a message?"

"Yeah. Could you ask him to get a brown loaf and two pints of milk on the way home, please?"

There was a pause. "Fine," I said. "Whom shall I say called?"

"His wife."

Steve returned to the office a minute later, performing a rapid, economical slide around the desk and into his chair, smiling up at me.

"Your wife rang," I said, as I grabbed the nearest hard object and hit him accurately — with the fire extinguisher.

I had wanted to move on anyway. All I needed was a really good reason to ask for a transfer. Now I had one.

They sent me to Peckham. To say that I was unprepared would be an understatement. I had done police work in the North London suburbs and this was South London, the inner city, the borough of Peckham.

There are a lot of ways to explain what this means, but they are all too complicated. The bottom line is that when you stopped a driver in Barnet you said, "Excuse me, sir, would you mind stepping out of your Mercedes/Jaguar/BMW?" In Peckham you dragged him out of his hopped-up Ford and threw him across the hood before he stabbed you.

The visible difference was skin color. I had literally never seen so many black people. Barnet was white. Really white, as in Pony Club and Gardening Center. White. My mum was, in fact, a racist — bigoted in the way only people who don't know what they are talking about can be. I am not racially prejudiced, and when I went to Peckham I had an open mind about who might be responsible for crime. The police, ironically, seemed prime candidates for the kind of criminal profile I'd come to recognize in Barnet: white with hair cut to a meaningfully short clip. This was South London. Or, as they said it with their accent, "Sarf Lunnun, aw'ri?"

They were "all right," as it happened. Somebody must have told them I was interested in detective work, because within weeks of arrival I found myself on the shoplifting squad.

Peckham is a huge huddle of Edwardian streets and 1960s "council" houses, built by the local government for cheap rental, strung along a mile or so of the main road to Dover out of London. To the west it bumbles into Camberwell, which is the same only smarter, and to the east it shades into Lewisham and New Cross, which are the same only duller. If you live in Blackheath or Greenwich, Peckham is where the help lives. It is a cheap place to live and shop because it hasn't got a metro station and the main street is constantly clogged with traffic.

It was my job to go out every morning and circulate in the mill of people going to work, returning from work, buying and selling. Pickpockets operated mainly at the more crowded bus stops, and gangs of kids stole stuff out of the Asian-owned shops. "Steaming" was in fashion at the time: three or four louts would swarm through a shop in a posse, taking exactly what they wanted, and get out while the staff wobbled with terror. Thieving housewives and professionals generally stole from the bigger stores.

I found I was good at this work. There were generally four of us in plain clothes out on the street at once, linked by radio. I learned how to spot a gang of pickpockets at a bus stop. If you watched for half an hour, the dippers, as we called them, were the ones who stood in line and then when the bus left were still there. They never boarded a bus. Number one would steal a wallet and pass it to number two, who would pass it to number three, who would then scoot round the corner, take out the cards and money and dump the empty wallet. If number one was grabbed by an indignant victim, he would be empty-handed. This was the late seventies, before the credit card boom. Many people in Peckham and places like it did not even have bank accounts. They kept cash in bulging purses. So, when the thieves dipped a bag, it meant rich pickings for one set of poor people and misery and the Christmas Club money gone for another.

I also caught a lot of shoplifters. You look at their eyes first; they give away their intentions. When they walked into a store, their eyes were everywhere. There were no security cameras in those days, and even the clothing stores did not tag their garments, so all the thieves had to look out for were strategically placed mirrors and casual nosey parkers who might point them out to the staff. As soon as I saw those busy eyes, I knew I was onto one. Then, I watched their hands. The hands of a shoplifter have a life of their own. While the thief is watching a huddle of gossiping salesgirls, his or her hands are busy sliding something expensive into an inner pocket or bag.

I loved the work, but it did not give me much overtime. It was a regular nine-to-five job, unless you nailed a thief shortly before five, in which case statements and other paperwork kept you at the station until ten. I was supposed to be living in police accommodations at Peckham, but I didn't. I stayed at home in Barnet and drove down every day. The gas was expensive, so was car repair, and police pay was crap. (Also, thanks to my parents, I had learned to like traveling overseas; yet now I could not even afford a decent vacation.) We all complained about it. There were articles in the police magazine, *The Job,* about low morale in the force and people muttered about getting a raise after the general election. But it would be at least six months before the election, nobody knew for sure that the Conservative Party would win, and I was impatient.

Somebody at the police station knew a sergeant at another South London precinct who recruited bodyguards. Not bouncers, all brawn and no brain, but trained men, ex- SAS or moonlighting police. He had happened to mention that one of the security companies was interested in hiring a woman for a special assignment. I called this sergeant, was interviewed by a couple of men who ran Special Operations out of the fourth floor of the company's office block somewhere on the South Circular Road that ringed London, and was hired. I would work for them whenever I was free; vacations, evenings and weekends. Moonlighting was a sackable offense, but I needed the money and this promised to be a whole lot more interesting than driving a cab or parking cars in my free time.

I had fifteen day's annual leave saved up. I took it and began work on a Monday morning. I did not know it at the time, but I was to become one of very few women who had ever worked on the Circuit.

THE ELEVATOR CARRIED ME TO THE TOP FLOOR OF THE Intercontinental Hotel, where its doors slid open to reveal a tall man wearing a suit. I was expected.

"Morning," he said. "Down there, door on your left, at the end."

The royal family of the ruler of one of the Gulf kingdoms occupied an entire floor of the hotel. Their suite was quiet, the carpets thick, all the doors shut. I heard a television somewhere, a childish shout from inside a room, and a dim, ambient hum. Luxury has a warm smell and a gentle soporific buzz.

In the security office, converted from a bedroom, with a desk, phones and a big fridge, a gray-haired man ran through the briefing as if he had said it all before. The family had taken up residence along Park Lane for the next three or four months. The sheikh was living in the Dorchester Hotel and each of his three wives in other hotels. Here at the Intercontinental, at Hyde Park Corner, eight of us were guarding the sheikha (number one wife) and her four children, daughters aged ten, eight and seven, and a son of five. I would be her personal body-guard. Placing myself between the sheikha and an assassin's bullet, should the occasion arise, was the non-negotiable aspect of the job. The only son was of course heir to the throne, so at five years old he also merited round-the-clock protection from a personal guard. Kidnapping being the main threat.

"You will be invisible until required," concluded the gray man dryly. "In other words, don't speak unless you're spoken to."

It was going to be a claustrophobic couple of weeks, I thought, as I sat outside the royal suite that first morning staring at one of the Intercontinental's immaculate walls. You were a flunkey on call and, short of any threat, you were expected to hang about in a kind of watchful coma unless told to do something by one of the royal family. As far as they were concerned, we were like the wooden figures on a Swiss clock, which exist only when visible and have no life when they are out of sight.

In each of the hotels the entourage occupied an entire floor. I wanted to know who everyone was, so one of the bodyguards came and stood by my chair keeping up a rapid-fire commentary out of the side of his mouth as short women swathed in yards of cloth scuttled past.

"Servant. Another servant . . ." People emerged from the lift. "That's the boy's tutor. Turns up every morning, poor bugger." And half an hour later, "Hairdresser. Comes Mondays and Thursdays."

Hours passed; chambermaids vacuumed and left; room service trudged past with laden trolleys; berobed women flitted in and out of the suites; some Arab women visited with a small boy.

Two little girls appeared. My companion had mooched off somewhere and one of the girls was frowning at me, so I nodded and murmured, "Good morning."

"Good morning."

They might be the princesses, and if so I should know them. "Are you sisters?" I ventured.

One girl scowled and raised her hand. Without warning, she smacked her companion hard on the head.

"I am Princess," she announced.

They walked on together, the second child with her eyes firmly fixed on the carpet.

Besides the bodyguard team, the sheikha was served by ten or twelve women and girls from some of the poorest countries in the world. These Eritreans, Filipinos, Sudanese and Tamils were personal nannies to the children, maids to the sheikha, and general gofers. They never left the building except as part of the royal entourage.

Neither did we. Some of the team were perfectly happy with the arrangement, especially those whose day jobs were based at West End Central, because elsewhere they could have been spotted by senior officers at any time. We were all a bit cagey about moonlighting, but coming from Peckham I felt there was no chance of being seen up here.

When the sheikha's door opened on that first morning and she emerged, in full going-to-Harrods shabbah, to see me standing opposite, her eyes widened above the yashmak. She stopped in shock on the threshold. The women behind her, clustered like crows, fell silent. I could see nobody had told her a woman would be guarding her.

"Good morning, your Highness," I said quietly.

She nodded and swept onward as I took up my position behind her.

Some deferential person always asked the sheikha what her plans were for the day, so in theory we knew when we would have to move. In practice we didn't because she changed her mind. The cars might be wanted an hour before or after the time she had said, so we always had to be fired up and ready to go. Usually we left the building at about twelve to go shopping somewhere expensive, like Knightsbridge or Bond Street. Our convoy of three limousines linked by radio consisted of a SAP (security advance party) team of four men in the first car, the sheikha's limousine and a back-up vehicle. The sheikha's limo contained whichever nannies, servants and children were going out that day, plus the lady herself, with me and a driver in front.

The other wives traveled the same way, and all the bodyguard teams kept in touch by radio. The sheikha used to listen idly to discover where the other wives planned to go, and if number two wife was on her way to Selfridge's department store or Harvey Nichols we would suddenly find that our sheikha had changed her mind and wanted to go there instead. Since she took priority, number two wife would have to eat dust and make do with Debenhams. I got the impression that this game was the most fun our sheikha had had in years.

I soon grew used to the routine. When we swept up to the front of the shop, three of the SAP team were already out on the pavement. The back-up team came to a halt behind us, I jumped out and one of the SAP team opened the limo door to let the sheikha step out. I strode quickly behind her and her entourage into the store. With two guards behind us and two ahead, we clove a path through the tourists and headed like an Exocet missile for the designer room, hoping that nothing would catch her eye on the way. Not that anything much could; we moved as fast as possible and since most of her body including her head was swathed in black cotton there was little opportunity to swivel and dither.

I loved all this. It was glamorous, there was no doubt of that, arriving with an exotic image of mysteriously acquired wealth at shops like Harrods and Liberty's when police pay in those days barely got you past the door of Kwiksave; but there was also a heightened sense of awareness. You were with people so rich and so politically sensitive that there was a genuine risk of an attempted kidnap. I got an adrenalin rush from these shopping trips. They were a lot more fun than having eggs thrown at you on the North Peckham housing project.

So when the Conservative party won the general election, Margaret Thatcher hopped into Number 10 Downing Street after her St. Francis of Assisi speech, and we humble and grateful guardians of the law were awarded a huge pay rise, I didn't stop close protection work. I kept on doing it, evenings and weekends. By now I had discovered that the men I worked with who were not police officers were freelancers working through a word-of-mouth network called, "The Circuit." They reckoned there were about two thousand men constantly in work. They seemed to do a lot of surveillance as well as close protection and undercover work, and most of them had worked all over the world. This was exactly what I had been looking for, only I couldn't put a name to it until I saw it.

I asked the directors of the firm I worked for if there might be regular work for a woman on the Circuit. They said there would be plenty, but only if she was properly trained. Most of the men had been trained by the SAS, the Parachute Regiment, or one of the security services, and additionally had done a special course in Herefordshire. No woman had yet come forward with the remotest chance of getting into this course. It focused on unarmed combat, outdoor survival skills, firearms handling, defensive driving, and surveillance and detection techniques.

It sounded exactly what I had been unconsciously preparing myself for all my life. As a schoolgirl I had won Amateur Athletic Association certificates for running and shotput; when I was about sixteen, Dad had set up a target so I could practice with an air rifle in the back garden; when I joined the police I had joined the gun club; and I had already completed a police driver's course. I hadn't been sewing a fine seam in my spare time; I had been getting ready for this.

On the other hand, I had to look at my chances of promotion through the force. The picture wasn't too rosy. If I stayed with the shoplifting squad I might transfer into the CID where I could plod along for years. They would not let me into a proper squad since I did not have the funny handshake that signified membership of the Freemasons. (A penis might have helped as well.) And the security services were as remote as they had ever been. Two years after joining the police, I was disillusioned. If anybody was going to be the first woman commissioner of the Metropolitan Police it would probably be some fast-track pen-pusher with a college degree.

While I thought about all this I kept on doing the day job.

One Saturday afternoon in November 1979, I arrested a kid (he looked about fourteen) stealing a pair of sneakers from a department store in Peckham High Street. I had just collared him and radioed for back up when the little bastard head-butted me. I kept hold of him, but there was blood everywhere and we were struggling and cursing, making people step into the traffic in alarm, which was a good thing as it made a local police patrol car stop. Out of it stepped a big blond policeman with an honest face, who grabbed the little toe rag and held him while I mopped my bloody nose with a handkerchief.

He took me to hospital and hung about while I processed the thief (who turned out to be nineteen), by which time it was early evening.

"You're in no state to go home," he said. "Let me drive your car, I'll get you there."

This was all a lie of course. Really he was brandishing a sword and riding a dashing white charger.

We had a long way to go, to Barnet, and all through the Christmas traffic. We drove well into North London and stopped at a pub for a drink. I was looking terrific: the full Saturday night drop-dead two inches of plaster over the nose, blood-encrusted hair and scruffy jeans. He did not seem to mind. We talked. We had hardly stopped talking since he drove me to the hospital. I told him I was thinking of leaving the force and after an hour or two I told him why. He turned out to have done some work for the same security company. We had a lot in common: he was a member of a gun club and played squash. In general it was all this that had attracted me more than his looks; he just seemed so straight and friendly, and he even made me laugh. I liked him more than anyone I had met for a long time. Well, ever.

At about eight o'clock he said, "Will you marry me?"

I said I would think about it.

"Well, don't think about it for too long."

"Umm . . . I wouldn't be breaking anything up, then?"

"Not a thing."

He finished his pint and we left. Twenty minutes later he pulled up outside my mum's home, which was a modern red brick house set well back from a quiet road. At regular intervals around our yard there were severely clipped cohorts of rosebushes, now leafless in the cold. On a Saturday night up here, everybody was at home, watching TV. Tim took the key out of the ignition and gave it to me.

"Have you thought about it?"

Drizzle slanted through the ice-white glare of a streetlight, and one side of his face was in shadow. He kissed me.

"Yes."

"And?"

"I will."

"Good. I'll be round to meet your mum and dad in the morning."

We got out of the car. He was putting an overcoat on ready to walk to the railroad station.

"Where are you going now?" I asked.

"Home to tell the wife," he grinned.

My face must have gone as white as the street lamp because he said, "Come here." He hugged me and spoke softly. "I haven't slept with her for a year," he said. "And yes, before you ask, we have got a baby. But the marriage is finished. The whole thing's kaput."

I said nothing.

"Jacquie, I've never fallen in love before."

I hadn't either.

M Y MUM AND DAD HAD ME WHEN SHE WAS FORTY-SIX AND HE was forty-eight. They had already brought up a family of three girls. The youngest was nine when I came along. These three, who were not far apart in age, had a much tougher upbringing than I did. We lived then in an ancient low-ceilinged house just off Barnet High Street, and before I was born there was not much money; Mum couldn't work when they were small, so there was only one wage coming in.

By the time I was old enough to appreciate nice things, the three eldest had left home and both Mum and Dad were working, so I enjoyed five-week holidays in Europe every year in their Winnebago with a friend brought along to keep me company, and riding lessons on Sundays, and ice skating with my own boots, and anything else I wanted.

For my sisters, I was the squealing brat who spoiled their teenage years. When I was five, Mum went back to work and my sisters had to drag me around with them just when they were growing interested in boys and clothes. I was made to feel their resentment and vowed that when I grew up I would never be dependent on anybody. I never have been. They went on resenting me, though, after they left home, because

I escaped the usual, "Take that muck off your face!" and, "You treat this house like a hotel!" and, "What time d'you call this then?" of growing up. By the time I was of an age to worry about, Mum and Dad had relaxed.

Dad never said he wished I'd been a boy but he always treated me like the boy he'd never had. I was a tall, athletic girl, a natural tomboy, and Dad got me out on a Saturday morning tinkering with the car, helping to change the oil and clean the sparkplugs. Both my parents were kind to me, but Dad was a friend in whom I could confide. He was a big man, six-foot-four and 250 pounds, dark, as he was of French and Spanish blood. I shared his true-blue Tory opinions and no-nonsense attitude to life; I had no self-doubt. By the time I was thirteen, I was subconsciously grooming myself to be a female combination of John Thaw and Dennis Waterman, the heroes of a popular TV cop show called *The Sweeney.* I wanted to slam doors and growl, "Right lads, let's get a ticket and spin this drum." I wasn't sure what it meant, but it sounded dramatic.

Given all this, when Tim walked in cocky as only he could be, grasped Dad's hand and said, "How d'you feel about me as a son-in-law?" it's no wonder Dad said, "Fine. But you should find out what it's like to live with her first. Set up house for a year or so and then get married."

That was on a Sunday. On Monday, forty-eight hours after we had met, we found an apartment in Mill Hill and moved in together.

Tim was gentle and good-natured. He shared the same go get 'em attitude to police work I had; in fact, he wanted to join the SPG, the Special Patrol Group, which even we called "Smash, Plant and Grab," but he did not bring all that home. He changed as soon as he was off duty and became considerate, teasing, a charmer; he had a persuasive way with him and I adored him more with every day we spent together. He made me feel desirable. Yvonne, his estranged wife, had already run to fat, he told me, and the fatter she got the less she appealed to him, so he had no regrets. I hardly spoke to her. She was not keen to let him have their son very often. She often said we could collect him on the weekend, and then she would change her mind.

What I had not been prepared for, though, was money worries. I had been doing quite well since the police pay raise, my agency work at the Intercontinental brought in a bit extra and I lived at home, paying my mum a reasonable rent, so I was able to maintain my own car. But now things were different. Although Tim was having trouble meeting his share of expenses, I felt that I was the one who needed to earn more money.

Promotion comes slowly in the police force, unless you are a high flyer with a degree. I knew pretty much all there was to know about catching the shoplifters of Peckham, and it was time to move on. I wanted to do undercover work, but there was no chance of that unless I got into one of the squads run out of Scotland Yard. Even the CID did not work undercover. At this rate I would be chasing toe rags through South London traffic for years before I got a promotion.

I went to see my employers at the agency again.

We sat down with a drink in a pub in Sutton. They were both in their thirties, knew the Circuit well and, more important, understood the police, squad, and services hierarchies. Over a beer-stained table set on a swirly brown-and-orange-patterned carpet, deafened by a pinball machine and occasionally cowering as the door opened to let in a great gust of wintry air from the street, I heard my future laid out for me.

"You've got three options," they said. "One: Stay in the job. You ain't got a hope in hell of getting into a squad. So you make detective sergeant in your forties, collect your pension. Two: Go for MI5 or 6. It'll be the same story for you: You got the wrong connections and you're the wrong sex. Three: Come on the Circuit full time. You've got to be ready to drop everything at a moment's notice, go anywhere in the world, risk your life. You've got to have the bottle to kill people in self-defense. You'll make a bloody good living and we'll train you."

I did not hesitate. I drove home rehearsing what I would say to Tim. *Have a good day, dear? Yes, my sweet pie. I have chosen to make a career shift. From now on I shall "drop everything at a moment's notice, go anywhere in the world, risk my life, and kill people in self-defense." Hmm. It might work.*

It went down quite well, actually. The money on the Circuit was good, and it dawned on me that that went a long way with Tim.

I did a deal with the agency: I would do one major undercover job they had lined up, and they would send me on a course before I returned to guarding the Gulf sheikha full-time during her annual visit to London.

The undercover job meant living away from Tim for as long as it took — six weeks, maybe — in a tiny apartment in a safe house in another part of London. My day job would be at Liberty's.

Liberty's is a rambling multi-level mock-Tudor department store in the busiest part of the West End of London, at the junction of Great Marlborough Street and Regent Street. Arthur Liberty, the founder, made his fortune catering to the arts-and-crafts taste of fashionable late-Victorian ladies. He sold a range of textiles influenced by Indian and Chinese designs, intricate florals and sinuous paisleys in cotton lawn and other natural fabrics. These same designs are the foundation of Liberty's fame today, reproduced on expensive scarves in hand-blocked silk and fine wool.

Even so, the scarf department had been losing money for months. It looked like an obvious target for shoplifters. The main entrance on the Great Marlborough Street side, a dark oak neo-Tudor lobby with glowing display cabinets, admits customers directly into the scarf department. They come in out of low light, low ceilings and carved black oak into a soaring hall resplendent with color. Orange, viridian, and ultramarine silks slither from every surface, and great swags of luxurious fabric hang from above. Idle shoppers can stare down on this opulence from paneled galleries on the upper floors. There is a temptation to steal. The scarves are folded and laid in overlapping rows, dainty as cucumber sandwiches at a garden party, and easily slipped into a bag. However, with up to three thousand pounds worth of scarves disappearing every week, the security department was sure it must be an inside job. So, I became a "sales assistant."

Monday mornings were the only quiet time in this retail business, and even then, customers emerged endlessly from the lobby. A "Sloane" (a well-heeled young lady) in an old Liberty headscarf, an American couple in Burberries, young office girls, a party of Japanese tourists, some German pensioners, a couple of preening black homosexuals, a group of chattering French housewives, a businessman, an African man wearing magnificent green and white robes and a headdress, a well-preserved grandmother with two whining children, an old rock chick — on and on they came, most of them looking as if they knew where they were going and then, dazzled by the scarves, hesitating, gazing. "May I help you, madam?" "The pink silk is forty-nine pounds." "That will do nicely, madam." Otherwise discreet, hovering behind the counter — don't make them feel under pressure.

You were discouraged from talking much while you were out on the floor, but as you trailed up the grubby back stairs at coffee time, past walls thick with dusty cream and green gloss paint and an inch of fluff on the pipes, you chatted.

"Camden's okay for now. When I've got a bit of money saved I'll move. Where do you live?"

"Don't even ask," I would sigh. "I've got a room in Archway. I went up to Birmingham as soon as I left school and it was a big mistake. I feel I've got to start all over again."

I had a false last name, a false social security record. The other women were friendly enough. The first time I told a glib lie, I held my breath; something irrational inside me was convinced that a voice would say, "No, you're not. You're Jacquie Courroyer. What are you doing here?"

They took the story at face value. It was so easy. I took care to stick as close to the truth as I could, and not to volunteer information I could not substantiate. They had no suspicions. I met about twenty saleswomen in the first few weeks and got to know others by sight. The core of the scarf department, who were always there, were five women in their twenties and thirties, and the buyer, Trish, a nervy blonde of about forty-five. I figured if anyone was "at it," it must be these six.

The surveillance team began to follow them from work. We swapped information in the course of long telephone calls most evenings.

"That one Paula, her old man picks her up from Bromley Station. Find out what he does, will you? They've got a nice house."

One lunchtime I walked down to Boots, the pharmacy, in Piccadilly with one of the girls. As we dodged delivery trucks in the narrow gulf of Kingly Street I wondered aloud if they needed staff in one of the bars we passed.

"You're not that broke, are you, Jacquie?"

"You must be kidding. By the time I've paid fares and rent, there's about enough left over for a pair of pantyhose. It's all right for you, you've got a husband working."

"My husband's not working. I make every penny that comes in. You should talk to Trish."

"She'll get me a raise after two and a half weeks? I don't think so."

"There are other ways."

"What? . . . Go on."

"Some of the scarves go out the back door. You can get a tenner each for them down on East Street Market. It's easy money."

"What, you mean carry them out? Don't they ever do spot checks?"

"No, none of us does that. Trish's got some guys in the stock department. You should see her spare room at home, she's got boxes of stuff round there. It turns over ever so fast."

Nothing more was said.

The surveillance team followed the six women and dug into their backgrounds. One woman's husband was collecting heavy brown cardboard boxes from the buyer's house on a Friday night and the next day in East Street Market the husband and wife were selling scarves that retailed for forty pounds for only ten pounds. We confirmed that much by observation. The others seemed to be in on it, too, and all six of the women had much more money than they should have had. All the same, we were becoming bogged down in the confusion of keeping so many of them under observation at once. Although we had indications of a conspiracy to steal, it was hard to work out who was doing what or to get pictures of them together doing it.

I knew honest staff at the store who were not in on the racket and worked hard for their commission. It annoyed me that these other women thought they could get away stealing.

The one member of the surveillance team I knew well was a bloke called Tommy, ex-SAS and recently split from his girlfriend. We all teased him because he fancied his target, and maybe it was the frustration of sleeping alone that drove him to have a brainwave.

One of the guys said, "We've got to get to know this lot better."

"We can," Tommy said slyly. "It's Jacquie's birthday, isn't it. Why doesn't she have a party?"

The birthday party was going like a train. The whole top floor of the safe house had been taken over. It was Saturday night, with blaring music and plenty of booze. The crucial guests were half a dozen policemen pretending to be lodgers or old school friends of mine, and all the targets, who were there without their husbands. A bemused fireman sprawled over my sofa and another was propping up my sink unit. The scarf department, faces glossy from alcohol, had had their pictures taken in a group, in hilarity, in a long-lost-friends embrace with the policeman. A constable from Barnet was even now snogging quietly on the landing with the woman who had walked down Kingly Street with me. As I repaired my lipstick in front of the bathroom mirror I thought the worst thing that could happen would be a complaint about the noise followed by a visit from a local police constable.

I knew now that I loved this work. I liked the edge that being watchful gives to life. I liked knowing that what I was doing was key to the whole investigation. I thanked my stars that I was on the Circuit now.

Next week I left Liberty's. We handed over a thick folder: six weeks of reported conversations, incriminating photographs of the suspects selling scarves, and observations of comings and goings. The buyer had been thieving from Liberty's for years. I do not know what happened to the guilty parties; Liberty's probably brought in the police. It was not my concern, because after a weekend with Tim I left home again, this time for the intensive training course.

The four weeks in Herefordshire changed my life. It was a sort of postgraduate course in policing. It was the foundation my career would be built on. I went back on the Circuit confident that I could handle anything that was thrown at me, quite literally.

Eight of us were on the course and I was the only woman. We lived in dilapidated pre-fabricated buildings known as Nissen huts, in an old army camp. We were up and out running at five every morning. A few hours of the army PTI (physical training instructor) course followed after breakfast; in the afternoon and evening we studied in a classroom or were out gaining practical experience. We learned reconnaissance, surveillance, map reading, first aid, firearms drill, protocol — everything from how to address a head of state to which knife and fork to use at dinner. I found out how to embus and debus a principal (getting your client in and out of a car, which is a little like formation dancing) and defensive and evasive driving techniques: how to spin a car 180 degrees and block a suspect vehicle when traveling in convoy. Every one of us felt confident enough to run a team or be a part of one.

At the end of the course we acted out a mock scenario. Our imaginary situation was outlined on a piece of paper: "An Englishwoman wants to buy a stud farm in Wales. The sons of Owain Glendowr see it as their business to prevent her. Your job is to protect her." The instructors would be playing the terrorists.

We were introduced to our principal, got her into the car and set off down the Welsh lanes to the address we had been given. We were in correct formation, the SAP team scouting well ahead of us, and close to the top of the lane where the stud farm was when we were flour-bombed by an ambush party. All eight of us and our VIP raced through to the stable yard, where she announced that she would like to have a look around. We surrounded her as we had been taught, and had started moving through the buildings when we heard an explosion.

We knew what to do — get out! The drivers were gunning the cars toward us; I grabbed the woman and threw her into the back of the car and hurled myself on top of her. Sniper fire was flying as the three cars skidded across the gravel and roared down the lane with a team of hooded "terrorists" in pursuit.

It was hard to follow that.

A few weeks later, still on an adrenalin high, I had my big wedding: hundreds of guests, yards of tulle, the whole bit. Our white-ribboned limousine was held up in a jam on Edgware Road on our way to the Hilton. I was staring dreamily through my veil at the Christmas shoppers — not looking for shoplifters at the time — when one of my sisters said reverently, "This is the most exciting day of your life, Jacquie."

"Like hell it is," I murmured.

S OON AFTER THE WEDDING, AT CHRISTMAS 1980, WE MOVED INTO A police apartment, one of a block of three in Chelsea. Our married life was exactly what I had been brought up to expect: I cooked, shopped and cleaned, and he checked the tire pressures and put the garbage out. I liked it this way. I would have sent Tim out mowing the lawn if we had had a lawn. The idea of a man washing up or making a bed shook me to the bone. Besides, my mum in her way was just as much a perfectionist as Dad, and as I wiped the work surfaces to a gleaming finish I was mentally rehearsing her nod of approval.

In our free time we played squash or went to the gun club, or socialized with other couples that were in the police force. That spring, Tim was moved from Peckham to Notting Hill. By now I was back working at the Intercontinental with the Gulf royal family.

I had taken close protection work seriously before the specialized training in Herefordshire, but with hindsight I think in a real emergency I might not have had the hair-trigger timing that comes only with training and commitment. Since the course, there was no doubt about it — the sheikha and her children had the best protection money could buy.

Money entered into every aspect of their lives without exception. Most people spend in order to save labor or impress their friends or amuse themselves, but all these ordinary things were so easily attainable that they were meaningless to the Gulf royals. Their buying decisions were on another level altogether. Money was a psychological weapon. When they handed it over they expected power, fear, and love in return.

One day I took the eldest girl, who was eleven, downstairs in the hotel to buy some candy. She stood in front of the display, choosing packets and bars and piling them on the counter by the cash register. An untidy heap of shiny paper packages accumulated and the kiosk woman, busily counting out change to a man for a box of cigars, said, "That's a lot of goodies. Can you afford all those?"

The child stared. "I can afford anything," she said icily. "I can buy all the candy in this store if I want to."

"Yes, dear," said the woman indulgently, and looked quizzically at me as I handed over the money. I remained stony-faced. Carrying the candy in a striped carrier bag, I escorted the silent princess back to the penthouse floor. As soon as we stepped out of the elevator she snatched the bag and ran into the suite, shutting the door behind her. Five minutes later she came out, flushed, carrying the same striped bag.

"You take me downstairs to the shop," she commanded.

The kiosk woman didn't see us coming. She was sipping a cup of coffee, and she nearly choked when a small brown hand once again began stacking chocolate on the counter. She looked at me.

"Her Royal Highness will pay," I said.

Mars bars, Twix bars, fruit gums, nougats, Bendicks mints, she made the woman put all of them into carrier bags. Boxes of chocolate pralines, Walnut Whips, marshmallows, humbugs, acid drops, chewing gum. She did not stop collecting until the woman had piled every last item of confectionary into a bag and climbed onto a set of steps to retrieve a couple of dusty boxes of crystallized fruit from the display behind her. Silently she rang up everything at the correct retail price. The child handed me her striped paper carrier and I counted out over

£2,000 in crisp twenties. As she handed me the change I caught a look pass between her and the princess. The child cut her eyes at the woman in utter disgust.

Carrier bags became quite a little feature of life with the Gulf royals after that. Money was just a meaningless token; they had no idea of the price of anything. One morning I had just arrived and had barely sat down in my usual chair in the corridor when I was summoned into the suite by the sheikha, who was lying on the sofa in a baggy pink garment while the hotel's manicurist painted her toenails.

"Good morning, Jacquie. My son is not well today. In five minutes a slave will give you some money. Go to Harrods' toy department. He wishes a train set and war things. Soldiers. You will find them."

I would. A skinny Eritrean woman all in white, her eyes downcast, scuttled out shortly afterward and handed me a shiny sage green and gold Harrods bag with £9,000 in it. I did my best, and like to think I bought the sheiklet quite a nice train set. Maybe when he grew up he would reproduce it full-size across the desert for the benefit of his people.

The girls had to be kept amused, too. To get them out of their mother's hair I took the two of them to Hamley's famous toy store one morning. They spent £5,000 in an hour, on Barbies and Sindys and wooden Pinocchio puppets; I had been handed the money in a Waitrose grocery store bag, and remember wondering who on earth had slipped out to Waitrose and why. There was certainly no need for extra groceries. Room service was called six or seven times a day, the waiters mincing out of the suite with a ten percent tip every time, having left a trolley laden with Lapsang tea and whole gâteaux which would remain untouched, except for the sticky depression left by a child's thumb, until half a day later when they mysteriously reappeared in the refrigerator in the security office.

The royal wife and children were bored witless. Inner resources were not in their repertoire. The sheikha spent tens of thousands on trunkloads of dresses that were shipped home, and some gaudy new toy or riotous action must be provided every day for the kids. The children soon tired of Hyde Park and throwing bread to the ducks on the Serpentine. For a short time they took to charging gleefully along the length of the corridor behind the food service trolley and ramming it into the bodyguard's shins. My legs were black and blue and I had to buy a new pair of pantyhose every day, but I put up with the little bastards in silence. Even that game bored them after a few days — maybe I should have winced more; they would have enjoyed that.

They were distracted when the princesses saw a funfair on television. The sheikha immediately commanded me to take them to one. It was late January, and phone calls all over London winkled out only one traveling fair, on Hampstead Heath. The carnival rides were locked up for the winter but another carrier bag with a couple of thousand pounds in it worked its magic. That gray London afternoon, eight bodyguards positioned themselves watchfully around four children shrieking past on a merry-go-round and waltzer, and peered into the dripping trees for potential kidnappers.

At least two of the girls usually accompanied their mother on her daily shopping trips. We would sweep into some toffee-nosed emporium in Bond Street, the advance bodyguard followed by the sheikha and myself, a troop of nannies and slaves and the two little girls, with two more guys from the close protection squad on watch outside and the drivers waiting in the limos on the double yellow lines that denote strictly no parking. Then the sheikha would point a scarlet-nailed finger out of her all-enveloping shabbah and demand and order while her daughters trampled about in calfskin stilettos or squealed and chucked handmade patent pumps at each other. The saleswoman could not have been more obsequious. The manager rushed out from behind a pillar, nose a-quiver like a nervous rabbit, as soon as our entourage arrived. She could smell commission.

"What delightful children you have, madam." A tiny flinch of the neck as a riding boot hurtled past her immaculate cheekbones. *Christ*, I thought, *you must be desperate.* She had said the right thing though, for the sheikha was a proud mama.

"Yes, My children speak three languages fluently." As the girls were now screaming like kindergarteners from hell in all three languages, you could hardly hear what she was saying. Disciplining these brats was evidently not in the nannies' job description. They smiled timidly as the girls wrecked the joint, the saleswomen gritted their teeth, the slaves made themselves invisible, and the bodyguards, as ever, looked out for a threat.

Meanwhile, back on a sky-level floor of the Intercontinental, the remaining prince and princess would be growing bored again. They might amuse themselves by painting on the wallpaper or carefully scoring their names into a leather desktop. When they finally returned to the Gulf, the resulting bill for damages amounting to twenty-five or thirty thousand pounds would be settled without question.

Their father, a petulant and chubby fifty-year-old in snowy dish-dash and Arab headdress, visited their mother for about twenty minutes at six each evening. He might occasionally see the boy. The girls were rarely brought to him. I do not, of course, know what he talked about with his number one wife during these interludes, but they can't have covered much ground. As far as I could see, they had nothing in common at all.

Though the team guarding the sheikh in his own hotel were mostly off-duty policemen, they had to turn a blind eye to a lot of things. The concierge of these places provided connections to anything that was asked for; they saw it as part of the job. Girls would be taken up to the suite, and cocaine delivered and snorted in the rooms, with open doors, allowing an unimpeded view. The management, who wanted their establishment to maintain at least the impression of a classy joint, looked the other way when it came to Arabs spending on this scale. As to the close protection team, they enjoyed the casino outings and ignored the rest.

Tim and I still needed all the work we could get, so I did close protection for the sheikha from eight until six and then crossed the road from the Intercontinental to the Hilton, where I had taken up an offer to work from six until two in the morning on the "tom squad."

All the big London hotels have a prostitute problem, especially the ones on Park Lane because they attract many wealthy, single male visitors on business. Tree-lined Park Lane with its empty sidewalks is a mecca for curb-crawlers and the huddled shops and cafés of Shepherd Market are only a few hundred yards away, on the Mayfair side away from Hyde Park. There have been toms in Shepherd Market since Mayfair was where they held the May Fair and, presumably, sheep ran through the back alleys. The Shepherd Market girls did not look bad — not at any rate as bad as the tired old tarts from King's Cross — but they looked enough like hookers to lower a hotel's reputation. The police had a tom squad to contain the problem on the streets, but they could not be everywhere, and if a hotel started to become notorious the police would warn its security department that they might oppose renewal of its license.

Security at the Hilton called in five of us: four men and me from the Circuit. Connected by radio, we hung about in the foyer or moved from floor to floor. Girls slipped in through staff entrances and up back stairways and went on the knock from room to room looking for "punters," as we call them. When we grabbed one of the girls, we would take her to the security office and see if there was a warrant out for her; if there wasn't we would caution her. Her picture would be added to the book, if it was not there already. "The Big Book of Toms" was compendious, and new snapshots were added and circulated around the hotels all the time, but the girls were not easily deterred. They could make a good living: one I got to know had two children at a fee-paying school, and the Williams sisters, who had both been on the game for years, had set up a carpet store in Leeds out of their earnings.

If the duty manager in the foyer saw a likely prostitute come in and go to the elevator with a hotel guest, he would radio up to us and we would be on that floor to see which room they went into. If he told us it was a single room, we would drag her out. Under an old English law called the Hotel Act, a hotel manager can be prosecuted for keeping a brothel if he lets two people share a room when he has any suspicion that they might not be married.

One night, one of us saw a girl go into a single room with a Japanese man. I arrived and put my ear to the door. She said she was leaving to buy some cigarettes, so two of us waited around the corner and nabbed her as she arrived at the elevator. We were on our way down to security when she remembered she had left her coat behind. I said I would go back for it, and as they disappeared into the elevator I set off down the corridor.

When I knocked on the door it opened a fraction, then a bit more, then wide.

"Ah, herro!" said a delighted voice, "Come in!"

I looked down. There stood the Japanese man, his head level with my chest, naked as a baby except for a thin gold thong thrust forward by the most enormous stonker.

"Hotel security," I said crisply. His equipment flopped sideways like a deflated balloon.

I got some laughs one way or another, but by March I was working such long hours to pay the bills, and Tim was doing so many broken shifts at Notting Hill, that I did not see much more of my husband than the sheikha did of the sheikh.

I had been suffering severe pain every month and suspected the cause: ovarian cysts had formed inside of me before. I first went into hospital to have them removed when I was about twelve years of age. In March 1981, not four months after our wedding, I collapsed and an ambulance rushed me from the Hilton to St. Stephen's Hospital on Fulham Road. I was told an immediate operation was necessary, so I signed the release form and went under.

I woke up staring at a white ceiling and thinking about Tim. It must be morning by now; he would be on duty. Failing Tim, I would have liked my dad to talk to, but he was not in great shape himself these days. He had had several heart attacks. He had been diabetic since before I was born, and lately he always seemed short of breath and walking had become painful. I promised myself I would go and see him before I went back to work. I raised my head and realized I was feeling rotten. A nurse saw me.

"Jacquieline? Mr. Dundas will be in to see you in a moment." (Surgeons in the UK are always referred to as "Mr." instead of "Doctor.") She disappeared to return within a few minutes with an elderly Scot in a white coat.

"Good evening, Jacquieline. Feeling a wee bit drowsy still? Well, I am glad to say you will have no further trouble . . . You are twenty-two, I see, Jacquieline. Is that correct?"

"Yes."

"However, I am sorry to have to tell you it hasn't all been plain sailing. It's always difficult — I'm afraid we found the trouble had progressed much further than we had expected. We considered what course of action to take, and I'm afraid there was nothing we could do except a complete hysterectomy."

I was still slow-witted from the anesthetic and did not understand properly.

"Is that what you want to do?"

"No, Jacquieline. That's what we have had to do. We had no option."

"Oh, you've done a hysterectomy?"

"Yes."

Something drastic had happened, but I could not quite take it in. I would never be able to have children now. Well, I had never consciously wanted to, though I had vaguely expected that would come later. My parents had been old, so none of their friends had babies, and I had never really seen the attraction of pregnancy and prams and all that.

The surgeon went away and I lay in bed trying to decide how I felt. Nice not to have to worry, in a way. But not thinking about having children and not physically being able to have them are two different things. I wondered how Tim would take the news.

I DID NOT CRY. THERE WAS NO POINT. I WAS MY USUAL MATTER-OF-FACT self when I told Tim. He held my hand for a minute and then he muttered something about how I did not seem very upset. So that was that. Visiting time left me feeling as if there was nothing to discuss.

An ambulance took me back to the Chelsea apartment, but I was not well enough to go to work right away. I fretted, I loved my work and was lost without it, but I had to lie down most of the time. I watched TV; Tim went to work at Notting Hill police station.

After a few days of this we did not have much to say to each other. We usually talked about work or the things we did together. Squash is not recommended after a hysterectomy, so we could not talk about that, or the gun club. We did not see any of the other couples we socialized with. Tim said he was too tired and I certainly was, even after three weeks. Then one night Tim came back looking more cheerful than usual, and said we should get away before I returned to work. Why didn't we, he said, go down to Devon with my mum and dad? That way, if anything went wrong he would know there were a couple of nurses around. (Mum was a nurse as well as Dad.)

Off we went, all of us in Tim's car, on the Sunday morning. Tim had taken annual leave and I thought that was nice of him. On the

Tuesday morning he had a call from work.

"Shit. I've got to go back. I'm due in court to give evidence."

"What d' you mean? You're on leave."

"Yeah, but there was a case due up before; I told you they deferred it, and now it's on tomorrow because one of the witnesses has to go overseas next week and he won't be back."

"How long will you be?"

"Couple of days. It should be over by Thursday."

I was disappointed, but there was not much I could do about it. I pottered around Taunton with Mum and Dad for a couple of days, admiring the sea view and eating restorative cream teas. I felt like a geriatric. The case dragged on and Tim did not come back on Thursday. He finally turned up late on Friday night. I felt sorry for him, having had to work all week and now spending most of Saturday driving us all the way back to London.

We dropped Mum and Dad in Barnet and it was three o'clock by the time Tim left me at the police apartments in Chelsea. He went over to Notting Hill to catch up with some paperwork, and I started to put laundry in the machine and unpack. I was taking some laundry downstairs to the washing line when I met my neighbor from the apartment above us, laden with shopping bags coming upstairs. She was a redhead married to a detective constable from Chelsea.

"Hi, Jacquie! How are you doing?"

"Fine. Much better."

"You had company anyway."

We knew each other to pass the time of day, but I did not know she knew I had been in Devon.

"My mum and dad, you mean? Yes."

"No, I meant that dark girl, is she your sister?"

"Sorry?"

"The girl who came over to your place with Tim in the week."

"What day was that?"

"Wednesday."

"A dark girl with curly hair wearing a leather jacket?"

"Yes."

"Oh, I know who you mean. No, she's not my sister." I went on my way to the clothesline, but my knees felt like jelly.

Tim had met Janine here; I had known it would be her. She was one half of a couple we knew. You register signs subconsciously. A look between two people or how they hand things to each other, or the way they pointedly sit apart. It is like recognizing a smell of gas; you smell it, but it is a while before you notice it. When you do, everything changes.

The color had drained out of everything. My life was spoiled. Tim had brought Janine here. Just the two of them. The apartment had never felt so empty. I walked into the bedroom and saw, now, that he had changed the sheets. I felt sick. My chest hurt with the pain of not crying. I started blindly cleaning floors. I was still polishing and cleaning when Tim came home in the middle of Saturday evening. He flung his jacket over the back of the sofa and sat down to take his shoes off in the living room. It was quiet in the apartment. He looked surprised by the silence.

"Nothing on telly? What's to eat?"

"You've had Janine here."

"What d'you mean?"

"Janine was here."

"So?"

"You never said a word. You got me down to Devon so you could bring her over here."

"That's crap. You're going out of your mind. Pull yourself together, Jacquie, for Christ's sake. The sooner you get back to work the better. I drove you all the way down there—"

"Well, what the fuck was she doing here then?"

Tim swore that Janine had only been at the apartment because she and her husband were thinking of divorcing and she wanted somebody to talk to. He became furious with me for questioning him and slammed into the bedroom.

I never brought the subject up again and we soon settled back into our routine of work, eat, sleep. It was at work I needed to mistrust people automatically. Not at home.

The sheikha had gone home, and to make up for the lost daytime earnings I worked six or seven nights a week on the tom squad. The long light days arrived and one warm evening I went for a walk just to get out of the bar. I wore a cocktail dress and high heels, wandering down a quiet street behind the hotel hunting in my bag for a cigarette when I saw a man coming toward me in half blues. He had a suit jacket on, but you can tell a police shirt, trousers and shoes anywhere. He gave me a sardonic, appraising stare. It feels great, being looked at like a prize horse.

"Want a light?" he asked.

"Thanks."

He took out a lighter. "You doing business?"

I put my cigarettes back in my bag. Then I took out my radio. All his facial muscles sagged. I smiled sweetly at him.

"Fuck!"

He turned and ran. I sprinted after him right through Mayfair to Marble Arch, and he was still dodging desperately between cars and down alleyways when I let him go. It served the bugger right. If I hadn't had heels on I would probably have nabbed him.

I was growing disillusioned with policemen. Not that Tim was like all the rest, of course; I had been letting this job make me paranoid.

I finally took the vacation I needed, although it was a working vacation. A highly paid executive had been injured at work, and had filed a claim against his employer for loss of earnings. It seemed he could barely walk since the accident and would be in constant pain. His employer's insurance company wanted him followed to the South of France. I jumped at the chance and spent five or six days at an expensive hotel with a glorious private beach. Wearing dark glasses against the hot sun, I shot several rolls of photographs of the target as he learned to water-ski and improved his diving skills at the hotel's pool. I had to admire him. For a man who could barely walk he was a bloody good water skier.

Not long after I returned, a couple of the agency's directors dropped by our apartment one afternoon to discuss a special project. The Ayatollah and his supporters had forced the Shah of Iran and his family to flee his country, and European capitals at that time teemed with rich Iranians. The shah's sister was in Geneva, but finding it difficult to leave because of some alleged illegal activities. For whatever reason, the Swiss did not want to let her go and quite a few other countries were not eager to have her as a visitor.

It would be my job to get her out of Switzerland: exactly the kind of challenge I wanted. It was risky and important and would use all the skills in undercover and close protection work I had learned so far. It would be my blooding; it would make my name on the Circuit. After this I would never want for work. I felt quietly exultant that they had chosen me for the job.

We sat working out how to do it without either her or me getting shot at when Tim walked in, still in uniform.

One of the guys was just saying, "Good thing it's a woman that's going—"

"Going where?" asked Tim.

"Geneva." They told him about the job.

"Dream on, mate. She's not doing that," Tim said.

"What d'you mean?" I said. "I bloody am. Butt out, Tim, it's got nothing to do with you."

"Oh, right. Who d'you think you are, some bloody cartoon character like Modesty Blaise? You must be out of your mind if you think I'd let you go out there and do that."

"Jacquie's good, Tim," said one of the guys. "She'll handle it fine. You don't need to worry."

"She's going nowhere."

"You mind your own business. It's me who's on the Circuit, Tim, not you. It's nothing to do with you—"

"Just go and make us a nice cup of tea, will you? Let me have a word with the lads here."

I was speechless.

"Go on, run along."

I was not willing to play out this scene in front of these guys. I just sat there, furious. Tim turned to them.

"Come on, lads. Would you let your wife go?"

"My wife's not Jacquie," said one. "Jacquie's trained. She knows what she's doing. If we thought anybody else could do it we'd ask them. We want Jacquie."

It was three of us, against him, and I knew I'd won. Tim turned to me, his face thunderous.

"I want to talk to you in the kitchen."

We squeezed into the kitchen together, and I leaned on the back of the door and got my word in first.

"You're being a total dickhead. It's my job."

"It's illegal. A lot of what you do is illegal."

"That's got nothing to do with it. I'm going, Tim, you're going to have to live with it."

Tim had gone red in the face.

"You stupid fat cow. I'll get you stopped. You'll never work again. All it'll take is one phone call."

I was not fat. He had never called me that before and neither had anybody else. He must have seen the twitch of anxiety in my eyes.

"What are you saying?" I stammered.

"If the Special Branch thinks you've got some idea of getting the shah's sister into this country, you won't have a fucking prayer, you stupid bitch. Not a fucking prayer. You want me to call them? Those guys in there won't know what's hit them."

I was silent. He knew he'd won. He looked triumphant.

"You'll thank me for this one day," he said, and pushed past me to pull the door open. "Come on. You're going to tell your friends."

We went back into the living room and he looked on while I wiped out my career. I could see it in their faces as they left: "That's the trouble with women . . . "

I was badly disheartened after Tim made me turn down the Geneva job. I knew word would go around and I would never again be offered the work I wanted on the Circuit. I could have felt embittered but there would have been no point; as I saw it (and I saw it the way I had been brought up to) marriage was for life, and if I had married a man who stood between my work and me I would have to change his mind. So I put my career on hold and convinced myself he would come around, given time. In the meantime I would stay on the tom squad in the evenings and look for a day job that I would do so outstandingly well that Tim would begin to trust me. I thought that must be the problem; he must think I could not cope. A few more years with me and he would understand.

One night, however, we had a particularly long and tearful argument and I demanded to know once and for all whether he had had an affair with Janine. He said yes, of course. It was all over now; she had been posted to Orpington to split them up. He spoke casually. They had started going to bed together in March, he said, when I was in hospital.

"When I was in hospital? Having a hysterectomy?"

"Look, men are different, Jacquie. You were away, she came on to me, what was I gonna do?"

"You could have told her to piss off."

"I hadn't had sex for weeks. You were in hospital. And to cap it all you'd just told me you couldn't have kids."

"So it was my fault, then?"

"You couldn't help it."

"If you want a divorce because I can't have children, then say so."

"No. You're my wife, Jacquie. For better or for worse."

In August, Dad fell ill again. He had had at least four heart attacks, was suffering from complications of diabetes, and this time when he went into hospital both legs were gangrenous and would have to be amputated. The horror of this was too much to think about. He was taken into hospital on a Thursday and the surgery took place on Friday. I went to see him on the Sunday.

There is really nothing you can say to anyone in that situation. There is none of the usual "Get Well Soon." From now on he would be dependent, and Mum would be caring for him. He would not be able to perform even routine bodily functions without assistance. Dad was somebody who had always had his own way. He ran things. He did not sit around waiting for something to happen. Now, white as the hospital sheets, he was literally half a person. I could see he could not cope. There were long silences after everything we said to each other.

In the end, he said, "I can't live like this, Jacquie."

"I can understand that, Dad." I took his hand. "I really can."

"I gotta do something, I can't go on like this."

"You do what you've got to do."

Because he had been a charge nurse, the nurses on the ward used to let him administer his own insulin injections twice a day. On the Monday, I received a phone call to say he had sunk into a coma overnight, and I was needed at the hospital.

By the time I arrived he had died. My mother and sisters were weeping, but I remained dry-eyed. I called the funeral director and organized what had to be done.

While the coroner concluded Dad had died of natural causes, a combination of diabetes and heart problems; I believe he deliberately forgot to administer an injection.

Dad had been my best friend. I felt desperately lonely.

TIM AND I FACED A BLEAK FUTURE TOGETHER, BUT WE COULD NOT admit it so we did what many people in the same situation have done: averted our eyes and aimed for a new goal. We began to save up for the deposit on a house. As he was still spending everything he earned and more, while my money went on the debts, and as I was not going to win good assignments on the Circuit for a while, I still needed a proper job. I applied for one I had seen advertised in the *Police Review,* and got it. A small family-owned chain of department stores in West London was losing five percent of its profits through shoplifting, and they had decided to take on a head of security, briefed to build up a small team. I knew a couple of policewomen who wanted out of the force; I advertised for more, and soon had a team of four floorwalkers.

Ealing, about six miles out of the West End of London and linked to it by subway, was a fashionable suburb in the early years of the twentieth century. It still has many trees, parks and large detached Victorian houses. Some of these are occupied by wealthy families, but most have been converted into language schools, retirement homes or apartments. Ealing sees itself as not quite London, somehow, but as a staging post on the way to lush Virginia Water or Weybridge. It definitely turns its back on slatternly Acton, with its seething polluted high street snaking from Ealing to London, and has nothing at all to do with Southall with its Indian-owned stores. Ealing thinks it has a touch of class.

The shop in West Ealing was an old-fashioned department store. It had creaked its way into the 1980s somehow, but many of the staff were elderly unmarried women who had been recruited so long ago that in their day, single salesgirls were expected to live in staff accommodations. There was another store thirty miles west of London in High Wycombe that trundled along and would soon be sold off. But the flagship, where I worked, was called Fields, in Ealing Broadway. The Broadway Centre, a new shopping mall, had just been built and a new extension to Fields store was inside. So were Safeways and Fields' main rival, Bentalls department store.

Fields was a well-organized store specializing in high-end women's clothing. The labels were there: Versace, Ralph Lauren, Armani, Donna Karan. They sold furs, too. At that time the Knightsbridge and Oxford Street department stores were reconsidering their position on the ethics of the fur trade. Some finally decided that they were losing more by alienating customers than they were by stocking expensive furs for those few women who still wanted to buy them. Out in Ealing, however, Fields still sold everything. My job, besides running the team of floorwalkers, included checking stock levels, and over the months it became pretty obvious to me that designer clothes and furs were disappearing fast. Profits were right down. It had to be an inside job, again. I put a couple of people on to it and waited.

In the meantime, I did the job I had learned so well in Peckham: I went out into the store and nicked thieves. We caught hundreds in the first year. One of the directors of the company was a magistrate, a judge who presides over local, low-level criminal cases. He told me there was some discussion of me in the courts. He could not sit on our cases, since he had an interest, but he heard what other magistrates said, and they were amazed by the constant stream of shoplifters I sent their way.

I soon realized most of the thieves were professionals. Even gangs all the way from Australia tried to steal from us. Luckily, all the women I had trained were as committed to catching thieves as these people were to getting away with it, so we scored some spectacular arrests. We did not let go. Thieves tend to move from store to store in a shopping mall, and sometimes we would follow a suspect out of Fields and into Bentalls or one of the other stores where they had closed circuit TV (CCTV). Their security staff would spot us on the monitors and one of their floorwalkers would sidle up, murmuring, "What you got?"

We did the same for them. We cooperated very well and set up regular meetings between the security departments of all the stores, and the local crime prevention officer, to pool information. Our detection rates improved still more. We had no CCTV at Fields, but we were linked by radio to each other through the switchboard and if a chase started, which it often did, the radio would switch straight to the local police station so they heard a live broadcast of what was going on and where.

One day Mick, my best friend at Ealing police station, said to me, "Your fame's spread, Jacquie."

"What d'you mean?"

"We turned over some houses last night, it was a bunch of kids; we caught one of them doing a burglary. Well, we were looking through their houses and one of them was full of electrical stuff from Bentalls, with the tickets still on, and John said to this kid, 'D'you ever nick stuff from Fields?' And he said, 'Not on your life, not since that bitch has been there.' "

Although I felt a complete failure with Tim, it was exactly the opposite at work. I took pride in my work. I behaved on the job like a lean, mean, fighting machine. Lean, especially. I hardly ever had time to eat because I was finishing work at five, driving over to the Cumberland or Hilton Hotel to work on the tom squad or occasionally to do close protection for a visiting rock star, arriving home at about two in the morning only to drive out to Ealing for nine o'clock. I kept going through the day on coffee and cigarettes and sometimes a sandwich. In the evenings, I usually had no time to eat at the hotel.

Abysmal profits in Fields women's clothing departments were now fully explained. The culprit was a senior sales assistant, at the center of a web of willing helpers. She was a dumpy, silent thing whose permanent air of anxiety concealed a truly criminal greed. She had shown her grown-up daughter and various friends how to go into one of the group's stores, choose some garments from the racks, and disappear into the changing rooms to stash stuff and walk out with it. (This was before the introduction of security tags.) I was watching when I saw one of her regular customers go in with an armful of fur coats and reappear with only one.

"Not quite me . . . I'll think about it."

The saleswoman had plenty of time to think about it in the end, because she went to jail. When I went along with the police to raid her house we found dresses worth thousands of pounds each, amazing creations in velvet and silk, and exquisitely tailored suits and jackets, just rolled up and stuffed in a corner or under the bed. She had sold some, but there were piles of clothes left, and I looked at the chaos and realized that this was a metaphor for her life. She had a problem. However, I had a job to do. When it came to court, the prosecution had worked out what she had cost the store in the course of her employment. It came to three and a half million pounds — that is more than five million dollars.

After this case I heard people say thieves always get caught in the end. They don't.

The senior sales assistant wasn't the only one stealing from fields. There was an old girl in the kitchenware department, she had been there over twenty years and if it had not been for me, she would have retired in her dotage with an unblemished reputation and a hefty nest egg.

One of my responsibilities as head of security was to check stock against takings. The cash register receipts never matched in kitchenware. I could see only one way to get to the bottom of this, so I collected all the department's cash register rolls for the previous two months and shut myself in my office.

By the end of the first morning I realized this needed weeks of work. I emerged still seeing numbers reeling past my eyes, went into the canteen and sat down to eat a sandwich. Little old Marjorie from kitchenware was in there, carefully carrying her tray, meat and two veg with apple pie to follow. I had my eye on her already, because I had asked my rather hoity-toity friend in personnel to let me know if there was anybody who worked in kitchenware who never took a day off. There was only Marjorie, and since she was seventy-two you would think she would want to put her feet up now and again and let somebody else sell kettles and cherry pitters to the good citizens of Ealing. But she never did; she came to work regardless of rain or snow as if her life depended on it. *Aha,* I thought, *hidden agenda.* I was right, but it took me weeks of poring over scraps of paper to be sure.

She was taking money out of the cash register more or less equivalent to the amounts received from Barclaycard credit card customers. She only got away with it because of the way the system worked. Credit card transactions were paper based at that time; there was no automatic link to a computer center. The salesperson placed the card into a mechanical press with two flimsy copies. Clunk. If somebody paid £25 on Barclaycard, the bottom copy was clipped to the back of the cash register receipt and put in the register. The salesperson had to treat the Barclaycard transaction as cash. The cash total for the day therefore would be the actual cash, plus all the Barclaycard transactions, minus the sum put into the register at the start of trading to make change.

I finally worked out what was happening. Somebody — somebody whose squiggled initials on the Barclaycard bottom copy looked a lot like Marjorie's, was saving old low-value, uncollected cash register receipts and clipping them to the front of big-ticket Barclaycard receipts. At first glance it would show a receipt for ninety-nine pence, and ninety-nine pence would be in the cash to match it, but on the back of the receipt you would find the Barclaycard copy showed twenty-five pounds, not ninety-nine pence. Somebody had pocketed the difference.

It was so obvious to me, but the records had been sloppily kept for years, in a way that skimmed over difficulties of basic arithmetic, and I could not be sure Marjorie was the only one responsible. I called in the other staff from the department; most of them were young girls. I took them through weeks-old transactions. I asked them why they had made this mistake or that. In nearly every case, the girl concerned had taken a day off when the mistake had been made.

I had all the staff checked out. They were all clean, but Marjorie had worked at Fields for so long that nobody could remember where she came from. An old personnel file dating from the 1960s, its manila cover crumbling, showed she had worked at the Co-op store for twenty-five years before showing up at Fields. I called them and they told me she had left under suspicion of dipping her hand in the cash register. At Woolworths, where she had worked as a young woman before the Second World War, moldering records revealed that she had been fired for the same reason.

I gathered up the entire case, crumpled receipts, cash register rolls, the old file, the lot, took it to the CID office at Ealing police station and said, "I've got this problem."

I explained about Marjorie. How she lived on her own, had never married, was seventy-two, and how I thought she was guilty of false accounting. She had been doing this all her life and had to be stopped. I intended to go for a prosecution.

"Come on, Jacquie." The chief inspector was shocked. "The poor old dear won't go down for that at her age, what's the use? You don't want to nick her. Get them to heave her out with loss of pension rights."

I shook my head. "That would be letting her get away with it. She's been at it too long. Look — I worked out that at the rate she's been going, in the last couple of years alone she's had fifty grand out of there."

He looked without enthusiasm at the bulging case notes I had brought with me. "She's an old woman. Have a heart."

"No. I came up here to tell you I'm going to arrest her. Just so you know. False accounting over half a century is serious. She's going to court."

The chief inspector looked grim. "You're a hard cow, Jacquie."

I returned to the store and had a brief meeting with the managing director. He told me he would back me in whatever I decided to do. I went back to my office. I sorted the case notes into neat piles on my desk, and I called Marjorie in.

"How long have you been working here, Marjorie?"

She told me.

"Can you tell me how the cash registers are reconciled at the end of the day?"

She told me.

"Do you know what this is?" I thrust a list of transactions across the desk.

"No."

"You don't know what it is . . . And this?" She was growing pale. "Can you tell me why this figure here does not match this one here?"

"No."

"Can you tell me whose signature this is?"

"No."

"Why did you scratch this out?"

"I don't remember." She took a small handkerchief from her pocket and started polishing her reading glasses.

"Have you ever pinned receipts to the wrong Visa copies?"

"I don't know."

"Why did you pin this receipt to this docket?"

"I don't know."

"You've made a lot of mistakes like that, haven't you, Marjorie?"

She was twisting the hanky and she stood up and said, "I'm leaving. I don't like you."

I stood up, too. "You're going nowhere. You're under arrest," I cautioned her, explaining her rights, and she sat down suddenly, in shock.

I called the police station, spoke to CID and told them to come down. "I've got a body," I said.

She hardly said a word when the CID arrived. We walked out through the store in a small silent group. Other sales assistants looked curiously at her. She was taken by car to Ealing police station, charged and, a few hours later, bailed. The next day at the magistrate's court she was bailed for another week. I knew it would take me that long to explain to the CID how the scam had worked and point out the crucial points of our case against her. Back at the store, I sensed hostility from many of the sales staff. Most people thought I had gone too far. They were sorry for her. I did not give a damn what they thought. I was proving I was tough. I was proving it to myself and especially to my husband, who didn't respect me as an equal.

Later that day the old lady's nephew came in to see me in my office. He was a short, fair-haired man, with a worried expression: a traveling salesman-type with a beer belly. He pleaded with me.

"She'll never get another job at her age; she's no danger to anybody. She's not a criminal. She's always wanted to do her best for the family. Look, my brother and I have been talking about this. Can we just pay it back and have no more said?"

"Have you got fifty grand?"

He looked stunned.

I added, "She won't go to prison. But she's been stealing from this store for years. People like her must not be allowed to think that we will let them get away with it."

The next morning I was on my way to my office when the switchboard operator told me the managing director wanted to see me. Richard was young to be the MD, only in his thirties. Standing behind his desk this morning he looked grave.

"Marjorie took an overdose last night. She's dead."

I did not know what to say.

"Are you all right?"

I gathered my thoughts. "Of course."

I went back to my office without a qualm. I knew I had done the right thing. All the same, the Marjorie saga did not do my relationship with the staff much good.

Half an hour later one of my store detectives caught the first shoplifter of the day. I had been fidgeting, putting papers away, and wanted to get out. I went to the police station with them. As we walked past the desk sergeant he muttered, "All right, this one, is it? No dicky heart?"

On the way up to the CID office I heard the chief inspector. "How old's this one, Jacquie? Hope it's not feeling depressed."

"Very funny."

I took it for months.

TIM HAD JOINED THE SPECIAL PATROL GROUP. MY GOD, THEY WERE unpopular! Even the police were wary of them, and anyone more liberally inclined, like radical students or militant trade unionists, put the SPG on a par with Nazi storm troopers. They alternated eight weeks in uniform with eight weeks in plain clothes, mainly doing surveillance work. Tim was a big man, but anonymous; he went unnoticed in a crowd, and he enjoyed spying on people.

Members of the Special Patrol Group were discouraged from discussing work at home, and the fact that he could not talk about what he was doing did not help our marriage. I would often drive off to work on a Friday morning saying, "Have a good day. See you tonight."

"Yeah, see you," he would say, climbing into his own car to follow me out onto the main road. When I came back in the evening I would find a note to say he would be away until Sunday. Called out on a special job, something's come up, anything. On other weekends he would be away on a course.

One Thursday night Tim came home from work and flung down his jacket and said, "That's it. They're sending us up to the miner's strike."

"Up to Derby? You're joking."

The coal miners, represented by Arthur Scargill and his National Union of Mineworkers, were in angry confrontation with Margaret Thatcher's government over the winding down of the industry. Some of the miners had rejected Scargill's position and formed a conciliatory union. They were regarded as scabs and blacklegs to a man. The wives of the Scargill miners were loud and photogenic and said their piece in the media constantly. Scuffles at the pit-head gained national television coverage, pickets arrived from all over the country, thousands of police man hours were expended controlling the crowds at the mines and hordes of extra officers poured into pit villages from the big English cities. But the SPG were something else again. They were armed and represented the State with its gloves off.

"It's a bit politically sensitive, sending you up there, isn't it?

"Ours is not to reason why . . . I've got to pack for two weeks. We're going up on standby and keeping a low profile in case we're needed."

He packed his uniforms and enough other clothes to keep him going for a fortnight, and in bed that night said, "I'll call you every night at eight o'clock."

"Okay. If I'm not here I'll be at the shop or down the nick or somewhere."

"You'd better be *here*. I don't want to be ringing and find my wife gallivanting about somewhere. I won't have time to mess about chasing you on the phone; they're gonna make us work all hours. Surveillance, if nothing else. Jesus, two weeks in Derby."

Every night the phone rang.

"How's it going?"

"How you'd expect, for sixteen hours a day? It's endless. There's nothing happening, dead boring. What a dump."

The first Saturday he was away, I felt really sorry for him. I saw pictures of Scargill bellowing at the miners on TV, and it was raining up there. In London the sun shone and I had a day off, and decided to take my dog, Boo, for a walk. Boo bounded across the park in Sutton with me in the morning while a nice old man walked alongside me and told me what he remembered about the war. It was peaceful, contented, not the kind of day Tim ought to be stuck up there working. When Boo and I walked down the high street on our way home I lingered at Dixon's window looking at all the little black boxes of electronics with special offers and discounts labeled in exciting colors. I thought about Tim and all this overtime and wished he were with me. On an impulse I went in, whipped out my credit card and bought him the top-of-the-range stereo system he had always wanted.

"I've a surprise for you," I told him that night. I felt happy, thinking what he would say and looking forward to his return at the end of the week. Only another six days.

I had settled on the sofa to watch the Saturday movie when the phone rang again. It was Tim's boss.

"Hello, Jacquie. Chief Inspector Griffiths. Sorry to call you so late. Is Tim about?"

"No, sir, why would he be?"

"I need to get a message to him. Would you tell him we're on standby for the miner's strike?"

"Er . . . Oh."

"He needs to be ready to go up to Derby tomorrow. Can you pass that message to him?"

"Oh, yes."

"Good. How's your annual leave going?"

"Well, I'm not on annual leave, sir."

"Oh, I see. Well, anyway, let him know we're on standby, would you? Good night."

The SPG work in twos. I called Tim's partner, Bill.

"Where is he?"

"Sorry, what d'you say, Jacquie?"

"I've just had Chief Inspector Griffiths on the phone. I know what's going on. Where is he?"

"You didn't say anything to him, did you?"

"Where is Tim?"

"He's in the West Country."

"Well, you'd better get hold of him, mate. Because you're all on standby to go up to Derby tomorrow. Which is where he's supposed to be already."

Bill did not know what to say to me. I did not sleep well. The next day, I was in the kitchen giving Boo something to eat when I heard Tim's car door slam and his key turning in the lock of the front door. He walked into the living room, dumped his luggage on the sofa and was taking his jacket off when I came in. He turned to look at me.

"Don't look so bloody tragic. I'm not going to have a go at you for phoning Bill."

"Where have you been?"

"Did you say anything to the Guv'nor?"

"No, of course not. What's going on?"

He shrugged. "I took Janine on holiday."

"Oh. Really."

"Yeah, really. And don't look at me like that. In the circumstances, what d'you expect?"

I minded a lot about Janine, so much I could not even bear to think about it, or about the scores of other weekends he had been "on a course" or when "something's come up." Now I knew exactly what that had been. But what I minded even more were the debts. He was spending money, *my* money from the Barclaycard account in my name of which he was the second card holder, on hotel rooms and candlelit dinners, cozy pub lunches, while I worked all hours to pay the mounting bills. I felt cheated because I had wanted a big strong man to look after me, and I was looking after him.

Tim walked out and stayed out for the rest of the day. After he had gone I slammed through the house in tears, muttering resentfully under my breath about women with stubby legs and freckles. I put on a show of world-weariness though I was terribly hurt, and yet, in a way I had resigned myself to his infidelity. I worked with the police all the time, I told myself I should have known what to expect. I knew how long hours spent in the front seats of an area patrol car usually end up with a recital of how the wife/husband just doesn't understand. I thought it was mean-ingless, but there was something about the way people avoided mentioning his name in my presence at Ealing police station. Something about the way he never turned up at the Christmas parties. People did not attend those parties with their wives, and half the male officers made it obvious they were having it away with somebody they worked with, so why should Tim be any different? Besides, my work brought me into contact with betrayal and deceit all the time, with liars and con artists and bullies.

One day, not long after the Derby incident, as I patrolled the ground floor of Fields, I saw a man in his fifties wearing a smart suit and looking as if he had come in to buy something for his wife. He sauntered alongside the handbags, then his eye ranged along the waist high display of gloves. He turned aside, but not before I had seen him slip a pair of gloves into his sleeve. There was something odd about the way he did it . . . delicate. He used his hand like a pincer. He walked toward the umbrellas and scarves, and as he looked at the umbrellas, with one deft movement he had ripped the sticky price label from the gloves.

I watched him return across the floor, urbane, assured. One long forefinger slid the gloves across the polished counter. "I bought these here last week, but they're not suitable. I'm so sorry. I've lost the receipt for them, but they haven't been worn. Do you think you could let me have a refund? I'll go and find something else."

As soon as the sales assistant had called the supervisor to fill in the paperwork, he was given forty pounds in cash with Fields compliments. He was on his way out into Ealing Broadway, light-stepping, head held high, when I stopped him.

"Excuse me, sir. You are under arrest. I am detaining you on a charge of deception."

Expressions, rapid as clouds on a windy day, slipped across his face. It is the same every time. Shoplifters scan the alternatives: break for it, punch her in the gut, brazen it out. He made his decision fast.

"I'm afraid you've made a big mistake, young lady."

I was already on the radio to Ealing, asking for a police constable I knew to assist. "If you'll just step this way, please. We'll be taking a statement from you."

In the office he began to bluster. "This is ridiculous."

"What's your name, sir?"

"My name is Dirk Van Cleef, and I am a professional of good repute. I am a heart surgeon. And I can tell you that if this goes much further you will come to regret it. You have already caused me serious embarrassment." He was leaning on my desk, his two mutilated hands in view. He had no thumbs and several fingers missing. "You may not be very good at your job, young lady, but that's a minor problem in view of the trouble I can cause. The way you approached me in public could be extremely damaging. This is defamation. I am sure your employers would rather avoid a lawsuit."

"Yes, sir. You can say it all in the presence of a policeman in just a moment."

The officer arrived in a car and took us to the police station. In cases of deception, the CID has to be involved. I took Van Cleef into an interview room and left him with them. Then went off to make my own statement.

Half an hour passed and one of the CID officers came up to me. He was a heavy man with a permanently troubled look, like an unhappy beagle.

"Are you sure about this one?"

"Not a shadow of doubt. He whipped the price off those gloves and got a refund."

"He has dozens of receipts in his pockets. One of them could easily be for those gloves."

"I know what I saw."

One of his colleagues entered the room.

"He lives in Ham, doesn't he?" I said. "You should get out there and search the house."

"What, for forty quid? For deception?"

"There's something else going on here."

"Yeah, well maybe you just got it wrong for once. He is a heart surgeon, you know."

"A heart surgeon?" I said with a slight smile.

"Yeah."

"He's lost two fingers off each hand, has no thumbs, and he's a heart surgeon?"

The detective's face crumpled into a frown. "You're right."

We piled into an unmarked car with the suspect and drove out to Ham. He lived in a large detached house with a gravel drive, tidy lawns and a protective fringe of fir trees. Van Cleef, or "Mr. Van Cleef" as the CID officers deferentially persisted in calling him, stayed with two officers in the parked car while another CID man trudged up to the door with me. A well-powdered smartly dressed woman, looking surprised, ushered us into the living room.

"So, what does your husband do, Mrs. Van Cleef?"

"He's a kidney specialist. At St. Stephen's hospital."

"I see. Mind if we have a look around?"

We could have waited for a warrant to be issued but she had no objection. We skimmed through documents in her husband's study and finally decided to take him in. He allowed us to take several boxes of paper away and slunk back to the station with us.

I had seen the look on her face when he came in with the two officers. She was devastated. I think she really believed she was living with a four-fingered kidney specialist. I felt sorry for her, and irritated at the same time.

A few days later, the CID told me what they had found. The man had been stealing things every day, and taking them back for refunds — that was true, no question; there were hundreds of documents to prove it. But there were other themes running through the paperwork: health insurance and South Africa. When they assembled the correspondence in order, they worked it out. He would insure himself for thousands, usually in London, against medical expenses incurred on vacation. A few weeks later he would make a claim, saying he had lost a finger when on vacation in South Africa. His London insurance company sent their request for confirmation to the box number of his doctor in Johannesburg, received the forms back duly attested and signed, and paid up. The box number belonged to his cousin. The two of them had repeated this over and over again.

The CID loved me. Two officers flew out to South Africa for ten days and when they came back, they brought a Johannesburg policeman with them and we had a party in the CID room at Ealing police station.

"All from one pair of gloves," Lynn said.

Later, at home in Sutton, we were eating dinner. Boo lay under the table with his warm chin on my instep. Tim never said a word. He did not like me making good arrests. He knew I secretly hankered to go back on the Circuit and he knew the more spectacular the crimes I unearthed in my job, the more often the guys from the Circuit would nag me to quit and go undercover for them again. I could not win. If I had done a lousy job at Fields Tim would have sneered at me; and now that I was earning huge Christmas bonuses, congratulations and invitations to join the chairman for breakfast, he sneered at me anyway.

Then one day I came home from work and he had gone.

HE HAD TAKEN ALL THE FURNITURE EXCEPT OUR BED, ONE RUG, and the kitchen table. He took my dog, the stereo I had so fondly bought, and the car my dad had given to him.

I knew where Janine lived. I called him there and told him he had twenty-four hours to bring it all back or I would phone his chief superintendent. Most of it came back, though not the things that mattered, like Boo. Nor my money; he had cleared out the bank account.

His first wife, Yvonne, called ten minutes after I had put the phone down on that first night. She wanted to know if we would have his son, Mark, for the weekend. I told her Tim had left me. I was huddled on the floor beside my bed and I must have sounded awful, because she said, "Hold on. I'm coming round."

She was very good. She made cups of tea while I sobbed into one tissue after another at the kitchen table. Yvonne looked as if she had been through it. She needed a good holiday; she seemed to be the type of woman always waiting at life's bus stop lugging a couple of shopping bags. She said Tim was a nasty piece of work, she had been glad to be rid of him, and what he had done to me was worse because he knew I loved him. It was exactly what he had done to Mark, ignored him when the kid needed a dad.

"Mind you, you're not much better," she said.

"What d'you mean?"

"Oh, come on, Jacquie. All those times he said you would have Mark, and then you put him off."

"But it was me who always wanted him! It was you that bottled out at the last moment."

"That's not the way I heard it."

We compared notes. Tim had been telling her I had to work and did not want Mark to stay over, and he had been telling me Yvonne was neurotic and would not let him have the boy.

At work the next day I did not tell anybody Tim had left. I stopped buying food, since there was nobody to buy it for, and worked long hours.

Outside Fields, in the shopping mall, there was a flower stall run by a known villain, somebody, Department C11, the organized crime unit, kept an eye on. One day I glanced out at him from the ground floor window and saw a tall, dark, thickset man who approached from our direction and slipped a leather jacket from under his coat to the man on the stall. Then he came back toward the store, headed for the men's department, and started riffling through the racks of clothes. The buyer had kicked up a hell of a fuss when I said the expensive stuff should be chained, so it was not. When I saw him steal a leather jacket I thought, *Right, I'm going to have you this time.* I followed him out of the main entrance on the ground floor, and caught up with him in front of the display window.

"Excuse me. I am a store detective. You've got something you haven't paid for. I'm arrest—"

He picked me up, but I grabbed his lapels and hung on grimly. *I'm not going on my own, you bastard.* As we hurtled together through the plate glass window I crashed painfully on my back. I lay on shards of broken glass and as tottering plaster dummies went flying I had all his weight on me. He scrambled to get up. I grabbed at the nearest moving thing, a tag on the heel of one of his boots. I looped one finger through it, when he wrenched his foot away from me, the finger snapped. I did not feel a thing, but, like an airbag, it inflated instantly. It was now jammed in the tag so he was lumbered. I was now like a ball and chain on his foot and as he twisted round I kneed him. He pulled out a retractable knife and slashed me across the knee, into the bone, blood everywhere and it hurt like hell! He crouched, lashing out with his boot aiming for my kneecap, but clumsily because I was attached to his other foot. He missed.

By this time the mall was in uproar, somebody had called 999, the British emergency number, and this had been broadcast over all police channels from Scotland Yard. Tim happened to be cruising around Acton in the SPG car. He heard that a store detective had been stabbed in Ealing and knew it would have been me.

His team tore over to the scene. When I woke up in Ealing Hospital hours later, the bloke who had cut me lay in the next bed with several broken ribs and a broken arm. Much later, in court, I demurely claimed that I had done it in self-defense.

I stayed in hospital for four months.

The nurses were curious; in fact they asked if I ever ate anything. I am five feet ten and due to bulimia, an eating disorder I battled then, only weighed ninety pounds when I went in — and not much more when I left.

Later, having gone back to work on crutches, I decided I had done everything possible and there was nothing more to keep me in the job. In my tenure as head of security, Fields' annual losses from theft had decreased from five percent to one percent. Some of the staff hated me, but they had stopped sticking their hands in the cash registers. I left feeling like the Lone Ranger. Who was that woman?

Without Tim's neuroses to restrain me, I joyfully went back on the Circuit.

A spring morning in Maidstone, in the county of Kent, early 1985: I had now been on the Circuit again for three months. I had never lacked for work and was enjoying myself. Outside the town there is an industrial estate. I swung my car into a space in the parking lot and set off for the front office.

"Hello again. Jacquie Moore, isn't it?"

"Yes. Hello."

The personnel manager was friendly. She had interviewed me last week. This first day, I was to bring my P45, my official record of employment, to her office and she would show me where to go. The P45 passed without comment. Nobody ever spots a fake. I followed her neat navy blue jacket as she bustled out of reception, through the warehouse piled high with pallets, to a set of offices at the rear of the building.

"You'll be working over here. The ladies room is that way; there's the water cooler. I'll just hand you over to Mrs. Richards, she'll tell you what to do."

My job was to be clerk to the manager, a colorless middle-aged man whose sole interest outside work was his garden. I mastered his filing system and bashed happily at the electric typewriter for a couple of hours until a coffee break seemed in order. Two stained machines in the corridor belched boiling brown liquid with lumps of powdered milk into paper cups. I hoped I would not have to hang around for too long before my target made her approach. I was in luck.

"It scalds, that one does," she said, sharp-featured just like the photograph showed, striding in from my left as I juggled a paper cup over the drip tray. "They should put a notice on it really."

"Or get it fixed even," I said. "Where do you work?"

"I'm in there." She jerked her head at the main office where half a dozen girls sat at computers. "I'm in marketing. You're Bill's new assistant, aren't you? D'you live local?"

"No," I said. "I don't know a soul really. It's a long story, how I came here and got this job. What's your name?"

"I'm Lisa."

Of course you are, dear. Ms. Lisa Mailer, with £1,392 in a current account. Mortgage arrears looking desperate until just before Christmas when two grand arrived, and another thousand sailed safely into port last week. Credit card debt £742 on Access, £598.74p on a Next store card. Pokey little apartment in the top half of an old back-to-back block, with two bedrooms and access to a flat roof above the kitchen downstairs, on sale at £30,000 with three realtors for the past nine months. Mum and dad divorced, both living in town. The same job since leaving high school. No known boyfriend, although somebody's stealing stuff out of the warehouse as if it is going out of style. And friendly Lisa has access to the company's customer database, which has almost certainly been provided, by a person unknown, to a rival firm.

"I'm Jacquie," I said.

Friendly she certainly was. She was all over me. By lunchtime that day, with steak pie inside us and only the horrible prospect of steaming brown tea from the machine at four to break the day's monotony, we were bosom buddies.

"So, how did you end up in Maidstone, then?"

"I used to come down here for vacations when I was a kid," I said. "You know, when you've been through a divorce, you sort of go to earth to lick your wounds. My parents are dead, and I've been an army wife for five years so I haven't got any ties anywhere else."

"So where are you living?"

"I'm in a hotel. You know, a residential hotel — I'm looking for a flat to buy, so if you hear of anything—"

"What sort of place d' you want?"

"Small. There's only me. A balcony would be nice, I like somewhere I can sit outside in the summer."

"I only ask because mine's for sale. It might not be in your price range—"

"Oh, I haven't got any money problems, the divorce will see to that when the lawyers get it all tied up, but I do want to start looking. I can go up to forty thousand I think."

Her pale eyes fixed on me with wonder. Here I was, the answer to a maiden's prayer.

"Well, come round."

"I'd love to."

She explained to me in detail how to find it. I had spent part of the previous weekend driving around Maidstone, paying particular attention to Lisa's address and the parts of countryside I was supposed to have known so well at age ten. But it was touching to find that she was so anxious I should not get lost on the way to her enticing apartment. Clutching my forty grand.

Lisa's social life began to include me. She asked me to join her and a couple of friends for dinner. They were both women and one of them worked for our firm in accounts. Nobody discussed work at all, except to bitch about the male managers. Lisa reckoned they were all as thick as pigshit. After demolishing two bottles of Valpolicella, Lisa and her friend from accounts collapsed into giggles working out which of the men would be most disgusting to sleep with. I said I quite fancied one of the blokes in the warehouse, but Lisa said he was a po-faced bugger, no fun at all, and did I want to go out with the girls on Thursday? They knew a club. I did, of course. But if we all planned to meet for a drink at seven, I would not have time to go home and change.

"Can I bring my stuff over to your place after work?"

"Yeah, course you can. You can have a shower there if you want."

On Thursday night I shut Lisa's bedroom door firmly behind me while she made some phone calls. There was no lock. The CD player boomed in the living room, luckily for me, it covered the low grinding sound made by her tacky furniture as I opened cupboards and drawers. In a shoebox in the wardrobe I found a roll of computer printouts and an unlabelled floppy disc. This was a client list, all right. Names, addresses, contacts, order value . . .

"You ready?" A voice spoke so close I jumped. She must have had her face pressed to the thin wood of the bedroom door.

"Nearly," I trilled. "Won't be a minute."

I swanned serenely out a few minutes later, done up for an evening in downtown Maidstone with the girls and looking as if I would not miss it for the world. Lisa was rolling a joint as usual, "skinning up" in English low-life slang. By now I knew she always smoked marijuana before she went out. I began humming the tune on the CD.

"I really like that song," I enthused. "That's what you miss when you live in a hotel. I've got to get myself a stereo. I was looking in Dixons on Saturday."

"You don't want to get them there," she snorted.

"What's wrong with them?"

"Well, nothing at all, except you work at our place. You don't have to pay for stuff like that, you can get anything you want out of the ware-house."

"You're kidding?"

"Nobody looking after it on a Saturday morning, is there? And you know what's in all those brown boxes. Seen one stereo, seen 'em all. They won't miss a thing."

The boxes, stacked high on the shelves, were generally accessible only to forklifts. I spent my days cataloging, filing, and storing lists of Japanese brand names and product code numbers for tape recorders and stacking systems, televisions and video recorders, all of them matte black and living on pallets in cozy molded-polystyrene shells within brown cardboard boxes.

"I wouldn't dare."

"Give one of the lads twenty quid, they'll get you one."

"Who?"

"Oh, any one of 'em. They'll all take stuff out if you buy them a drink."

By now I had my own ideas about who to buy drinks for. I called somebody I knew in the Regional Crime Squad and asked him to meet me in a pub. Len had been a sergeant at Peckham when I worked there, and I knew he would be interested.

"The clients asked my agency to suss out who is selling their client list," I explained. "You know, counter-industrial espionage. I have evidence; I've seen the lists in her flat. But that's not all. We can get her and a whole ring of other people for pinching electronics out of their warehouse. And there's drugs involved as well."

"What drugs?"

"She's always got hash, and she's started asking if I want to score a gram of coke before this party she's having. Look — are you interested?"

Len sipped his beer thoughtfully.

"Not in doing drugs, personally. When is the party?"

It was to be on a Saturday night. I stayed out of Lisa's way the week before. She kept calling the hotel; I kept having to go and see my lawyers after work, or whatever excuse sprang to mind. I did not want to give her a definite no on the cocaine, because I wanted to see if she would offer it to me on the night, and in any case I did have some co-ordination to do. The Regional Crime Squad told me they would raid her flat at exactly 10:30 on the Saturday night. I promised them I would arrive at 9:50.

When I drove into the street where Lisa lived I passed Len and a woman sitting in a parked car. As I opened the front gate I could hear a faint thump of rock music, growing louder as I climbed the stairs. I do not know who heard the doorbell when I rang it. They all seemed a tad preoccupied. A small fat girl who seemed to have just got up opened the door. She wore leather jeans and matching brassiere exposing a roll of midriff as white and firm as a lifebelt. Behind her stood a woman holding a whip. It was all like that. It got worse. I looked wildly around for a man. This was a party for God's sake. There must be at least one! A skinny vegetarian cyclist with a beard — anybody, anybody would do as long as he was male and sane. But wherever I looked I saw Amazonian females in rubber fondling lady partners. One of these, wearing crimson lipstick and a PVC skirt, was the giggling man-hater from accounts. She swayed suggestively toward me in time to the music only to be intercepted by Lisa. I did a quick double take at Lisa and hoped that 10:30 was galloping toward us. Quiet conservative Maidstone of all places!

Lisa, her mousy hair newly streaked blond, wore a kind of cat suit and smoked a joint in a long holder. "Jack, sweetheart," she murmured, hooking an arm around my neck. "Here, I got you some punch."

Punch! It probably had hallucinogenic drugs in it. I took the glass, batted my eyelashes, chucked Lisa under the chin and said something to the girl from accounts. Lisa, close up, had gaping pores on her nose. I could see the kitchen clock from here and it was only five past ten. I could also see into Lisa's spare room, where two girls were engaged in violent love play on a creaking fold-a-bed.

"Come into the bedroom for a minute," Lisa breathed close to my ear. Her mascara was caked like a tide line on a beach, and she had drawn a thick brown border around her unpleasant lips. Ten twenty. Time drags when you are in a state of panic. I disengaged myself from Lisa's sweaty embrace and headed for the bathroom, where I stood watching the hands on my watch creep on for five minutes before people started banging on the door.

"Okay, okay."

I opened the door and had just got out when two women squeezed past and bolted themselves in. I hoped they stayed there, preventing Lisa from throwing her stash down the lavatory when the Regional Crime Squad charged in. Where the hell were they? Why did they have to be so bloody punctual? Why not come in at 10:29?

"You look gorgeous, Jack."

Lisa had just made a desperate lunge across the sofa when in the nick of time we heard an uproar in the hall. The front door crashed in and the room filled with men in uniform.

"Everybody over there. Get over there."

There were twenty or thirty women at the party, and we were all taken kicking and screaming to the police station. It was perishing cold outside, if you were not wearing wool next to the skin. I felt suddenly cold and very tired in the police van. *The things I do,* I thought. *Well, it's a laugh.*

Lisa screamed abuse at the officers and never stopped, even in the cells. Hours later, it must have been two in the morning, most of the others had been bailed but she was still yelling. Maybe it was the cocaine.

"You there, Jack? You all right?"

I huddled in a blanket in the next cell, but she could not see me. "Yeah, are you all right, Lisa?" I wished she would go to sleep. Heavy footsteps descended the stairs.

"You sad bastard, you leave my friend alone!" She shrieked at Len. He walked passed her and made for my cell.

"Get up, you bitch. Get off the floor."

"Fuck off," I said.

"Right, that's it, you're comin' out of there." He unlocked the door.

"Where you takin' her?" Lisa screeched, frustrated. Len wiggled his eyebrows at me.

"It's all right, Lisa! I'm all right!" I shouted. "Gerroff, you bastard!"

He hustled me upstairs in my trailing blanket to the police canteen.

"Len, I thought you'd never turn up," I said, gratefully sipping a mug of tea. A female sergeant at the next table gave me funny looks. Prisoners are not usually invited to the canteen.

"What you got, Len?" I asked.

The raid had been a great success. They had everything at once: stolen electronics, client lists, cannabis in dealing quantity and some cocaine. We had a good laugh about the state of the guests and then the time came for me to be returned to the cell. On the landing we began the sound effects and by the time I passed Lisa's cell, Len and I were exchanging fierce abuse.

I was out by breakfast time and so was she. Later that morning she called me at the hotel.

"What you being done for, Lisa?" I asked.

"Conspiracy, theft, theft employee. And supply. They're right pigs, aren't they?"

It always seems the same to me. People do greedy things, acts of betrayal, cruel things, and then they are aggrieved when they are caught, as if the police are the ones at fault.

"I gotta come over, Jack, I gotta see you, I want to talk, you know, get it together — we've got court tomorrow," she whined.

"You don't want to come over here, it's too public. I'll come over to you. Stay where you are, I'll be right there." I had already packed. I picked up my things from the bathroom, stuffed them into an overnight bag, and had my luggage taken to the foyer. I checked out. Within fifteen minutes I was on the freeway back to London. I gazed coldly into Lisa's future. When she heard my witness statement read out in court, maybe she would get some sense of what a piss ant I thought she was.

MOST OF MY UNDERCOVER COUNTER-INDUSTRIAL ESPIONAGE OR investigation jobs lasted six or eight weeks. The agency provided an information pack on the people concerned, the location and the background, and I had to make up my own cover story. After that, all I had to do was make the target trust me enough to talk.

I was really into it, pretending to be someone I was not. Partly because it made the job easier, for it was much easier to get close to contemptible people if I was not being myself. Partly because it reassured me that I was superior to them; I had a secret. And partly because it set me free. Being in the police force restricts your behavior in unexpected ways. You are always watching your back.

Now a job came up that meant I had to behave as I never normally would. I had to be vaguely leftie, malleable, and a bit of a slob. It repelled but fascinated me at the same time.

The Greenham Common Peace Camp was famous. It was set up to protest the US Air Force keeping ground-launched cruise missiles on the Greenham Royal Air Force Base, near Newbury, about forty miles west of London. Hundreds of women, announcing that they were in favor of non-violent direct action, had been living in makeshift accommodations on land adjacent to the base. This had been going on for several years, and many of the women were troubled. Our client's wife had taken their children there and refused to communicate with him. My job was to find the children and their mother, so the husband's lawyer could serve an injunction to make her return the children to the family home. Of course, it was crucial that she not suspect anybody was on her trail or she would disappear again.

I watched video that had been taken of the camp and read various news clippings. It was not going to be easy to fit in. I am tidy and organized and have no interest in politics. The arguments bored me, but I did my best. I even tried to sort out, without much success, what the tiny new Social Democratic Party and the Liberals stood for. I had never heard of any of these people. I had seen Brenda Dean on television, the first female leader of a big printers union, but nothing else had really registered.

In the end, I decided I would just have to wing it. I got up one Sunday morning, pulled on a pair of grubby jeans and unearthed the sleeping bag I had last used on a camping vacation when I was fourteen and asked a friend to drop me outside Greenham Village.

The air base was across a field, on the other side of a small wood. It was a bright, beautiful morning, cold, and a hare sat up fifty yards away and stared as I tramped through his field. Halfway across I smelt the camp. It was like the worst public lavatory you have ever been in. By the time I got through the trees I was inwardly reeling with disgust.

Thousands of tents in all colors had been erected as far as the eye could see. They were mostly low, slumped shelters for two or three people. Possessions littered the ground outside: camping stoves, old carrier bags, toys, battered radios. Trampled mud paths ran between the tents, and women and children ambled along as if in no particular hurry to get anywhere. The women wore droopy clothes or dungarees, with no make-up, a lot of jewelry and dirty necks.

I picked my way across guy ropes until two gray-haired women offered me a cup of tea. They were brewing it in an enamel pot singing over a wood fire. I thought it was probably the kind of tea soldiers must have drunk in the trenches in the First World War, nearly black but with sweetened condensed milk added to the churning mass of leaves and water so it poured out in an opaque stream. Good grief! It was worse than the drinks machine at the Maidstone job!

In this role I played a soulful girl who did not talk much. I stared meditatively, smoked cigarettes, and listened. I squatted on top of my rucksack on a thin patch of grass studded with cigarette butts, and when they asked politely why I was here, I told them I had been traveling since I dropped out of college and had decided to come and lend my support for a few weeks.

They were unquestioning in a well-mannered way. They assumed that because I was a woman and had found my way to the camp, I was automatically a part of their system of values. I felt they were kind, yet foolish.

They offered me a space in the tent, but I said no thanks. Three women already slept in there. It was dim, it was clammy, and the fetid stuffiness when it was packed with people must have been over-whelming. So, they showed me where I could sleep near their dying fire.

On the icy-trodden earth of early summer I zipped my rucksack into the foot of my sleeping bag and climbed in after it, shut my eyes against the stars and tried to ignore my freezing feet. I woke up in the moonlight with a hot shower coursing around me. Steaming liquid was splashing on my face. I sat up just in time to see a sniggering pair of Ministry of Defense (MOD) policemen zipping their flies as they trotted back to the perimeter road. I yelled a curse at them and got up in disgust. I had to rinse my hair and sleeping bag in icy water from a standpipe at three in the morning. I was not pleased.

My new friends were very sympathetic, but . . . *They might have bloody well warned me,* I thought, irritably, maintaining my vacuous smile. It seemed these MOD idiots did it all the time. They smeared excrement on the tent poles and urinated outside the tents.

Two of the women, Beth and Linda, and their friend Dorothy, had no objection to my staying in their tiny patch of territory within the camp. Using it as my base, I spent several days wandering about trying to figure out whether there was any pattern to the camp. There was not. There were water pipes, field latrines that stank and, apart from that, nothing but sagging tents. I saw hundreds of children, none of them identifiable as the two in the photograph I carried in my money belt.

The days slipped aimlessly by. People woke early, largely because sleeping was so uncomfortable, washed in cold water, lit a fire and made tea. Outside most of the tents' radios would be tuned in for the news. We ate cereals and porridge and then the morning stretched ahead with no relief except dog-eared books, conversation, washing up and attempts at doing laundry. It was amazing. These women came from houses as I did, with central heating and hot baths and lives, if they had chosen to lead them. I mentally slapped my own wrists whenever I felt irritation rising. It was all so passive and uncomfortable and dirty, as if we had traveled back to the Stone Age. I felt filthy. None of my outer clothes ever got washed, and my underwear could practically stand up by itself. I tried rinsing it under the standpipe once or twice but nothing ever dried properly so I gave up. We all reeked.

After two weeks, during most of which we huddled in the tent to escape the pouring rain, I realized I had head and body lice. I scraped lines of minute white eggs out of the hems of my jacket and sat shivering while it hung on a tree, and I hoped the problem would somehow be blown away. This seemed exactly the course of action a woman like me would take.

In role, I was not what you would call dynamic. The others urged me to claim social security benefits from the Department of Social Security in Newbury, and I sloped off a few times announcing that I planned to sign on, but when I came back I always told them there was a long queue and I could not be bothered to wait.

Having hung out and tramped around and made my inscrutable face familiar for weeks, I discovered a school at the camp. I did not want to become suddenly conspicuous, but I found my way over there most days. Yet, still no sign of the children I was looking for.

It was not all boring and dirty. Oh no. Quite often we would mosey on over to the perimeter road and wait for the trucks entering or leaving. A folk music group turned up sometimes to lead a sing along. All very earnest, and if you joined in with some all-purpose lyric about flowers and the wind, you were all right. If you grew bored you could go and tie a length of ribbon to the high-wire perimeter fence, giving it the same slightly loopy, trailing look that the camp had. When the trucks growled toward us, some of the braver spirits would lie down on the road and have to be dragged out of the way by the MOD police. There was a lot of exhilarating shouting to do on these occasions and sometimes I would clamber up a post of the fence and scream foul invective at the MOD men. I really meant that part of it. That was not acting. The way they behaved toward these women was totally unprofessional.

I never needed to worry about showing my political ignorance in conversation as there was no need to discuss the issues. Since anyone who had tits and turned up must be on our side, there was nothing to say. Apart from the crew-cut girls with big earrings and spangly leggings who would keep banging on about the Socialist Worker's Party, everybody wanted to talk about themselves. Not themselves in relation to the cause, just themselves. It was easy to let it all wash over you; I felt like a therapist.

When this palled, some of the women told stories to while away the long, crowded evenings. I sat cross-legged while joints passed around, watching the storyteller and out of the corner of my eye seeing one woman take a nit comb to another's hair and thinking this was the worst place I had ever been in. I loathed sleeping in the camp. Nearly every night some dyke would prowl up and try to touch me up in my sleeping bag. In the end I put about a story regarding my girlfriend in the Royal Navy and most of the advances stopped.

It seemed odd how these women were so conventional and respectful of the idea of possession. In my view, the camp was one big lesbian lust fest that carried on for years, full of impressionable housewives too polite to tell the more predatory women to sod off. I saw outright exploitation of battered wives who were lonely, but scared of men in general and their husbands in particular. But a lot of the wealthier women who used the camp as a refuge from suburbia had never had a good time when they were young, and they were just catching up with the sixties. They were into "finding themselves" and could not, therefore, reject any of life's possibilities, just in case they missed out on an inner discovery. They said things very gently, like, "If that's what seems right for you, that's fine." The worst words they could use about you were "confrontational" and "judgmental." So you could pass killer judgment on the USAF, but if some smelly bitch chose to unzip your sleeping bag you were supposed to allow her to express her true feelings.

I walked past the school every day and finally I saw the kids. They looked fairly clean and happy, but you do not argue with a client, and his wife had no moral right as far as I could see to remove their children from a secure background to this dump. From a phone booth in the village I told my handler the best time for the injunction to be served. The lawyer's clerk would present her with it on the Tuesday after a national holiday, so I made plans to leave on the Sunday. I promised Beth, Dorothy and Linda I would be back. I said I was going fruit picking for the summer.

I walked to the main road and began hitchhiking. Normally I would not risk it. This time, I could have safely hitched a ride with a man who had not had sex for a decade. Nobody with a working sense of smell would have gone near me. I saw the poor bloke's nose wrinkle as I climbed into the cab of his van. He drove me home to Barnet leaning against his door, with the window wide open. He dropped me at the end of my mum's street. I had called her the day before to tell her to buy some nit shampoo, so, whatever she thought, she did not expect me to arrive as if I had spent six weeks at Claridge's five-star hotel. Still, I was not prepared for her reaction. She opened the door about four inches and peered at me with one eye.

"You're not coming in here in those clothes," she said firmly. "You go around the back and strip off before you come in here." So I had to do just that, huddled outside the back door. While I had a bath in four changes of water, followed by a shower and several shampoos, she burned my clothes in the backyard.

A few months later, I came face to face with Beth, Dorothy and Linda in different circumstances. I was at Wapping in the East End of London by then, on a picket line, and having them recognize me by name helped my cover no end.

Rupert Murdoch, the Australian owner of *The Times, Sunday Times, Sun* and *News of the World,* had moved his company's operational base out of Fleet Street, the traditional home of British journalism, to Wapping, beside the Tower of London on the banks of the River Thames, and announced that from then on, News International papers would be produced using state-of-the-art technology direct from the journalists' desks. The printers had had it their own way literally for centuries. Their union was one of the most powerful, founded on the simple fact that it had been born in a time when most workers were illiterate, while printers, by their very profession, had to be able to read and write. Articulate and wealthy, they were a powerful adversary for Murdoch. Whole families had passed on lucrative jobs from generation to generation, laboriously setting out lines of type in a way that had become rapidly redundant with the advent of computerized production. They were not about to take the loss of their jobs lying down and set up a mass protest outside the News International headquarters.

The plant was now located behind high brick walls beside the River Thames at Wapping. A cobbled street ran alongside the walls, and other streets gave off it and led back up a slope to Ratcliff Highway, the arterial road running east from the Tower of London parallel with the river. Many crumbling old dock buildings lie between the Highway and the river, with some other land waiting to be developed in those days. It was here, and in the streets that ran up to the Highway, that most of the action took place.

The crowds filled the side streets most nights near News International: pickets by the gate, food vendors and the union trailer further back. A team of three, we were asked to mingle with the protesters to try to get proof that SOGAT, the main printer's union, was paying non-members for support. Once Beth and the others had greeted me like a long-lost sister, I was confident I passed as a right-on supporter.

As usual, the protest took on a social angle as well as a political one. People were enjoying themselves, in their way. The dreary folk group from Greenham Common arrived, and I stood and joined in with the familiar song of woe on a patch of waste ground outside the crowd. All the same, Wapping was rough. In most respects it was nothing like Greenham, which was one long picnic. This was a war, with real hate in it.

Scuffles erupted every time the trucks went in and out with newsprint and printed papers. Although all you had to do was yell, "Filth!" every so often at the police, or, "Scab!" at the truck driver, and claim to be a sacked social worker with a hatred for the Tories, you knew that if anybody sussed out that you were a plant, you would not be let off with a verbal reprimand. Heavies guarded the SOGAT union trailer and nobody could get near Brenda Dean, their leader. And the language was violent, the language of the Socialist Worker's Party and other militant groups: "Smash Murdoch" and "Kill the pigs."

A confrontation was planned for Saturday afternoon. I heard blokes in the crowd muttering, "It's going up tonight." I saw a man pick up a half-brick from the waste ground and stuff it in his coat. A mob of protestors milled along the Highway. The road had been closed to all traffic except the trucks that News International used, and they could not get through the throng. I had slipped toward the back of the whole heaving group when we started moving slowly westward toward the

Tower. We were singing, a good few thousand of us had moved out onto the highway and we had a plan. The crowd would tail off behind us, the police Special Patrol Group and mounted police would follow, then another group that meant business would come up behind the police and then the rear of the crowd in front of them would turn on them. The police would be surrounded.

That plan turned into the Wapping Riot. I was close enough to the rearward group to turn and find myself facing a barrier of police with linked arms. People were chucking marbles from behind, knowing the police horses would skid and go crashing down. They threw darts at them to madden them. Horses whinnied and reared, half bricks and lumps of concrete flew overhead and buckets of urine were hurled into the police lines. Some of the militants in the crowd were so high on adrenalin that they tore forward and laid into police officers with the strength of four people.

I found myself staring straight into my husband's face. I saw the look on Tim's face, and contributed my own very personal abuse to the uproar before a raving miner elbowed me out of the way in order to chuck something. I was driven back from the front line by men who wanted to fight without a woman getting in the way (Bloody typical! Nothing changes whatever side you are on), but not before I had been seen by several very surprised pals from Ealing police station. None of them said a word until the following day, when they all called on the phone to ask if I had changed sides. I think I reassured them.

Toward the end of 1985, I spent many dull days sitting in a series of different cars, watching a woman in the busy London suburb of Golders Green. I did not know who she was. She had streaked blond hair, drove a Jaguar XJ6, lived above a realtor's office on a main road and wore the tom's uniform of miniskirt without pantyhose (time is money), fake fur jacket and chain link purse. All I knew was that she was the target, and she stayed in all day and drove over to Belgravia or Ealing most nights. In Ealing she went once or twice into a small terraced house in a back street, where a black man answered the door. In Belgravia, she always visited a house in one of the ritzy squares. I did not see how long she stayed, but by the time I quit at midnight she had never come out.

I was doing the job for Tony, a bloke I had worked with, who was being paid directly by the client, an acquaintance of his. After a few weeks, Tony bought me a cup of coffee, and told me he was going overseas for the next three months on a job. He wanted to know if I would take over and deal with the client. I had no objection; I would get the whole fee.

The client lived in a square in Belgravia, one of the most desirable properties in London, four floors, all shiny cream stucco and geraniums outside. And there was a housekeeper and a manservant, acres of pale carpeting, mirror glass and gilt with a living room on the first floor. The client was a short, fat, balding Scotsman in his fifties. Very charming, he could not do enough for me, but he had an oblique way of referring to, "The Young Lady." The young lady might be receiving visitors at the Golders Green apartment, Jacquie, and he would like to know. Did I understand him correctly?

"Ian," I said, "I can't really help you unless I know what I'm looking for. Who is she and why do you want her followed?"

"You see, Jacquie, it's like this. She is my girlfriend, but I think she might be seeing somebody else."

"Right." Some girlfriend. "If you want round-the-clock surveillance I can't do it on my own. It needs a team of three or four people at least. One person sitting in a car is bound to get noticed sooner or later."

"I don't want to spend a fortune," he said cautiously. "What I'd like you to do is watch her from, let's say, ten in the morning until midnight. Don't worry about cars. I've got five, you can have three of them. The Roller and the Aston Martin are a mite conspicuous. But you can always hire more cars, it's not a problem. Just you bill me once a fortnight, Jacquie. I'm generous and I always pay on the nail. Oh, and I want you to put a bug in my bedroom telephone. Just to keep a record of what the young lady is up to, you understand me?"

I checked her out the following day and, as I suspected, found that she had been cautioned for prostitution. So I called him the next day and told him. My God, but men are full of surprises! He knew. He had hired her from an escort agency in the first place. "There's something I'd like you to hear, Jacquie," he said. "Come over tomorrow."

At his luxurious house the next day I relaxed in an armchair sipping a glass of spring water while he played an audiotape for me. The microphone must have been six inches from the bed. Either he was a great lover or she was very good at faking it. He was the client, so I was not about to decide which. Instead, I fixed him with a beady stare and he took the hint. He fast-forwarded the tape to the part where he gave her £500 afterward.

"Ian, I don't get it. You give her money for sex, but you say she is your girlfriend."

"She needs living expenses. I got her the flat and the car, you understand me, Jacquie. All I expect is that she will be there when I want her, but she keeps telling me she is spending more time with her mother and stepfather. You see, Jacquie, she's had a sad life. Her mother has a drinking problem. They live on some terrible council estate in Willesden."

She was not driving down to Willesden in the evenings, but to the house in Ealing. She saw Ian and got the £500 about twice a week, and nearly every other night she was in Ealing. After a while, she stopped leaving the Golders Green apartment in the evening and headed into town direct from Ealing, where she was spending nights. I had checked the electoral roll and there were several names down for that house, but I did not know who she was going to see until one day when she drove from Golders Green to a car repair workshop near the Ealing House.

Out came the same black man, wearing mechanic's overalls. He spoke to her briefly through the car window, disappeared, reappeared in ordinary clothes and jumped into the Jag beside her.

I followed them to High Street, where they parked and went into the local branch of the Abbey National Building Society. They were inside for forty-five minutes, somewhere out of sight, seeing a manager I assumed. I was pretty sure they were making a mortgage application, and I had a contact at the Abbey National. Within a couple of days I had the information I needed and went back to Belgravia.

"She's applied for a mortgage, along with a man called Hunter," I told him. "They want to buy a house in Alperton. Hunter is a mechanic who lives at a house in Ealing. He's got a previous criminal record for dealing drugs."

Ian was beside himself with rage. He called her every name under the sun, most of which reflected accurately on her profession, except for the bits about being cheap. At this stage he seemed to have overlooked my own last bill, so I was anxious to tie the whole thing up and get paid. His obsession with this mercenary little tart was getting on my nerves. A rational man would have called a halt to the affair weeks ago. But not Ian. His urbanity was sliding off him like oil off a mirror. I was beginning to see the raw man underneath.

"I'll settle the little bitch," he fumed. "She's not going to get away with this. Give me the Alperton address. I'm going to buy that house."

"You're what?"

"She's going to find herself well and truly shafted if she thinks she can buy that house with my money. I'll buy it over her head."

"Ian, there are a lot of houses," I said. "If you do that she'll just get another one."

"She's a fucking tart," he muttered. I could see he had taken my point.

"Are you going to stop seeing her, then?"

"No, I'm going to get her into serious trouble. It's only a matter of time."

So she went on sleeping with him for money, and I went on watching the Ealing house. I was beginning to see why Tony had made a diplomatic exit. Making Ian pay me for those hours of boredom was like getting blood out of a stone, only more embarrassing. Whenever he finally shut his eyes, gritted his teeth and signed a check, he wanted me to come to his house to receive it in person and listen to another tape. They were all the same: sounds of ecstasy as performed nightly by pros everywhere. In the end I said, "You're really not impressing me, Ian."

"Just you listen to this." He spun the tape forward. She told him she wanted a thousand pounds to buy a mink coat. He asked her why it was so cheap and she said it was stolen. She knew the bloke who had done it. She had a load of them at her Mum's apartment in Willesden.

The following day she called Ian to tell him she had crashed the XJ6 on the way back to his apartment. I checked that and found that she had actually had the accident near Ealing, at 6 AM. Hunter had been a passenger in her car.

Ian spat vitriol as before, but still refused to stop seeing her. It was as if she provided the drama he needed. She gave him an emotional fix. He now insisted that I should have her prosecuted for receiving stolen goods. He was a hypocrite. I knew he had made a fraudulent insurance claim the year before. I had once admired his watch, and he boasted that he had claimed to have been tied up and robbed in his own house and the insurance company had paid compensation for stacks of stuff he still owned.

I knew I had to do something, if the apartment in Willesden was a stash for the proceeds of burglaries, but the way Ian kept on at me to get the girl arrested made me sick. Behind all his front, he had the mind-set of a petty crook. He called me every day. She had said this, she had said that, when were the police going to raid the house? By Christmas all I cared about was getting paid and getting out of the job.

I went with the police on the Willesden raid. She was taken to the police station and bailed for further investigations. On Christmas Day, Ian called me from the ocean liner, the QE2, where he was on a cruise, to ask whether she had been arrested yet. She had not been charged yet, because she told the police that Ian had given her the fur coat, but he was going to have to make his own decision about whether or not to back up that story.

"Leave that with me," he said." "I've got another little favor I'd like to ask of you, Jacquie. You know I told you I was once married. Well, my ex-wife has got a boyfriend. I don't like the man. He is not good for her, you understand me, don't you? I want you to have him arrested for drinking and driving."

His spite was unbelievable. I felt tainted. He was making me feel like an accomplice, not an employee. I did not mind having somebody arrested for dishonesty, but I was not in the business of wrecking people's lives.

After endless nagging, I received his final check and deposited it, avoiding taking his calls until it cleared the bank. When he contacted me at my mum's house, with some new plan for making "the Young Lady" suffer, I said I was busy on another job.

"I'll make it worth your while."

"Sorry, Ian. No."

"You're making a big mistake, Jacquie."

I lost my patience. "For Christ's sake, give it a rest, Ian. She's a cheap hooker living with a drug dealer; you pay her for sex, what the hell do you expect?"

I was away working when he started leaving messages. My mum was always calm, she never asked me what I did or showed any sign of worrying about it, and I found that very supportive. But I was outraged when she took a call from Ian.

"Tell Jacquie not to back me into a corner. She won't like what I'll do."

"Are you threatening my daughter?" Mum said.

"Just tell her," he said, and rang off.

Ambulances started arriving. They had been ordered by a caller in the West End. I finished the job I was doing and called my mum to tell her I was on my way home.

"I've just had another ambulance here," she said. "They were looking for somebody at this address who's had a heart attack."

She had been through the real thing with dad. I was furious. I called Ian and left a message on his machine. "If I hear that one more pizza delivery, one more minicab, or one more ambulance has arrived at my mum's house, somebody'll get a phone call. And they'll be told exactly what allegedly stolen goods were still in your house last time I looked. Do not threaten my mum."

He was a nasty, vindictive little man. You can choose your clients, but most of the time, you don't know if you are working for the wrong side until it's too late.

I HAD NOT TAKEN A WEEKEND OFF THE CIRCUIT FOR OVER EIGHTEEN
months. It was nearly all undercover work in lowly jobs, counter-
industrial espionage or working out who had their hands in the till.

People who do menial jobs are often in the best position to see
fiddles going on. Managers credit you with all the powers of observation of a potted plant. They treat you as a commodity, "the girl" who
posts the mail and washes the glasses. They assume you are thick. The
workers assume you would go, "on the fiddle," given half a chance.
After all, you are in the same badly-paid boat as them, and they would.
They like to use the quaint English slang expression, somehow
"fiddling" does not sound as bad as stealing or cheating, but it is still the
same thing in my book. But anyway, one way or another, everybody
reveals their secrets.

Through 1985 and 1986, I lived under different names, with
different background stories, without a break. Most people who go
undercover take time off between jobs. I did not. There was so much
work for a woman. Anyway, I had nothing else — no husband, not even
my dog anymore. My sisters were housewives and had never shown the
slightest interest in what I did. We did not have much in common. Mum
was busy with the Women's Institute, the Spiritualist church, and her
own circle of friends. I enjoyed seeing my own friends, but I was never

quite ready to, at the end of a job. I felt I should wind down first, and get back into my own personality, but there was no time because I always had to write up the report and open the folder on the next case.

"That's Beryl. You don't want to get on the wrong side of her." A thin girl of my own age was pointing out the other members of staff. We all wore blue serge overalls and sat at island cash registers in a big airy store beside racks of paint and wallpaper. It was the autumn of 1986, and home buying was reaching frenzy. All the home improvement chains were making money. Even so, one of them, a family-owned operation with a hundred "shed" outlets (called that because the stores were like giant sheds on retail parks) in the southeast of England was seeing a loss every month at its store in Lewisham. I attended a crash course in operating their cash registers and appeared at the store one Monday morning as Jacquie, the new cashier.

"Is Beryl the fat one with gray hair?"

"Shurrup, she'll hear you."

Beryl, a hefty-looking matron, was barely able to squeeze behind her register. I had seen her staring at me when I arrived. She had been buttoning her overalls in the staff room, so I already knew she had gold chains looped across her ample chest under the blue serge.

There were about twenty of us: checkout girls, warehouse workers to log in the deliveries, and half a dozen assistants who were glorified shelf-fillers. The shop opened seven days a week from eight to six with a late night on Thursday and a complicated system of days and half-days off. We ran the place. There was a manager, but the two assistant managers were the only ones who came on the shop floor. The manager cowered in his office drinking mugs of sweet tea and filling in the time sheets.

Beryl was married to a policeman. You would hear, "Did you see Crimewatch last night? Seen your old man was on it—"

She made it clear with heavy hints that, as we say in England, he was "bent as a nine bob note." In the old pounds, shillings and pence currency, we only had a ten "bob" note, so you can imagine how honest her husband was! Nobody dared cross her. I was informed, after I had been there about a day, that she was a friend of the notorious London gangsters, the Krays. She loved letting you know it. The "Twins," as they were known, were in prison for good, in fact the mad one had, by that time, been committed to Broadmoor, a secure hospital for the criminally insane, but you would never have known. A whole industry had grown devoted to their violent exploits and somebody was making a film about them. Beryl would talk with grisly relish about Ronnie and Reggie cutting people up. She basked in the notoriety. You would think she had a face that made the entire Blind Beggar pub (the scene of one of their brutal murders) reel back in horror, the way she carried herself. The rest of the staff lived by what Beryl did and said.

So I was not surprised when not a week had passed before they showed me how to "fiddle" the cash register whenever Beryl's pals came in. They would take a thousand pounds' worth of goods; I would ring up a hundred. Then, I was offered meat from the butcher's shop next door. A bunch of them had a neat barter arrangement: steaks for cans of paint. I reported that one to the clients as well, but avoided getting involved because, although I told the other staff I lived in a room in Peckham, I was actually staying at the Clarendon Hotel on Blackheath and did not fancy traipsing through the foyer with bloody parcels of beef.

A surveillance team followed key staff to their homes and snooped around. Their houses were like little palaces. They had half the stock of the store, from unopened boxes of vinyl tiles in their potting sheds to planks of hardwood flooring stacked, ready to lay, in the garage.

None of what I saw in the first few weeks explained losses on the scale at which they were running. I had been told that takings for paint were particularly low. There was a stock check every Saturday and everything was more or less where it should have been, so staff theft was not the biggest problem, yet the figures were down. There was some scam here that I did not quite understand, and the clients were still mystified.

I was cautious, kept very quiet, and played a waiting game. Beryl was a bully, but conceited, and I was sure her big mouth would catch her out in the end. I made sure I reacted with the same awe and wonder as the rest of them when she said her old man would see the manager "sorted out" if he ever snitched on her. I could see she was busting to let me know how clever she was; it was only a matter of time.

I had been punching out barcodes for wallpaper, putty and paint-brushes for two months before Beryl graciously permitted one of the others to drop a word in my ear. It was a scam that eight of them were running: a couple of the warehousemen, some of the shelf-fillers and the checkout girls. Every Tuesday, a truckload of white and magnolia emulsion paint turned up. I used to see loads of it pass my checkout; it was cheap. It always sold out by Saturday. On Wednesday, the Dulux consignment arrived. This being Lewisham, where people will not pay top dollar for anything if they can help it, the high-quality Dulux brand never sold at all until the cheap stuff had gone. When the stock was checked on Saturday hardly any of the Dulux had been sold. On Sundays it began to go. However, the directors of the firm did not even know they were selling cheap paint, because it was all off the books — coming from a friend of Beryl's.

That explained a lot. The surveillance team took photographs of the paint delivery and, what with the loot in the houses, my own state-ments about fiddles on the cash register and the bartered steaks, and the evidence of the paint scam, the clients were keen to prosecute. I met with the local crime squad, and we discussed exactly when they would carry out simultaneous raids on the homes of the eight staff. I also explained, poker-faced, that they would find themselves face to face with Beryl's husband, a sergeant in the force. That was their problem. The date was fixed for the following Thursday.

I had been staying at the hotel in Blackheath for about six weeks and knew now that I would be leaving for home on the night of the raid, so I called my mum from a phone booth. It was a Thursday night: exactly seven days to go. I heard a number unobtainable tone, so I called my sister, who lived in Barnet as well. My sister said mum had become fed up with the phone ringing when she was trying to watch TV so she unplugged it.

"Could you pop down?" I said.

"What for? She's okay, don't worry."

"You only live five minutes down the road—"

"Jacquie, there's nothing wrong with mum. She's fine."

So I called again on Friday and Mum's phone was still unobtainable. I called my sister.

"Look, for God's sake, there is nothing wrong with mum. I'm going up there tomorrow, all right?"

On Saturday morning the store was just starting to get busy and most of the others were still having their first cup of coffee of the day in the staff room. I was at my checkout, but an assistant manager came out and took over, telling me to go to the phone in the staff room.

"Your brother-in-law's on the phone."

I went in and they all stared at me. Nobody had taken a call in the staff room in my time there. They were all puffing a final cigarette before going out on the floor of the shop, but lingered nearby to see what was wrong. Nobody said a word. I picked up the receiver.

"Hello, Jacquie, it's me." It was my handler from the agency.

"Hi, everything okay?"

"No. You probably can't talk right now. I've got bad news."

"Yeah?"

"Yes, I'm sorry to break this to you, love. Your mum's died."

"Oh," I said. I caught somebody's eye, fixed my gaze on the telephone, and absently took a cigarette one of them offered me. "Right. Right. Well, I can't do anything about that now."

"No, it's difficult. You know what to do then."

"Yeah. Fine. Thanks for telling me. Bye."

I put the phone down. Lit the cigarette. Kept my hand steady.

"What is it, Jack?"

"My sister's been taken to hospital. He wants me to go and see her on the way home."

One of the assistant managers said I had better go home early. I muttered agreement. I drove up to Barnet. The milkman had found her. Everybody was crying. The sister who had ignored me when I asked her to go check on mum could not look me in the eye.

It was a terrible weekend, and I had to go back undercover on Monday. The coroner's hearing revealed that mum had been dead since Thursday.

The next Thursday I left the hotel knowing that the raids were already in progress. Mum's cremation was the following day. Then I went back to work on another job.

A few months later, it was Christmas. I was fighting with my sisters all the time. Mum had been the one person still alive I could trust; in the last year I had only seen her between jobs, and there had been too many jobs.

If you asked me what my name was, or where I lived, I hardly knew. I had spent so much time being different people, in different parts of the country, that I was a wreck. At the time I blamed the agency I worked for, because they continually sent me off on new assignments. I see now that I could have refused, taken time off whether they liked it or not, but it was years before I understood that, and understood why in those days I compulsively took everything they threw at me.

All I knew, by the New Year, was that I was no longer able to weep, even in private. I was a zombie — emotionally dead. My family were the only ones who saw even a part of the real me, and the part they saw was not very nice. I snapped at anyone who crossed me. I was even lying to them. It was as if nothing mattered. I was desperate, and I knew

I was cracking up.

I went to see my doctor. She told me to take a few weeks off and think about what I really wanted to do. It was the sort of advice I could have given myself, but I was so weakened by this time that I needed an authority figure to tell me. So I took a few weeks off. I turned down all requests from the Circuit.

And I applied for a job.

SHEERNESS IS DEAD FLAT, A LOW TOWN HUDDLED ON A VAST MUD bank at the mouth of the River Thames. So, even before I drove into it, I could see the Olau Line's M.V. *Britannia* in dock. She was 500-feet long and eight-stories high, a massive vessel designed to fulfill the task of luxury cruise ship and car ferry that sailed every other day from Sheerness to Vlissingen, in Holland, with up to two thousand passengers on board.

White paint sparkled, decks gleamed green, and portholes glinted in smart maritime style as I dashed up the gangplank through driving sleet. Six of us had been called back, after preliminary interviews, for the ship's police force, to make a cross-channel trip on which we would find out more about the job. When we disembarked we would hand in our own written reports about how we thought security could be tightened up.

Olau ships sailed under the German flag, and under German law any ship above a certain size had to carry police officers who were also trained paramedics. The successful candidates would also sign a contract in Hamburg and become members of the Olau Schiffpolizei, the ship's police. The posts had been advertised to English speakers, through the *Police Review,* because forty-five percent of the passengers, and some of the crew, were English.

So we rolled off across the roaring January-lashed Channel to Vlissingen and back. A few days later, I heard that I was one of three applicants accepted. They liked the references supplied by all the Circuit agencies, but even more, they liked the fact that I had taken a walk around the ship at two in the morning and had noticed, as I pointed out acidly in my report, that the engine room was wide open to terrorist attack.

I did not tell them I had been violently seasick.

This was just what I wanted, travel and meeting the public and, above all, being myself again, a police officer. There was nothing to keep me in England anymore but I could not be happy without the adrenalin my work provided. I was good at law-keeping and, at this point, lived for it; a dangerous state of mind. If Olau had known how dangerous; they should probably have given the job to somebody else.

By now I knew that, for me, the pinnacle of achievement was never going to be reached by becoming commissioner of police or the longest-serving agent on the Circuit. I was a lot more desperate than that. The pinnacle for me was to risk my own life in the course of protecting somebody else's. I was not exactly looking for trouble, but very deep down I wanted something to happen. When I heard that blowsy Beryl from the home improvement store, having seen the prosecution's statements, had been shooting her mouth off about what the Kray twins were going to do to my face, I thought, *Oh yeah? Come and get me if you think you're hard enough.* Subconsciously I wanted to be a hero, or be in a shoot-out or engaged in some death-defying act of bravery. Since I believe in Spiritualism, a faith that makes worries about the temporal body pretty irrelevant, I have never been physically afraid. But now I was almost reckless.

If I were to survive with all limbs intact it would be largely because I was armed to the teeth. Aboard and on duty, German ship's police carry revolvers, stun guns and PR24 sidearm batons that are nearly two-feet long. The gun would be of precious little use where a bullet might ricochet, but the stun guns, which put a 60,000-volt charge through an offender and knock him to the floor, were used all the time.

Before I went onboard as an officer I was required to learn inter-national maritime law so that I would know piracy and mutiny when I saw them. I also learned some German law. My knowledge of the German language was slight, mostly phrases remembered from family camping vacations. I got by somehow, and the law seemed fair enough. I was particularly keen on the rule that said I could collect on-the-spot fines. "The more you argue, the bigger your fine will be." I could hear myself saying it already.

At twenty-eight, and with more police experience than my colleague, I was quickly promoted to sergeant. I was answerable only to the captain, a nice middle-aged German man who worked alternate fortnights with other captains. The officers were also German. The crew were mostly German and English and the receptionists, pursers, bar staff and so on who dealt with the public were Dutch, German or English. There were 120 of us working onboard. I found myself looking after a small multinational town. It was a small town in which, every weekend, many of the English visitors acted out the Oktoberfest beer drinking festival.

The crew greeted the arrival of a female police officer with deri-sion. On my first day I heard one of them sneer, "She'll last till Friday night when she gets her first smack in the gob." He was dead wrong. Physical fear was not one of my failings. I collected plenty of smacks in the gob — black eyes almost every weekend; my nose was broken five or six times in two years; I got broken fingers and was kicked black and blue. At first I suffered with bouts of seasickness, but I waded in there and made arrests.

The ship boasted several bars and restaurants, a sauna, a solarium and pool, a duty-free store, a playroom and nursery, a disco, a boutique and a casino. It was a nicely-decorated ship — a lot of money had been spent on the interior — it was efficiently and politely run, and the food was excellent. You would have thought all these facilities would be enough to keep most young English working-class males occupied for the nine hours it took to cross the English Channel. Not a bit of it. All they ever wanted to do was get a skinful of beer and start a fight.

I had been onboard about a month and was scribbling notes in the office when, at two o'clock on a Saturday morning, a couple of skinheads lurched in. They were slightly-slurred. (As opposed to vicious-drunk, staggering-drunk, puking-drunk or dead-drunk. I could already assess all these from half-a-deck's-length away.)

"'Ere, darlin'," said the bigger of the two. His forehead was wrinkled like a bulldog's and "c.u.t.h.e.r.e." was tattooed across his throat. "This bloke's just come in our cabin."

"He tried to touch Darren up," said his mate indignantly. "And he had a uniform on, didn't he?"

"Yeah, he'd a uniform on," confirmed Darren.

"Where did he go?" I asked.

"Dunno, do we, fucking pansy, he was feeling me up under me blankets, said they were looking for summat, didn't he? He just gone off."

"Well," I said carefully. "Looking at you two, I'm surprised he's still walking."

They were able to identify the man, who was a German purser. I had had a complaint about him before, so I took statements from them and the watch officer woke the captain. He agreed I should arrest the purser for indecent assault. The skinheads strutted about all puffed up with righteous indignation, the purser was quickly booted off the ship, and I found myself suddenly popular with the crew, who had disliked him. It did not last.

During the week, two of us were enough to police the ship. On weekends during the soccer season, there were always four and some-

times up to twenty police. Olau did their best to prevent soccer hooligans from coming aboard by the busload, but they were regularly
outmaneuvered. Hundreds of pig-faced, drunken louts created mayhem
most weekends from October to May. As police, we were always
outnumbered and abused, but we dealt with them. If necessary we
drafted in a support team of officers who were lowered to the deck from
a helicopter off the Belgian coast.

Besides the usual run of Friday-night fights, I had to deal with
hookers, pedophiles, illegal immigrant rackets, porn smugglers,
suicides, attempted rapes and at least one stabbing. But, what the hell,
I had wanted to meet the public. I had just begun to suspect that there
was a drug-smuggling racket going on among the crew, and was
thinking about how to tackle it, when a ferry like our own, the *Herald
of Free Enterprise,* keeled right over on its way out of Zeebrugge
Harbor in Belgium and hundreds of people died. The skies were full of
news helicopters taking aerial shots, and for the first few weeks the
Britannia played host to ghouls making day trips to see the flooded ship
lying in the Channel. An eerie shell, the *Herald* was salvaged and
towed into Vlissingen within a month.

The public were appalled by the way the accident had happened:
the ferry flooded and capsized because the bow doors to the car deck
were open. This was against maritime regulations but had become unre-
markable. Turnaround times for a ship in dock are extremely tight. In a
few hours they have to offload two thousand people and their cars, plus
dozens of eighteen-wheelers, and get another couple of thousand on
board. Every member of the crew has to work flat out to make this
happen. Unsurprisingly, it had become normal for some cross-Channel
ferries to shave minutes off the schedule by sailing out of port before
the bow doors were fully shut. The *Herald,* like the others, was a tall
ship and unstable if a big wave crashed in and started heaving the vessel
from side to side. A heavy sea had surged so far over onto the exposed
car deck that the whole tower, the cars, the container trucks, the decks

and bars and restaurants, mums, dads, children and crew keeled over into the icy Channel.

The crew of the *Britannia* were gutted. Nearly all the English crewmembers were from Sheerness or Dover or one of the other English coastal ports, and had lost a relation traveling as passenger or crew. They came from a close community of small towns, full of people who were only a generation or two away from the East End of London, and if you did not have a dead brother-in-law, or wife's cousin on the *Herald,* you were a rarity. The accident cast a pall of gloom over everybody.

The maritime authorities saw with hindsight that what happened on the *Herald* could have happened on many cross-channel car ferries, so safety procedures were suddenly enforced with zeal. Ships no longer pulled out of harbor with bow doors open, diamond-tipped hammers became standard equipment so that porthole glass could be broken in an emergency, and crews rehearsed lifeboat drills until they could launch boatloads of people into the water within minutes.

We had all drawn together, over the week or two during which the disaster was headline news. Maybe that was why a seaman stopped me one afternoon as I was leaving my cabin and asked for a quiet word ashore.

We met one afternoon in a pub in Sheerness. I had seen him on the ship. He was a fat little middle-aged cook with a ready smile under normal circumstances, but there was something on his mind. . . .

"Tell you what it is," he said awkwardly. "I don't want to grass nobody up, but if you see something you don't agree with you've got to speak out."

Large quantities of cannabis and cocaine were being smuggled onboard at Vlissingen and sold in England. He named two bar staff he knew were involved.

"I've got nothing against 'em," he said. "I've got nothing against 'em at all. I don't like drugs, that's all, and I can tell you there's more involved than just those lads."

"How many?"

"Maybe eight or nine. I couldn't tell you who. I'm telling you nothing, right? We never had this conversation. I just don't want my kids to get offered no gear, I don't agree with it at all."

I did not agree with it either, but I would need proof, and if at some stage I intended to arrest a large contingent of the catering staff on board I thought it might be a good idea to let the captain know. I resolved to tell him as soon as I could. As tomorrow night was Friday night, there would be plenty to report.

Early next morning at Vlissingen I stood watching the foot passengers trudge up the gangplank. I spotted a few I had seen before, but when a tall, good-looking fair man in a well-cut suit came up to me and said in a soft German accent, "You must be the new police officer?" I was so surprised that I just nodded and muttered yes, I was. I was surprised because I caught myself thinking, *Whooah, he's nice.* It had been a long time since I thought that about anybody, and I was overwhelmed.

But I quickly relegated lustful thoughts. It was Friday, and I had to try and get some kip before tonight: I needed to be wide-awake. I had only been aboard for a month or two, but I knew what to expect. We turned the ship around in Sheerness late on a Friday afternoon. Busloads of soccer shits would roll onto the car deck, already tanked up and roaring for the bars to be open as soon as we put to sea.

It was the same most Friday nights. The fights began at about midnight. I would start arresting people for assault and criminal damage and if they declined to come quietly, I would grimly knock them down with a stun gun. A typical hooligan would slide to the floor with his eyes open, I would flip him over, cuff him, drag him down to a cell and let him lie in his own mess. The 60,000-volt charge relaxes all the muscles, including the bowels. We would keep ten people in each of the two cells, and sometimes up to a hundred cuffed to the rails outside. The ones in the cells were hosed down with icy water at intervals through the night. I suspected that the crew enjoyed that part of it the most.

When the drunks woke up I fined them all their money. It is not possible to land on Dutch soil without a nominal sum for accommodation for every night of your stay, so, having confiscated their passports, and knowing they were potless, it was a simple matter to visit the Dutch Maritime Police on landing and have their passports stamped "deported." The hooligans, still in the cells, would travel straight back to England. Back in Sheerness, after the nice family passengers had disembarked, police vans would back up to the ship waiting to take the damp and shivering scum to the magistrates' court.

This particular Friday night, somebody had blackened both my eyes, and my nose swelled up and bled. I had not been in the job long, but long enough to recognize that I would have black eyes more often than not. It is odd, the effect of a uniform on a drunken English yob. After a certain number of pints you become the sexiest thing they have ever seen in a skirt. You approach them complete with badge, gun and severe uniform, and they are all glee and hands and, "Wahay! I could give you one, darlin'."

"If you've got one like this, come and see me," I used to say sweetly, whipping out my two-foot rubber truncheon. "Otherwise, sod off!"

This approach worked only during drinking hours. As soon as the bars shut they became less predictable. I once hauled a roaring, blood-covered sot out of a bar, cuffed him to the bed in the sickroom, and stitched up his face. His nose hung off sideways. I had just shut the door on him and turned into the narrow corridor outside when I came face to face with the four blokes who had beaten him up. They indicated their intention to get past me into the hospital room and finish what they started.

"Uh-huh. We can talk about this," I began, one hand on my radio and the other on my nightstick. I could see the uniform was going to have a negative effect, which is: if she's in uniform she's a cow. The four of them decided as one man to give me a good kicking. On the floor, curled up, you jam your finger on the radio button that transmits everything that's happening to fellow officers so that they will come down and get the bastards off you. They did and I survived. Uniforms do not reassure everybody, least of all the person who has to wear one.

So early this Saturday morning, with my suspicions about the crew newly confirmed, when I climbed all the way up to the bridge to hand in my sidearm at the end of my twelve-hour shift I was not feeling full of benevolent thoughts about humanity in general. Surly, would have been the word. First there had been cheating Tim, my husband. Then the professional thieves at Fields', then the greedy little toe rags with their miserable scams in industry, and now these oafs who broke my nose and vomited down my skirt. It was a normal weekend and I had made over eighty arrests since midnight. Did I like people? Hardly.

The bridge was a wide low room with inward-slanting windows revealing the black morning outside. The captain and senior officers sat on swivel chairs at a console winking with electronics. Conversation was intermittent, hushed and in German. I had to call the captain "master," it was the German custom. I was getting used to it; and this week the senior captain of the line was to be on duty. He turned when I came in.

"Good morning, Sergeant."

"Good morning, Master."

He was tall, he was fair, he was very good-looking and he was the dish who had approached me on the gangway. I almost felt a smile breaking out.

B UT YOUR EYES! YOU MUST GET TREATMENT."
"Oh, don't worry. It'll go down."
"But—"
"It's fine, really."

Thomas, the fair-haired captain, stared at me for a minute. "I've never had a woman before."

"You poor devil," I said.

"No. I mean — I mean, I have never had a woman police officer. You know what I mean," he said, grinning.

Lovely smile. Oh, crinkly eyes when he did that. I controlled my urge to beam back at him and handed him the arrest reports. As he locked away my .38 Smith & Wesson and ammunition I murmured, "There's something I need to talk to you about in private."

Early next morning, in brilliant sunlight under a huge blue sky, he drove me from the car park at Vlissingen dockyard to a fishing village ten minutes further north. Veere is a lovely place, cobbled, quaint and, at eight o'clock on a breezy Sunday, deserted. There was a coffee shop on the quay, one of those dark brown Dutch places that give you cheese and ham and toast for breakfast, but it did not open for another twenty minutes. We sat on the pebbled beach, and I told him what the cook had told me.

"I thought it might be so," he said. " I didn't know it was so big, though."

"It's on quite a scale. Do you think it's been going on for a while?"
"Maybe."

"But there was a police officer on board before me?"

"Ah, but a man."

"So?"

"I have known the two previous sergeants on this ship and both of them were making love to women from the crew. Both of them were married. That sort of thing makes a policeman vulnerable."

"Yes, I suppose it does." I agreed.

"Are you married?"

"No."

"Good." Thomas smiled.

As it happened, I was lying. I was, technically, still married, though separated. This may have been a factor when Olau Line gave me the job. As Thomas said, police officers onboard a ferry are even more vulnerable if they are married. They are working in an exciting atmosphere, with most people off the leash and looking for a good time. Affairs are not expected to last because circumstances will drag people apart. The ship's police live cheek by jowl with the crew; but the crew are suspicious as hell because ultimately the police officer is on the side of authority. He or she shares experiences with them, but will never be one of them. It is small wonder that, quite often, police onboard ship cannot stand the social isolation and "go native."

If you are a female working on the ferries, any male officer with limbs and features arranged in conventional alignment is the most practical catch. A man with authority can protect you. All the women onboard are repeatedly propositioned. They want to be known as the girlfriend of somebody high up in the hierarchy because then they will be left alone.

Having a lover on board also changes the police officer's attitude to the job. Policemen are, of course, more inclined to turn a blind eye to smuggling if it is tacitly understood that the crew will not tell his wife about the girlfriend. But there is also the dependence on social contact. Very often the lover is the one person the officer can talk to in a hostile community. People get possessive in those circumstances. They will compromise themselves rather than lose their lover.

Watching and listening to Thomas, as we talked in the coffee shop and walked around the village, I was attracted by him, and I knew he felt the same way about me, two black eyes notwithstanding. But I was under no illusions. Thomas had good looks, status and oodles of charm. If I fell in love with him, he could very easily break my heart. I was not going to let that happen a third time. Under the spell of a man like this, I thought, I could screw up my job. That was not going to happen either.

"So, about these clowns and the illicit substances; I'm going to have to keep Special Branch informed."

"Jacquie, I am the captain of the ship, and I know how to do my job; and you are a police person and you know how to do your job — come and see me when you have got all your evidence, and I will back you up."

"Okay."

"I mean that for everything. You police the ship; I won't interfere. I drive; you don't interfere. And we'll be fine. Tell me about yourself, how is it you are here?"

I told him about working undercover and how I felt I had burned out, how I had almost forgotten who I really was and wanted to go back to meeting the public. He looked wryly at my bruised face.

"But not meeting like last night."

Thomas was forty-one and lived in Düsseldorf. He had entered into a marriage of convenience to an Indian woman who wanted her parents to believe she was the devoted wife of a German sea captain. (She actually lived with an Indian businessman her parents knew, and disliked, in Dortmund.) Her father was a senior civil servant in New Delhi, and he and her mother came to stay for two weeks in Düsseldorf every year. Thomas stayed with his wife for the duration and together they played Captain and Mrs. "Happy Couple."

Before this there had been a first wife and a divorce. He was on good terms with her, and their two children who were now at university. They also lived in another part of Germany. As a young man, Thomas had been a refugee from East Berlin. His mother still lived there. His father's life had been a tragedy: he had worked in the salt mines of the east right through the Second World War. On his return in 1945, Thomas was born, an only child. By now the little family was trapped in the poverty of East Berlin, cut off from the western world by that cruel concrete wall. Thomas and his father had talked about getting out. His mother was nervous. At fourteen, Thomas had made his way to a Baltic seaport and stowed away. A tall, strong boy, he found work as a sailor and survived. Eventually his father had made a break for it. He was shot dead as he climbed the wall that divided Berlin.

I had not dated anybody since my marriage ended three years before. I had not given myself time; I was always working. Also, nobody had been anywhere near good enough. If a man appeared he would have to be riding on the bridge of a very tall cruise ship or I would not notice him. Now my dreamboat had sailed into harbor, I was being wooed, and I was flirting right back. Every morning we met, either on the boat or ashore, and had coffee. Thomas showed me the countryside and the little towns and ports around Vlissingen. People smiled at us; Holland glittered proudly with crimson tulips and aquamarine and white paint in the spring sunshine, and we were absorbed in each other.

"Only another four days. I have to go off duty on Friday," he said sadly. We were sitting on the beach in deckchairs; we were never far from the sea he loved so much. The sun warmed my face. We gazed at the long white yachts moored in the harbor.

"Maybe I should stow away on a yacht," I said dreamily. "Sail somewhere warm and exotic."

"The Caribbean. Have you been there?"

"No. Have you?"

"Many times. In a few years I shall work there."

"Tell me."

"Tell me first how you will stow away."

"I'm talking to an expert. You tell me," I said.

"I don't think it's right for you. I don't think you are the stowaway type. A hijack would be more your style. Piracy. With drama and gunfire. You could leap onto the yacht with a black scarf over your face and frighten the captain. He would put his hands up at once."

"But you've got to come onboard, too."

"Of course. Smoking my pipe. I am the calm one. I shall take the controls after you have stolen the boat."

"And where shall we go?"

"I think a little detour to the Mediterranean first."

"Cannes, maybe. Or Monte Carlo. We'll break the bank."

We planned our escape. We went round the world together, sitting on that beach in Vlissingen, and when it was time to leave and go back to work we both felt utterly happy in one another's company. We always left the ship and returned to it separately. This time I headed for the *Britannia* before him. He grabbed my hand as I stood on the beach dusting sand off my skirt.

"I forgot, it wouldn't work, Jacquie," he said, smiling up at me from his deckchair. "You would be seasick."

That night I bought a card at the ship's shop and slipped it under his cabin door. "Thank you," I wrote. "I have had two wonderful weeks and you have been so kind. Do you know a cure for seasickness?"

The next day, a little note invited me to come to lunch in Thomas's cabin. It seemed he knew just the cure I needed.

Our affair was a secret. The crew would have made all sorts of capital out of it, had they known, and with a very few exceptions they never did. I did not socialize with them; I talked to the girls in the duty-free store and the beauticians and the hairdressers, but for the most part I ate in the officers' mess rather than the crew mess. I did not know how the English sailors thought I spent my spare time. If they discussed it at all they probably told each other that any woman who was willing to risk getting her teeth knocked out twice a week was probably a dyke or a masochist or both. The truth was, before I met Thomas I was aggressive outside and depressed inside. And without the elation of those first months of the affair with him, I would have found the rest of that year very difficult, because, suddenly, things began to go wrong.

The cook, my informant, met me again at Sheerness. He now knew to within a week when a large consignment of cannabis was due to come onboard. He knew who was picking it up, where it was going to be stashed and who would take it off the ship at Sheerness. What he could not say exactly was when it would come aboard. He would know very soon, but I would not be around for him to tell me. I had to appear as a witness at Maidstone Crown Court and would be on shore for five days. I told him that Craig, a colleague who had been appointed soon after me, would be told what was going on. As soon as the cook had reliable information he should speak to Craig.

I put Craig in the picture. I had not told him anything before because until action had to be taken, there was no point. He was a color-less character, but efficient enough. Then I left the ship.

Five days later, when I walked up the gangplank at Sheerness, I knew something was wrong. I stopped a man I knew on his way to the car deck.

"Where's Craig?"

He shrugged and hurried on without meeting my eye. The chief purser, a Dutchman, saw me before I reached my cabin.

"Jacquie, I think we may have a problem." He guided me into a corner. Passengers were pouring up the stairs between decks making considerable noise.

"Craig is not with us anymore. Captain Harman has sacked him."

"He what?"

"For his own protection. On Tuesday night Craig started drinking."

"He doesn't drink."

"Oh, doesn't he? Believe me, once he starts he does not stop. He got blind drunk. Rat-arsed," he added firmly, in case I had missed the point.

"And?"

"And he told Derek, the English barman, that you had told him Derek was smuggling drugs. Captain Harman has also got rid of one of the cooks. The English are talking about nothing else. Derek is still here but . . . I don't think you are very popular."

Oh. Right. I got to my cabin at last, opened the door of my wardrobe and found all my uniforms dripping with engine oil. My bed was full of cut grass. Odd to think somebody had gone ashore, mown his lawn and returned with a bag full of clippings. I bet his wife thought it was Christmas, having her old man come home and mow the grass.

There had been eight conspirators in the pathetic little plot to smuggle hashish, and there were at least seventy English crew, but they were all on the same side when it came to treating me like shit. For the next three months, nobody except the Dutch receptionists and the German officers would speak to me. If I went into the crew mess to pick up a meal to eat in my cabin and put down my orange juice, later I would find salt in it; at other times I would turn just in time to catch somebody spitting on my food. At first I found the perpetual silence unnerving, but I did not resent it. I thought they were a sad bunch, imagining themselves loyal to a stupid code and too scared to step out of line.

Maybe I felt indifferent because Thomas and I were in love; we had our own life, which mattered much more to me than the crew's attitude. The only effect their vendetta had on me was that I hardly ever had shore leave. I was on duty more or less single-handed for about five months. Replacements for Craig quickly found out that when fights broke out in the bar, when thieves tried to rob cabins or drunks fell through doors at three in the morning and attempted to rape women passengers, nobody, not the cabin staff nor the cleaners, the barmen nor the lowliest of the sailors, would help. I would be trying to handcuff a man while another one took a swing at my nose and as I peered through the blood already coursing down my forehead the crew would all turn away. Police colleagues did not stay long.

IF I WAS PARANOID, IT WAS HARDLY SURPRISING, BUT ONLY SOMEBODY with Thomas's maturity could have put up with me in those months. I was in love with him, but I was determined to trust nobody, not even him. He said he loved me, so I had his background checked out: career history, bank details, credit references, everything. He seemed respectable enough, but I was convinced he must have a hidden agenda. After all, he was a man, and I knew what happened with men. Sooner or later they turned and attacked you. I was damn sure I was not going to let myself be trampled on again. And he worked on the ferries. I knew what temptations ferry crew were prone to — he could have been smuggling porn on a large scale, or drugs, or turning a blind eye to any of a hundred rackets that would making dating the ship's police officer a great idea.

It was not that anything in his behavior made me suspicious. Exactly the opposite. He was unfailingly kind. Too kind. My problem was that his affection made no sense. I could not believe it was real. When your lover sees you with a black eye nearly every week, your arms and legs covered in bruises, and you wear a plaster bandage on your nose the way other women wear sunglasses, it is easy to feel outclassed by the competition. As the captain of the ship, he could have made love to any of the glamorous women aboard — the croupiers were always dressed to the nines, for a start — or any rich, cultivated, beautiful creature he met on shore that might find herself attracted to a sea captain who had sailed the world. He met interesting women all the time. Why me?

You could say my self-esteem was shaky. I was certainly confused. Our passion for each other was growing. I had taken a house in Vlissingen, a sweet little town in those days with a windmill, cobbled streets and a boardwalk, and we spent as much time together as we could on shore as well as at sea. But there were still whole months during which we could not be together and I missed him. At such times, in self-defense, I deliberately made myself assume Thomas was insincere. If he could stand being away from me for a month, then I could stand life without him.

I could even clear up outstanding business. When I was back in London for a weekend, Tim rang me. He wanted to discuss divorce, he said. I told him I would think about it.

"Janine's gone to Spain for a week. I am at a loose end, can I buy you dinner?"

It was a nice dinner.

"D'you want to see where we live?" he asked.

"Sure," I said. "I'd like to see what I paid for."

It was a nice house. Boo was fine. The bedroom was okay. The bed was not, but worth it to have a good look around.

A week later, when Janine was due to return from Spain, I dropped her a line. I thought it was high time I said my piece to the woman who had slept in my bed while I was in hospital having a hysterectomy. *You've got a cream carpet in your bedroom,* I wrote, *and you keep your knickers in the top drawer by the window. Have a look behind the wardrobe. You'll find my name and address. I left it there last Saturday night when my husband was in the shower and I was putting my clothes on again. Funny, he's had so many women in that bed and he's still not much good, is he?*

I did not hear from Tim for a long time.

As the months passed, and Thomas and I stayed together as often as we could, he showed me it was possible to be gentle and tolerant without giving up your principles. I thought lawbreakers were contemptible, and I said so. I was unforgiving and censorious. He was not. He disliked anti-social behavior, he hated cruelty, but he taught me that not everyone operates to my standards and values.

"You shouldn't see everything in black and white," he said. "There are shades of gray."

He said sometimes people have to dump their ideals in order to survive. Knowing what his life must have been like when he was a boy sailor, I thought he must know what he was talking about and I listened to him. Also, I was impressed by the way he treated his crew. As a boy he had been victimized by a string of sadistic captains, and he was determined never to be unfair. Apart from anything else, he said, you do not often change people by unkindness, but you can sometimes make a difference if you show you trust them.

"And you should trust me," he said one night, as we lay in each other's arms in his cabin.

"You think I don't?"

"No, you don't. I've got a song I want you to listen to."

He rolled over and pushed a CD into the player with Billy Joel singing *An Innocent Man.* I listened to it, sleepily. All about a man whose girlfriend is angry at him for something he has not done.

"Well?" he said when the music stopped.

"Well what?"

"Don't you see? You've got to stop blaming me for what somebody else did to you."

I wanted to, I really did. I wanted to trust him. But I had been trapped before.

After the storm over Derek, the barman, the crew knew they could not turn me, but that did not change a thing about their attitude to the law. There was a hard core of lads from in and around the Isle of Sheppey, the vast mud bank Sheerness stands on, and as far as most of them were concerned you scraped every ounce of fat off a job on the ferries. There were so many scams going on, in and out of my line of sight that I could not begin to deal with all of them. I could walk into any pub on Sheppey and see two-liter bottles of vodka and cartons of cigarettes all marked duty-free, and I knew it had all come from the bonded store on the ship. But it was not my problem. Unless they started to take the piss by walking off the ship with stuff under my nose, I did not bother talking to the customs officers about it. I just kept on doing my job on board and let the excise men worry about the rest.

Eventually people started talking to me again. I sat with a female crew member for twenty-four hours feeding her fluids while she had a bad attack of gastroenteritis, and people came round a bit. Then a barman suffered a twisted gut and had to be taken off the ship to Holland by helicopter, and I gave his wife and kids the keys to my house in Vlissingen. After that we were almost back to normal. In fact, within a year of my starting the job, I was getting messages from local villains via the crew, which was progress of a kind.

"Jim drinks wiv me bruvver an' 'e says to tell you if he ever sees you again, you're dead."

"You don't say. And, would you credit it, I'm still here. Is it that hard to come and find me?"

If I got the chance I would go up to these idiots in the courthouse when they were shuffling, booted and suited, clean collars biting into their thick necks, in a huddle with their lawyers waiting for the magistrates to call them.

"I believe you've made a threat against my life. Is that correct?"

A fleeting look of panic shot across from the lawyer, every time. Their clients could be done for threatening witnesses if they rose to the bait. They never did. They were all mouth with a rabble around them, but scared little boys on their own.

Olau Line went to a lot of trouble to distract the British on vacation from beating the living shit out of each other. As soon as passengers came onboard, they were plied with invitations to dance in the disco or recline in the hot tub or lose their money playing blackjack. Most weeks in high season there were live bands. The trip from Sheerness to Vlissingen was not long, but it was more than just an interlude on a journey; it was an outing. Even the staff at Buckingham Palace get outings.

One day I was watching passengers come up the gangplank when a man broke away from a party of visitors and introduced himself as an officer of the Royalty Protection Group. He was here with some maids and footmen of the Royal Household, off to Europe on a "jolly." He said if I needed any help I must call him. I thought that was nice of him, especially since it promised to be a fairly rough Friday.

We had a live band playing in one of the bars that night, and I saw one of the royal maids, a pretty blond of about twenty, hanging around the drummer all evening. She must definitely have had a thing about older men. They were just the right kind of band to have playing on a family outing, but they were not exactly babe magnets — they had been famous for about three weeks in the mid-sixties and the singer was going bald. What remained of his hair was scraped into a scruffy ponytail. I scrutinized him carefully because he had another girl at his feet, and she was even younger than the royal maid. I asked how old she was because I did not think she should be drinking alcohol, and she muttered that she was sixteen and it was only orange juice. Grandfather complex, I supposed, but that was her problem. He was lapping up the attention and leering down her blouse. *Maybe,* I thought, *she was a hooker.* If so there was not a lot I could do about it. Under German law I was to let hookers go about their business. They had to carry evidence of a recent medical check-up, and I could ask to see that, but that was all.

When the bar shut, I dealt with the usual run of fights and rowdyism through the small hours. By about four in the morning all the passengers were safely tucked up in a cabin, or in a cell sleeping it off. It was a warm night and I went outside, scanning the rail out of the corner of my eye. I hated seeing lone figures near the rail in the middle of the night. Plenty of people came onboard intending to plunge into the seething black water, and many succeeded. Only a few weeks before, I had spent four hours dissuading a bloke from Newcastle from making the final leap. He wanted to do it because of his credit card bills, he said. They were about half of what Tim's had been, but then Tim was not burdened by a conscience.

We tore through a calm summer sea, the engine's low thrumming constantly audible, other ships' lights glimmering in the distance across the Channel. I patrolled *C* deck, under the lifeboats, when a pale figure moved in the shadows and made a small moaning noise. I approached cautiously. *C* deck is far above the sea, but sheltered, with high metal walls that conceal dark corners popular with snogging couples.

The blonde maid from the royal party was shivering, weeping and cowering alone in a corner with not a stitch on. At once I tore off my jacket, put it around her and led her inside. She was staggering and reeked of vomit and booze.

"Wuz raped," she gasped.

Here was my nightmare. A member of the queen's household raped onboard the *Britannia*. And she was so very, very drunk.

"Who? Where?"

"Dunno." She lurched on her feet, slumping sideways and rolling into the sides of the corridor.

"Okay," I said slowly, thinking, *Oh Christ, newspapers, official enquiries* . . . "First I'm going to take you to the hospital cabin."

In the sick bay I gave her a white sleeping gown, and she fell into the bunk dead asleep. That was the best thing she could have done. I wanted her to sleep it off before I could get a statement out of her, and the ship would have to dock before I could get a doctor on board to take swabs.

It was now a quarter to five. This was going to be a very long day. I had to marshal my thoughts. I had to eat, because I would not get another chance. I could smell bacon and coffee wafting from the cafeteria. That would be a good start. One of the waiters called to me on the stairs.

"Cooee, Jacquie. Can I have a word, dear?"

"Sure."

He skipped over to me. "I think I'd better tell you this. There's a girl's clothes in my cabin."

Despite the situation I could not help grinning, "There are? Have you been trying on this season's fashions?"

"No. But you may well wonder — I went out on deck for a ciggie at about three this morning and there was this girl, crying drunk, wandering about. She kept pawing my arm and saying she was lost, she didn't know where she was, so to cut a long story short I couldn't leave her on her own, I thought to be on the safe side, I'd put her in my cabin to sleep it off. So she comes in and we take her dress off and she flops into the bottom bunk. I'm in the top one, and as far as I know she's asleep. And I wake up with the lark this morning, and she's gone! But the dress is still in a heap on my floor and so's her bra, handbag, everything. So where is she? The vanishing lady?"

"What did she look like?"

"A very pretty blonde."

"Short, tall, long hair or short?"

"Average height, about twenty, you know, bobbed hair. And all I can say, darling, is if I was a girl I'd be jealous of that figure."

He pursed his lips and put his finger against his cheek. Sex with a woman simply was not on his agenda; he was gay as ninepence, there was no way he was the rapist. A horrible progression of events trooped across my mind's eye.

"Is there any ID in the bag?"

"Nothing, only a purse with about three quid in it and a lipstick. But James thinks he saw the girl last night after the bars shut. You really should talk to him."

James, a cook looking half asleep, fried bacon and talked. "There was a blonde in the corridor necking with that drummer from the band. Then she went into his cabin with him. They sort of fell in there when I came past, and then they shut the door. They was both giggling."

In two minutes, swallowing the last of my bacon sandwich, I was banging on the drummer's cabin door. He opened it, bleary-eyed, and I told him to get dressed. I arrested him and escorted him in handcuffs down to the cell. He looked stunned.

"I never touched her," he kept saying.

It was five-thirty now and, with Julia the maid in hospital and Ron the drummer in the cell, it was time to inform the Royal Protection Group officer. I ran up to the bridge to let Thomas know what was going on and then, my heart sinking, went to wake Alasdair from the RPG.

An hour later, with Vlissingen and its neat houses twinkling half a mile away, Alasdair and I took Julia some coffee. By a quarter to seven the ship was making those slow shifting movements that tell you it's nosing into dock. We could still get no sense out of her. She was completely incoherent. I left Alasdair in the hospital cabin and was first off the ship. I ran across the dockyard to the office of the Dutch Maritime Police.

"Gotta make a phone call."

I told Special Branch at Sheerness what had happened. "I'm getting a doctor to take swabs from her."

The Special Branch officer in England sounded as if the sky had fallen in. "Don't envy you this one, Jacquie."

As I went back onboard the first passengers were disembarking. I poured more coffee and took it down to Alasdair. Julia was sitting up now, crouched on the hospital bunk hugging her knees in the white smock. She was slurred but comprehensible.

"Can you talk?"

"Sorry. So sorry. I'm really sorry. I went to Ron's cabin with him. I jus' need my clothes. That's all."

"Did he rape you?"

"No. Nobody raped me. He never raped me."

"So what happened?"

"Only remember bits. I remember going to his cabin and lying down. I wanted to go to the toilet. So I went in there. Then I was on deck."

"Did you have sexual intercourse?"

"No. I'd got my dress on."

"Were you fully clothed?"

"Yes, yes, I'd got my dress on. Then I went to the loo."

The door from each cabin's bathroom opened in such a way that a disoriented person could easily find themselves in the corridor. Drunks were always doing it. This was probably what had happened, twice, to Julia.

"And?"

"I was on the deck . . . then somebody helped me get my dress off, then I was back outside on the deck with no clothes on. Where are my clothes? I don't know what happened — and you put me in here. You gave me this to wear. That's all I know."

The whole sequence dropped into place: She had fallen into Ron's cabin with him; he was probably too drunk to take advantage of her anyway and had most likely passed out. She had staggered to the toilet, and then pitched out into the corridor thanks to the tricky door fitted to the bathroom. Lost and confused, she had blundered around until rescued by the kindly gay waiter. In his cabin, in her drunken state, she had finished undressing, fallen asleep until woken by the demands of her overworked bladder, then repeated the same performance with the bathroom door, but this time she staggered out on deck stark naked. That is when I found her. If the consequences had not been so potentially serious it would have been downright comical.

I gave her a piece of my mind. "Do you have any idea how much trouble you've caused with your drinking?"

I phoned Special Branch again — panic over. I released the

drummer from the cell, which he had shared for two hours with a farting, snoring drunk, and apologized to him. He was quite reasonable about it, seemed to understand my predicament perfectly and was more relieved than anything else. I felt much the same. I left Alasdair to worry over Julia, who was by now sniveling about how she did not want to lose her job, and went to my office. My head still buzzed from all the coffee. One of the receptionists dropped by with some lost property: a pair of trousers somebody had found in the corridor. I logged them in the book along with the rest of the night's paperwork and crawled into bed at ten in the morning.

It seemed like only minutes later that somebody was banging on my door.

"Yeah?"

"There's a bloke down at the police office. Say's he's got to see you before we go home."

I peered out of my porthole on *B* deck. Vlissingen was still down there. It was 11:15 and we were leaving at twelve. I showered, dragged a comb through my hair and went downstairs in uniform.

Mike, the balding singer from the band, was hanging about outside the police office looking agitated. I unlocked the door and let him in.

"I've had two grand in cash stolen out of my cabin," he burst out.

"Was anybody in your cabin other than you?"

He looked shifty. "No."

"Where were you keeping the money?"

"It was in my trouser pocket. I can't find my trousers either."

"Right." I took the lost property out of the desk drawer. "Gray trousers labeled Austin Reed, waist size 38?"

"Yeah. That's them. Is my wallet in there?"

"Your wallet was in a pocket. Brown leather wallet, empty."

"Shit."

"So what's the story?"

"Eh? Well, I want somebody nicked for this. It's a lot of money. It's two thousand pounds."

I took his passport. He was fifty years old. He began to make a statement but I stopped him and said, "Are you married?"

"Yeah."

"You had that girl in your cabin last night, didn't you?"

"What girl?"

"Mike, I'm tired. Short, dark, jailbait — that girl."

"Well, it happens."

"And you had your trousers off."

"So?"

"So I'd say she nicked your two grand and dumped your trousers and got off the ship this morning, wouldn't you? I don't think there's a lot I can do to get your money back."

"You can't let her get away with that."

"All right. Let's say I make a full investigation. Police time and money in two countries. It goes to court. Witness statements. Medical reports. Press coverage. At the very least, correspondence sent to your home address. One way or another your wife is going to find out that you had a sixteen-year-old girl in your cabin."

He looked thoughtful. I could see he was coming around to my way of thinking.

"Give it a rest, Mike. Just call it the most expensive shag you ever had."

THOMAS AND I HAD TO SNATCH TIME TOGETHER AS IF WE WERE both married to somebody else. In a sense we were; we were both married to our work. These days I did not feel the sort of death wish that had made me undertake a violent job in the first place, but I was still getting a lot of satisfaction from policing the *Britannia*. And Thomas lived to go to sea.

When we got time ashore we always had too many things to talk about and places we wanted to go. We even took pleasure in the domestic chores like shopping for food. When he had to spend the annual two weeks in his apartment in Düsseldorf with his Indian wife and her parents, I knew I would not want to stay on my own in Vlissingen. I drove down to Marbella in Spain to see some friends.

Two weeks later, I was on my way back. I drove the convertible I had brought from England; the weather was balmy and little towns in the north of Spain slumbered through a late afternoon siesta in golden sunshine. As the car climbed toward the Pyrenees and I breezed along with warm herb-scented wind on my face and rock music on the radio, it occurred to me that I had not been so happy since before Mum and Dad died. I was going back to Thomas, and wherever he was seemed like home. I had not felt since Mum died that I had a home anywhere;

now I did. My rented house in Vlissingen was ordinary enough. It was Thomas's attitude to living in it that was a revelation to me. I took housewifery seriously. I was the sort who had to have matching side plates and no balls of dust under the washing machine. Whenever Thomas caught me wiping a work surface he grabbed me around the waist and said I should stop wasting time and come to bed.

"But these things matter," I said one day. I was worried. I had proudly produced a mug tree after a shopping expedition and he got the giggles.

"Jacquie, you don't need all this stuff. We do not need a life full of coffee mugs. We don't need ionisers or hair dryers or any of it." (I had recently bought these items for the house.) "If we have each other all we need is a tent on the beach."

I was starting to see life his way. It left so much more time for making love, for a start. I had probably gotten a soppy smile on my face as I drove along thinking about this, or maybe it was the British license plates, but for whatever reason, when I rounded the next bend on the mountain road a policeman appeared out of nowhere and flagged me down.

There was a turn out just ahead, with a Guardia Civil van parked in it, on the edge of a drop to a green valley below. I pulled up behind the van, quietly swearing. It was dusk already, and I wanted to cross the border before dark. I still had sixty miles to go. I had been pulled up by these types in Spain before and held in a time-wasting bureaucratic tangle. In fact, because I spoke no Spanish, I had once been conned into paying sixty quid for a non-existent traffic offense. (I was still bewildered when a Spanish-speaking friend later read the ticket that said I had been going up a mountainside in second gear.) And then there were girlfriends' horror stories: rape at the police station, when they had gone there to report a rape, for instance. But you never really believed it. At the end of the day, the Guardia were policemen.

This one was fortyish, clean-shaven, and he wore his black hair a little too long. I watched in the rearview mirror as he approached my car from behind. There were only a few feet of gravel between my driver's door and the drop to the valley. He stood on the edge of the precipice, under the mauve evening sky.

"Get out. Out!" he said, stabbing his baton in the air. Pathetic. As I got out another policeman appeared. Hatless and gaunt, he leaned on the back doors of the van to watch.

I turned my back on him and faced the first one with professional severity. "Is there a problem?"

"You go too fast."

"No, I don't. I am a police officer."

I heard the gaunt driver creeping up behind me. This was all wrong. By now I should be getting asked for ID, passport, car documents.

"You. Stand here. You are bad girl."

I felt a finger on the back of my neck. The bastard was playing with my hair. I shook my head angrily, and they both laughed. The one in front said something with a snigger to the one toying with my hair. Footsteps crunched. I heard the van's suspension creak as he climbed back in.

The man in front of me was armed. I decided to leave and made a tiny movement in the direction of my car, but he suddenly grabbed my arm, hard. His left hand dropped to the holster of his gun.

"There."

"What?"

"You go there." Gripping my arm he pulled me a couple of feet along the edge of the precipice until I stood at the back of the car. I glanced down. There was a thirty-foot drop to scrubby trees on a slope. He was pushing me to the ground, on my knees.

"Down."

Oh, I understood.

"You go down."

My goodness me, but that gun was a great persuader. I slid obediently to my knees with my hands behind my back. Except for the noise of my feet on the gravel there was not a sound. *Christ, but the other one could creep up with handcuffs.* I was listening desperately for the approach of a car. The man's fingers were on both my shoulders. Scuffling my feet around I knelt at right angles to the precipice. A kestrel soared through the cold valley sky behind him; and then the policeman was close to me, the felted cloth of his trousers smelling like warm parsnips. He unzipped his fly and stuck his erection in my face. I looked up at him. Not circumcised, yellowish and none too clean. I took a breath, took it in my mouth. His knees forced against my shoulders. His hands were around his dick. His eyes looked shut, from my viewpoint.

I might go over the edge. But I had nothing to lose. *They are not going to let me drive on after this.* I bared my teeth . . . and bit hard.

It was like snapping a big carrot. A wild scream rang out. I forced his legs sharply toward me at the knee and heaved. The scream pitched up as he disappeared. I saw the soles of his boots vanish. I scrambled to my feet, dashed to my car and, grabbing the heavy steering lock, tore around the van, yanked the driver's door open and swung the steel bar violently at his forehead. As he lunged at me I smashed his head hard between the door and the metal side. He slumped. I stretched past him, snatched the van keys, and ran to the edge of the precipice.

The ignition keys hurtled out over the valley, a tiny black arc in space. I drove like a maniac, the first few zigzag mountain miles without lights in the dusk, hoping that this would make it easier to hide. I scrabbled around in the back seat as I steered, trying to grab rolling cans of Coke to wash out my mouth.

The bastards. The policewoman part of me wanted to drive to the nearest police station and report them. I saw myself rushing in, distraught. "I've just bitten one of your bloke's knob off, and shoved him over a cliff!" That would go down well.

I would have to switch the headlamps on soon. It was sixty miles, well over an hour on these roads, to the border, and ahead of me were several towns big enough to have a police station. The creep in the van was probably only momentarily stunned. He might make a radio call within minutes. They would send out an army of Guardia Civil. I had seen what they were like when they had no quarrel with me; I could not bear to think how they would treat me if they had.

I made it, but did not stop until I was ten miles inside France. When I got back to Vlissingen, Thomas told me I should have shot them. I told him I would have if I had had a gun. I guessed I was in trouble enough in any case. For weeks afterward, I expected somebody to come and arrest me for murder. I would telephone English police friends in Marbella and casually interpose, "Umm . . . Nothing in the paper about Guardia Civil in the north of Spain, is there??

"No. What sort of thing?"

"Oh, you know. Accidents. Deaths."

"No-o. What have you been up to?"

"Nothing, just wondered."

I was convinced that somebody must have seen my car, with its British registration plates, and taken the number. I imagined how they would prove it had been me and realized with horror that they would do it from my teeth marks. As an ever more gruesome series of events unfolded in my imagination, the days passed, and, after a while, I dared to think that he must have survived the fall. If so, his wounds would have healed. He would be a whole man again.

He must have had a few awkward moments explaining his injury to his wife, but maybe this sort of thing was a regular occurrence in police marriages in Spain. I should not be at all surprised.

Tim called me. Again, he wanted to discuss a divorce. My letter to Janine had made it all the more important that he should be free to marry her, he said. I would have thought that Janine, having seen written proof that he routinely knocked off anything in a skirt crossing his field of vision, would have refused him at any price, but it seemed nothing short of matrimony would cement their love. He was welcome to a divorce. I told him I had no time to talk about the details on shore, but if he would like to bring a few mates for a free cross-Channel booze cruise we could meet for an hour. He was delighted with that idea, and so was I. I could have fun with it. The endless rivalry between police, Customs and Immigration at ports could be exploited if you knew how. The Customs at Sheerness had recently arrested an Immigration officer returning from Amsterdam with the trunk of his car stuffed with hard porn, and in their current frame of mind they would have searched Mother Theresa if they had even a whisker of a hint about a breath of suspicion. I told them that Tim, of the Territorial Support Group, would be bringing his car. It should be searched.

"How searched?" enquired my nice friend in the Customs office.

"Mmm . . . searched," I said.

I kept wandering into the Customs shed.

"But, I'm a police officer," I heard Tim protesting. He was standing helplessly by as they wrenched the passenger seat out. Later in the afternoon they had a sniffer dog nosing at the wheel arches, and next time I went in they had the engine on the floor.

I could not bear to look after that. It was all so greasy and dirty and they were under no obligation, of course, to put any of it back.

I was always wary when somebody went out of their way to be nice to me because, as a police officer, you get used to the idea that the public does not like you much. So, when a middle-aged man with a child approached me as I stood on the gangplank watching foot passengers embark at Sheerness, I did not know quite what to make of him. I had certainly seen him at least once before. He was tall, fair, slightly hunched over, with a London accent and held a small boy by the hand. He was a quiet little boy.

"My nephew," the man explained, but I was almost sure he had been with a different little boy the last time I had seen him. Three weeks later, I was certain. Again he greeted me, again he had a boy with him, and this time the boy was red-haired and freckled.

On the way back from Holland a fight broke out in the bar. The man was on his own, though I had seen him take the child down to a cabin earlier.

"I witnessed that fight," he said to me. I stared into his pale, eager eyes. He wanted me to like him. He wanted me to think he was a righteous citizen. He was trying too hard.

"Good, I'll take your statement," I said. "Come into the police office and bring your passport."

I copied down his details: Dennis Michael Harris, aged forty-five. When we berthed, I had Special Branch check him out. There was nothing in Criminal Records about him. I asked around, and one of the barmen said he had sold Harris alcoholic drinks that he had taken down to the cabin. He had shared the cabin with the nephew. Whether he had given the child anything to drink, of course, I had no way of knowing.

Next month Harris was back again with another child. As the *Britannia* rode out of the Thames estuary I spotted them in the line for cabin bookings.

"Hello, Jacquie," he smirked, glad to have the surrounding trippers see he was on familiar terms with the ship's police officer. I decided I needed to get the little boy alone to ask him what was going on.

"Hello," I smiled, and squatted on my heels next to the latest little nephew. He had a sweet face, freckles again and floppy hair. Harris glared at me.

"What's your name?"

"Paul."

"How old are you, Paul?"

"Ten."

"Are you having a nice time?"

The boy nodded.

"Do you want to come up to the bridge and meet the captain?"

"Yes, please." He beamed for the first time.

I took his hand and stood up.

"We're just going up to—"

"No, he's not going without me," snapped Harris. Suddenly agitated, he grabbed the boy's shoulder.

"But — don't be silly, we're only going to the—"

"No. I promised his mum I wouldn't let him out of my sight. Sorry."

"Suit yourself, " I murmured. "I'm sorry, Paul."

I had to do something. However, it was Friday night. The usual uproar commenced and hours slipped by. At about midnight as I hurried along a corridor the radio burst into life.

"The bar's gone up again!" I could hear screaming in the background. A bar steward raced toward me.

"One of your lot's getting beaten to a pulp in there."

I tore up a flight of stairs and was about to climb another, two at a time, when a middle-aged German woman seized my elbow.

"Yes?"

"There is a man in the elevator with a boy—"

"And?"

She was confused. She could not find the words. I could imagine the policeman upstairs having a broken glass shoved into his face while I stood there.

"The little boy. He's . . . he is—"

"I'll deal with it in a minute," I yelled, dashing upstairs.

When I got back to the spot an hour later, the woman was nowhere to be seen. But the following morning I saw the little boy. On deck with Harris, he looked petrified. He would not meet my eye when I spoke to him. They were going to disembark at Vlissingen together, however, and there was nothing I could do to stop them.

When we docked back at Sheerness I went to the Special Branch office. "I really need help with this," I pleaded. "I can't prove anything. I don't care if he hasn't got a record, there is something wrong. That boy was scared. He's not the first one either. He always takes them to Holland for two days and brings them back and they never have a word to say for themselves."

"Nothing you can do about it, love. No evidence. You should know that by now."

"Well, thanks for your tireless support, guys." Flabby bunch of useless piss artists, I thought, splashing angrily across the dockyard in the driving rain. As far as I was concerned, the Sheerness office was the elephant's graveyard of Special Branch.

Once I had bought myself lunch and got over my resentment I began to think constructively. I went to a phone booth and made an anonymous call, to the Child Support Unit of the Kent police.

Next day, in dock at Sheerness, there came a knock on the door of the *Britannia*'s police office. A man and woman introduced themselves as a detective inspector and a detective sergeant from the Child Support Unit.

"And how can I help you?" I asked.

"You made the phone call," the detective inspector said.

"Did I?"

"What do you want to tell us?"

"If I had called you I couldn't admit to it," I said. "I would have to go over the heads of Special Branch to do that. You know I could be in deep trouble."

I told them what I had seen. I had the child's name and address, from his own passport, and they interviewed him and his parents at home in Chatham.

Harris had met the boy's father in a pub about six weeks before. He was looking for lodgings and they offered him the living-room sofa until he found some. And then — and it happened this way every time, it had happened with all the boys — the bloke and his wife were arguing and Harris said, "Look, mate, you need some time on your own. I've got contacts on the ferries, I can get free tickets." (He could not, he paid.) "Why don't I take the kid away for a weekend?"

The Child Protection Unit interviewed the little boy. At first he said Harris had tickled his tummy; and then he told the truth, which was that he had been sexually assaulted in the cabin. Harris was a known pedophile. The records had somehow been mislaid. He had also been interviewed about the murder of a homosexual twenty-five years before.

I had to go to court to give the main evidence. The jury looked at me with utter contempt. I felt like a worm. I had made a split-second decision to sort out a fight instead of going to defend a child, and it had been the wrong decision. The prosecuting lawyer tore me apart; he was right.

I have to live with my mistake. Harris was sent down for two years in jail.

THE BAR HAD JUST SHUT, AND THERE WAS A FULL MOON. SIX OF them stood in a noisy group on *D* deck, all about twenty years old, all male, with a good few pints inside them. The seventh man was strung spread-eagled between them, slumped like a sagging wineskin and yelling his head off. They were clutching his ankles and wrists and swaying back and forth with the rocking of the boat, roaring, "We are sailing . . . We are SAILING . . . "

The seventh man swung around, his T-shirt riding up over his paunch, and they were hoisting him higher and higher toward the rail against the windy night. The Channel churned past sixty feet below.

I had dived off that deck twice as part of my training as a police officer and paramedic. Yet, I had dived into a calm harbor from a stationary vessel with no bother. Once out to sea, if you went over the *Britannia*'s side, night or day, you were fish food. If you survived the fall, the water temperature even in summer was so cold that you would be dead in eight minutes. The ship would have traveled about three miles before it could be slowed enough to turn back for you. Not that it would turn back. Nobody was ever seen going over — that was half the problem; we lost people over the side, but the first I would know about it would be when three or four hung-over white faces would announce when we docked, "Our mate's missing."

We lost a boy scout that way once. He was only eleven and disappeared around the time of the pedophile case. I was very upset. Dennis Michael Harris had made me depressed. Or maybe it was the fact that I had failed to help. Whatever the reason, it was the last straw. I was no longer happy in my work.

Of course it could have been something to do with being beaten up every weekend. I was getting sick and tired of having the same drunken yobs vomiting all over my uniform, doing things they thought were funny. Like grabbing one of their mates and threatening to chuck him overboard. And now here I was again, Friday night, grasping my radio, ordering the six of them to stop arsing about. I was near the stern of the ship, a cold wind ripped across the deck and it had just gone midnight. Other people hovered in little anxious knots of twos and threes.

"I'm a police officer. Put him down."

"Oh!"

They were giggling, they continued to lift him but when I shoved into the middle of the group with a baton they dropped him. I was close by them now, close by the rail, handcuffs at the ready. I spat a few choice and vehement words at the two ringleaders.

"We wouldn'a done nuffink."

One of them caught somebody's eye over my shoulder and sniggered. The other four moved behind me now, crowding me. A sixth sense told me what to expect. With a surge of anger I snapped the cuffs onto my wrist and the rail and turned to them with my thumb on the radio button, but I was too late. They had got me by the knees.

"Wo-aaAH!"

I was over the side. One hand grabbing the rail. Christ, but I wanted to let go that radio. But I resisted. I screamed into the transmitter. The cuff was holding, but my hand was sliding on the rail and my wrist felt like it was being cut. My legs dangled in space. *Christ . . . let that cuff hold.* Crewmen grabbed my arms and hauled me back on board. Oh and didn't those bastards get a few choice remarks.

Not long afterward, Thomas took me out to dinner. He knew I was growing increasingly fed up with the violence on board. Thomas himself now had the chance of the career move he had wanted for a long time. He could spend the winters as the captain of a cruise liner in the Caribbean, and summers sailing from Hamburg around the Baltic and Norway.

"I think it's time I left the ferries," he told me.

"I won't stay when you go," I said. "I think I've paid my dues on the *Britannia*."

"Come with me, Jacquie. We can do what we always said we would. We'll sail around the Caribbean together."

"You know I can't. What would I do?"

"Be a Hausfrau for a change."

We smiled at each other. It was impossible and we both knew it.

"I'm thirty-one. I'm too young to spend the rest of my life baking apple pie."

"What do you want to do?"

"I want to go back on the Circuit."

"I will never know where you are. They could send you anywhere."

"I don't want another job like this one, Thomas."

"I don't want you to have another job like this one. I hate to see it when you are hurt. I want you to be with me, where you are safe. The Circuit isn't safe; you get menaced by nasty people. Look at those criminals the Krays. You had threats."

"Most of the time I shall be sitting in a car following some boring businessman. It's a lot safer than the *Britannia*."

He sighed. Neither of us had any appetite, and our glasses of wine stood untouched.

"When will we see each other?"

"We can meet six or seven times a year. We can call each other, you know we can. I can come to you in the Caribbean. I've got to do this, Thomas. I can't stop working at thirty-one."

"But when will you stop? I want you to promise me. You must stop one day; we must be together all the time."

"Yes, I want to be with you all the time, too. But not until I'm ready, and I'm not ready yet. I've thought about it. I'll do five years on the Circuit, and then I will come to you for good."

"You promise me?"

"I promise."

A few months later I left, and so did he. When we gave up the house in Vlissingen I very nearly cried.

All the same, something in me returned to the Circuit with guilty delight, like a woman returning to a secret lover.

I had been only too right about sitting in cars. The first jobs I did were mainly surveillance. I like surveillance because, however well trained you are, there is usually something to learn. People's behavior is unpredictable, technology changes. And you are working in a team. Eight of us on to one target, more if there is a group to be watched. Everybody can do everybody else's job. Some are better at undercover work, some at desk-based investigation, some at bugging phones. All of us can do any one of these things if required. We are used to taking orders as well as giving them, and can judge when to take the initiative.

It's expensive. A team following a target in London is generally two or three cars, a cab, an observation vehicle (the obbo van) and a motorbike. I watched Roger Levitt, for example, a businessman who was on bail for allegedly defrauding various individuals of millions of pounds, though he was later acquitted. And a boring life he had too, stuck in his apartment in Maida Vale with nothing to do but pop out for a pint of milk and sign on at the local police station once a day. But we had a typical team: a couple of guys in a scruffy construction worker's van parked near his apartment, myself and a few other cars around the corner, and a cab that would conveniently appear if he wanted one. My job was to wait for a radio message that he had driven away in my direction. Then I would pick him up, stay a couple of cars behind, and see where he went.

A target might go to the airport. In the trunk I would have a bag packed. I would have my passport with me. Other cars would follow in formation, taking over from each other at intervals. When you first do surveillance, the least hint of a dodge and you think the target is on to you. They never are. Partly, because they are intent on what they are doing. Mostly, it is because surveillance techniques have been honed over the years to be relatively unnoticable and pretty well foolproof.

You start from a point where you want to see, and often hear, everything the target is doing. Let's say you are putting the audio part in place. A phone can be bugged in various ways. You might have a hard-wire tap from the junction box in the street; there are people on the Circuit, as well as moonlighting telephone engineers, who do this. Or you have a scanner in a parked car or a room nearby, and a pair of head-phones, and you listen in to calls to and from the target's cell phone. Maybe the phone in the house or the hotel room has been bugged. Inserting the tiny bug is a purely mechanical job; simply a matter of gaining access in advance with the result being one can listen in from up to half a mile away. Then again you can leave a bug in almost any office without it being detected. One three-way electrical adaptor looks much the same as any other. Or you can replace a wall-socket, leaving a bug behind it. Let's say the target leaves his office and takes a cab. If you know — because you have been listening — that that is what he is going to do, then your own cab turns up. It has a microphone in the back seat, so he would be well advised not to entrust any confidences to a companion there.

If you spend enough time and money you can overhear just about anything, unless the target whispers into a confidant's ear in the middle of Dartmoor or a lead-lined room. The more money you spend, and the more advance warning you have of where people will be, the less likely it is that you will be flying blind in an investigation.

By "flying blind," I mean getting surprises. You do not always know by bugging or other means what a target is up to. You might be following somebody along a four-lane highway and suddenly they make a U-turn. Have they just remembered the central heating was left on and now they are going back to turn it off, or are they surveillance conscious?

Suspected drug dealers are usually surveillance aware. Sudden unexpected moves are a dead giveaway that they have something to hide. You find out on the first day. If it happens, surveillance might be abandoned for the day, while a bigger team is brought in: more frequent changes of car, another cab, another bike. People tend not to suspect bikes. They always think they are couriers.

If you are following a car, you do not want to be right up his chuff, but in London, with traffic lights and lane changes and pedestrian crossings it is almost inevitable that you will be, some of the time. In the countryside, following a car presents a different set of challenges. You are more conspicuous if you want to pull out behind the one guy who leaves a sleeping village at exactly 06:40 every morning. You just plot up and lay plans for it. There will be team members on all the roads out, probably lying in a ditch while their cars are hidden behind a hedge. Everybody is in radio contact. Before the team is in place, in fact before they are hired in most cases, the desk research has been done. Where the target works, who his wife is having an affair with, the number of his offshore bank account — it's all known. So when your colleague hidden in the woods tells you over your radio that the target is northbound on the M2 freeway, you probably know where he is going and who he is going to see.

Roger Levitt had months to wait for his trial and led a blameless life, outwardly at any rate. As one of his watchers I was well paid for sitting in a car in a street in Maida Vale. That was it. If Levitt did not go anywhere, I did not budge. Maida Vale is a smart residential area just north of central London, with wide tree-lined boulevards of stately mansions and massive Victorian, terraced houses. The street I was in had parking down the middle as well as both sides. Day after day, I admired the architecture, ate my regular breakfast of four Mars bars and a chocolate milkshake — a girl, even a thin one, needs go — and scanned the paper. I kept radio contact with the obbo van. I learnt the dog-walking habits of various old ladies and Filipino maids. I listened to the racket coming from the house across the road — the thump of a bass guitar, and a singer in there somewhere. The noise began about eleven in the morning and was still banging when I quit in the evening. I watched a parade of frazzled blokes in jeans and shades trailing up to the front door. Well, it takes all sorts. I was beginning to worry about whether the garbage truck was late collecting this week. It was that interesting.

A man with designer stubble and dark glasses tapped on the window. I slid it down.

"D'you mind telling me why you're here?" He had an Irish accent and a pleasant manner.

"If you've any worries, just call the police station. They'll set your mind at rest."

"Oh. Fine." Looking taken aback, he returned to the house across the street. I thought it likely he would call the police station. The local nick is always forewarned by surveillance teams. You will explain which streets you are "plotted up" in, so if the Neighborhood Watch do any curtain twitching they do not get too bothered — but you cannot do much about traffic police. They are inclined to ask you out to dinner in return for going away. Always accept, is my motto. You can cancel later.

Next day the designer stubble came out in a woolly hat with a cup of tea and some muffins. I declined the muffins, but the tea was very welcome.

"I made the cake meself," he said. I hoped I had not offended him. I gulped my tea. The din from inside had stopped, briefly.

"What are you doing in there anyway?"

"Practicing."

"Is that what you call it? Ever thought of getting a proper job?"

He grinned.

I wished somebody had told me that he was Bono from U2, but I did not find out for days. It keeps on happening to me, that sort of thing. When you are working, you absorb everything around you without being consciously aware; you are entirely focused on the job in hand.

The secret of good surveillance is in the details. For instance, learning to dip headlamps, then put them on half beam, or full, and back again, when you are following a vehicle at night; that way they think it is a different car all the time. Keeping a bike or a cab closest to a speeding car in town so that it can run a red if it has to — couriers and taxis do that all the time anyway, so the driver of the car in front will not be suspicious. On a freeway, a target who is not surveillance aware can be followed in any lane, you do not have to be behind him. If he pulls into a service area some of the team can keep along the highway, get ahead and be ready to pick him up when the team in the car park say he is leaving. Radio and telephone contact is constant.

In cities especially, most of the team may be on foot. There are signals you give each other, to tell each other to move up, take over, get back in formation; you can form a triangle behind the target, or a box shape, or any of a dozen others. You will take your hat off, or scratch your ear or make a sign behind your back to indicate where you are going or to tell one of the team to take over from you. Often you are after somebody who runs down to the tube. If there is a crowd at the ticket booth, you can get right behind the target, find out where he is going, and tell the rest of the team by cell phone, all the while following him down to the platform. You will not be seen as long as you stay close.

Also, personally, I find it easy to disguise myself. I am tall, thin and dark-haired. Like many women, I can make myself unnoticeable or turn heads when I walk in a room simply by the way I do my clothes and hair. With make-up on, I suddenly have a face; without it, you could pass me by. And stance and deportment are everything. In my time I have worn a wig and aged up to sixty. The trunk of whatever car I have contains day clothes, nightclothes, evening dresses — you have to be able to run into a loo or a bush and change. Once I was pulling on my pantyhose on the floor of a surveillance taxi in Park Lane when a punter in a hurry yanked the door open yelling, "South Kensington!" at the driver. We stared at each other in mutual amazement. Another time, I was plotted up in a parked car waiting to serve an injunction on a notorious gambler when a radio message told me he had taken a room at the Ritz and had ordered a call girl. I was into my party frock and eyeliner like lightning, and up to his door. A couple of guys were positioned either side, out of sight. I knocked.

"Hello?" came a cautious voice from inside.

"Good evening. You sent for me."

The door opened and he stood there smirking and scratching his chest. I smirked right back and thrust the documents into his hand.

"You're served."

Thomas and I met, whenever we could, all over Europe in the first few months. I set the rules of engagement early on — I did not talk about work. I learned very quickly that it would only make him uneasy. He had no basis for sexual jealousy, and I do not think that it ever bothered him. He knew me well enough to realize that as far as rivals on the Circuit were concerned, I had already tried the insecure aggressive type, and would not do so again. I valued Thomas because he was kind and wise. The longer I worked on the Circuit, the more I appreciated how rare these qualities are. However, if I talked about work Thomas started to think I might get hurt. So I never mentioned it, except for once when I needed his help.

I had been asked to fly to Nice, where I would stay in a little town on the Côte d'Azur and be part of a large surveillance team subcontracted to one of the international security companies. On jobs like that you do not get the whole picture. I vaguely understood that a credit card company was suing our target for millions and he was pleading bankruptcy. The investigation we were part of was supposed to lead to the seizure of his fraudulently acquired assets: assets that included a yacht, cars, houses and works of art. The sort of trinkets we all overlook in moments of crisis!

I envied him, living here, sun sparkling on deep blue water, bougainvillea in the garden and platefuls of fruits *de mer* on snowy tablecloths in dockside restaurants every night. What a life! His wife was an art dealer, and it seemed that he had obtained valuable sculptures that were now held in her name. When the bailiffs turned up, the sculptures were not in their villa; they were on permanent loan to the Principality of Monaco. I was told to retrieve them. Three brass sculptures, said the brief, and at least one of them was easy to get at as it was on public view in the open air, on a traffic circle near the casino. Ever obedient, I cleared the trunk of my trusty rental car, nipped along the Corniche and whirled around the traffic circle a couple of times. The sculpture was there all right: a solid brass abstract, probably of deep artistic significance, but it would have to stay right where it was. It stood about eight feet high and twenty feet long. I called my handler and told him he would have to conceive Plan B.

"One more damn thing," he said gloomily. He was having a hard day. He had just heard that goods were being loaded on board the yacht in the marina as if it was about to leave. It looked as if the swindler had decided to shift his possessions somewhere we could not find them.

"They might sail away tonight. It's a lot of bloody sea to lose them in."

"You want the yacht followed?"

"We want the yacht kept here. Don't suppose you know how to disable it, do you?"

"No, but I know a man who does."

I called Thomas and explained the problem. He was in Southampton in England, berthed for two nights, and he sounded lonely. I wished he was here. But we talked business, just this once.

"To make it stay? A chain around the propeller shaft. With a heavy chain, it will go nowhere."

One of the team bought about four meters of chain from a ship's chandlers. After dark, with scores of wealthy yachtsmen and their consorts carousing on shore, the water in the marina was as quiet as it got. Portholes bounced long glimmers of light onto the inky Mediterranean. There was nobody to see me slip into the water. The target's yacht was about 150 yards out. I had slung the chain over my shoulder. It was not so heavy in the salt sea, and I crawled out to the yacht doing the side-stroke. I felt safe once I was in the shadow of its sides, took a huge breath and dived down, following the line of the hull with my fingers until I found the propeller shaft. I quickly slung it around as well and tightly as I could. Which was not very tight, as once I had it half on, I got my arm stuck. Refusing to imagine what would happen if they started the propeller while I was floundering about, I tugged, wrenched and tore my bruised arm out from under, broke free and burst up to the surface for air. Bad move! I saw turbulence near the surface and as soon as I broke cover I saw a much more impressive yacht almost on top of me. I squinted through salt water long enough to read *Trump Princess* written on the side before I had to dive again. When I staggered back up the beach I was not in the best of tempers.

F OR AT LEAST A YEAR, JUST BY COINCIDENCE, I KEPT GETTING
surveillance jobs around Maida Vale and Little Venice. They are
pretty much the same place, Little Venice being the swanky part
of Maida Vale, with canals, cherry blossoms, lots of cream stucco and
even higher property prices. I was staked out there to watch a divorced
woman whose ex-husband suspected that she was getting entangled
with a bizarre religious cult. No doubt he would not have minded, but
they shared custody of their ten-year-old son and the cult members were
rumored to go in for pedophilia.

She certainly did not look like a Moonie or a member of any other
recognizable cult. No headbands, thonged sandals or floating silk frocks
here. Toward lunchtime most mornings she would swan down the
elegant steps of the Victorian villa I was watching, a vision in Chanel
and Gucci, and step daintily into a BMW. From then on it was one long
exhausting round of getting one's highlights done and one's nails
painted, massage therapy and light lunches with friends. Often there
would be a hard afternoon's shopping at Harvey Nichols upmarket
department store, or an evening supper at San Lorenzo. Oh, the endless
search for a parking meter. Such a strain.

Occasionally, on the alternate Friday nights when her son was spending the weekend with his father, she would have a bit of a bop at Annabel's nightclub in Berkeley Square. The rest of the time she did not socialize much. The little boy boarded at a prep school Monday to Friday. She had male company, however, in the person of a society masseur called Jonathan Clark. He counted a royal princess as one of his clients, so he must have been checked out by the security services. He did not fit the usual profile of a pederast.

Clark never stayed the night. He lived nearby in Hampstead, and the two of them spent many an afternoon trekking up and down the high street, nipping into bookstores. They were in each other's company most evenings, and on weekends they took the boy out walking on Hampstead Heath, or to the zoo in Regent's Park. I watched them. The child appeared cheerful. They looked like a happy family group.

For the first couple of weeks, watching this woman was very dull. Parking was difficult, and we had to be plotted up by six in the morning or we would never find room for the obbo van. The back of that airless, windowless metal box was usually occupied for eighteen hours a day by Dave, an old pal I had worked with on dozens of jobs, plus the listening equipment and cameras, and an old ice cream bucket for a toilet. The heat built up in the van. You could see out, though nobody could see in, but there was not much to look at since our girl rarely left the house until midday. However, one Wednesday evening there came the breakthrough that would make it all worthwhile. (For me, at any rate. I like a good laugh.) About ten people, including Clark, turned up at this woman's house in ones and twos and stayed until eleven o'clock.

They came every Wednesday night after that. We took photographs of them, and their car registration numbers were checked out. All of these individuals were found, at some time, to have had links to minority religious sects. They looked as conventional and well heeled as the target did. But we had established that at least part of the rumor seemed to be true, so the client decided to proceed. We had to get closer to our target.

Everyone concerned turned to me at this point for two reasons. One, I was a woman. I could get my back professionally rubbed by Mr. Clark and try to define exactly what his charms were. Two, I was a spiritualist. I have always been a spiritualist. My mum and dad were, and so was at least one of my grandparents. I am also psychic. Everybody on the Circuit who knows me knows this about me. And as far as they are concerned, most of these alternative religion freaks are vaguely heading in the same direction and it takes one to know one. I was going to have to play a major part in the infiltration of this cult.

I made an appointment to see Jonathan Clark. Frozen shoulder, I explained on the phone to his receptionist — which was true enough. He had a nice house, with a consulting room upstairs, and he seemed pleasant. He was a holistic masseur, he said. His long fingers pushed and palpated my shoulders while his voice, soothing as he hovered above the nape of my neck, instructed me to cleanse my system from the inside out. He was a skinny, tall, ethereal man in his late thirties, with curly brown hair; not my type, but you could see what some women saw in him, because he was unctuous. He flattered. He was so slick, you could have slid off him. He came a cropper with me, though. He spent twenty minutes telling me to rid my body of coffee and cigarettes because it would clear my cellulite, he said. My tranquility hit the floor like a rock. If there is one thing I do not have, it is cellulite; never have had. After that I did not volunteer to buy any of the balms and aromatic oils ranged on the shelves in the consulting room. I could see how, after a session with him, a woman with regular alimony and nothing better to do would find herself parting with good money for whole racks of potions.

The religious group had not come up in the conversation, but one of the other watchers had come up with a brainwave. He had been muttering since the first Wednesday that he knew one of the women visitors from somewhere, and now he remembered where. He had briefly worked on an investigation in the States that indirectly involved a cult, and he had seen her then. She was a Chinese American who gave talks and conducted seminars on inner spiritual health and mind over matter. She was a professional spiritual leader and, like any other sales-person, she did exhibitions. One was coming up very soon: a psychic fair at a West End hotel. I bought a heap of magazines on the subject and found a ticket offer.

Two of us went, me and Mike, the guy who had recognized the woman in the first place (though he looked bemused by the experi-ence). We wandered between the stalls that genteelly promoted every-thing from incense, ouija boards and crystals to six-month courses and weekend retreats in Northumberland. It struck me as all a bit rarified. I went into a side room and listened to the Chinese-American woman, Louise Tan, giving a seminar. She used the usual brainwashing tech-nique of repetition, but I heard no sinister references to small children. My only concern was to find out if the group involved children. So far, I had seen no hint of malpractice. After the seminar I told her how inter-ested I was, how inspiring she had been, and she invited me to the group's meeting in Maida Vale. We were in.

The following Wednesday I turned up at the house. The lads stayed outside in the van and a couple of cars. Inside, the wide marble-floored entrance hall gave an elegant impression, with tall mirrors and a huddle of potted palms. The target lived on the first floor. I was ushered into the living room, all vermilion paint and soft furnishings in flickering candlelight with a drift of incense. There I was introduced to the other guests by their first names. Most of them were women in their early forties. Everyone was conventionally smart. It could have been a rather repressed dinner party anywhere in North London, except there was no food or alcohol. Jonathan Clark recognized me and said he was glad I could come. He must have thought he had invited me himself.

We perched on chairs, sipped mineral water and listened with rapt delight as Mrs. Tan held forth for a while. Then we began to chant with our eyes shut. I sneaked a look at the radio mike taped to my chest; still firmly in place. The guys would not have made much of what they had heard tonight. I needed more. After the chanting there were prayers, and then mingling. I mingled hopefully.

"Will you come again?" an earnest woman asked me. "Will you become integrated?"

"Tell me, what's involved?"

They could not wait to explain. I would be "born again." I would be "returned to the nakedness in which I was born," boomed one of the men, and "released into the world as a baby." "A joyous rebirthing," he called it. There was enough of a hint of some connection with children to make me wonder. I said I would think about it.

"Well, will you do it?" asked my handler on the phone. "I think you should."

"If you want," I said cautiously. "But you know what I said about returning to nakedness and all."

"Yeah?"

"Where shall I put the mike?"

There was a thoughtful silence. Finally we decided that my purse was the best place for a microphone and transmitter.

Next Wednesday I turned up again. It was a hot night and, as I drove past the obbo van in the street I knew that at least four of the team were huddled in the back, probably stripped to their undershorts.

My integration was to be the highlight of the evening. There was no sign of any children and everybody greeted me warmly. The more I saw of these people the more I thought they were perfectly decent. Sad and daft, maybe, but not child molesters. Tonight, like last time, there were three or four men and the rest were women. We began the evening cross-legged on the floor, with silence, relaxation and a few mantras chanted around a Persian rug. Joss sticks wafted pungent smoke from the hearth. After half an hour of this I was timidly invited to go to the bathroom and remove all my clothes, jewelry and make-up so I would be in my original, unpolluted, childlike state. I reappeared, a modest neophyte ready for integration, wearing a kimono and clutching my handbag.

"Take off your robe and lie on the carpet," commanded Mr. Clark. I put my purse on the sideboard. The others had already started chanting soulfully. I hoped the lads in the van were enjoying this. Everyone stood up around me. Two of the men rolled me into the carpet with only my head sticking out. Twelve pairs of eyes gazed down at my startled face.

"Allelujah."

"Allelujah."

My inner being was then commended to a higher power. Everyone said "Ommm" and lit candles and swayed about a bit. The carpet was horribly scratchy and chanting doesn't half get tedious. Just when I was daring a wistful hope that they would suddenly form a line and start dancing the conga, I saw signs that the process might be coming to an end. The two men stepped forward smiling. I was now integrated. With a flourish they unrolled me. I rotated one more time to make sure I was face down on the carpet. My eyes were watering, I could feel my neck going crimson, and I was getting a pain between the shoulder blades from the effort of stifling my hysteria. Hefty male feet in sandals tramped around me in a sort of dance. I could tell who was who by their toenails. The women kept on chanting and the men pulled me to my feet. I rolled my eyes to the heavens, sucked in my cheeks, waved my arms sinuously and swayed to and fro. Good thing I had shaved my armpits. This carried on for a few minutes and, squinting through half-closed eyes, I could see the others seemed to be attaining a trance-like state. I loped gracefully along the wall toward the door, swiped the purse and kimono from the sideboard and headed for the bathroom.

"I'm getting dressed," I hissed into my purse. "See you in the pub in half an hour." They offered me a reviving mineral water in the kitchen and showed me back into the living room, where I lay down with others who were now all prone, staring at the ceiling. Jonathan

Clark sat cross-legged contemplating his hairy toes. I remained motionless for five minutes. At last Clark trod softly to my side of the room and knelt beside me.

"How do you feel, Jacquieline?"

"I feel so cleansed. So pure, it's amazing."

The others sat up.

"That's exactly how I was. It's really weird, how you get rid of all the baggage."

"You're reborn."

"Gosh, yes," I agreed. "It's so wearying, though. You feel you've sort of plumbed hidden depths."

"It's like soaring up from the bottom of the ocean."

"Yes." I yawned.

"Is it too much for you?" Clark asked sympathetically.

"Well, it's rather a lot to take in all in one evening. It's an amazing experience. I'm going to sneak away. I need to be alone to take it in properly."

"That's so true."

"It's all about growth, isn't it? You need to rest. It's kind of strenuous."

With their well-meaning cries of encouragement ringing in my ears, I went off to deepen my spirituality down at the pub. The lads appeared, sniggering, ten minutes later. What an insensitive lot they were.

I was glad when a job ended without the client's suspicions being proved right. It did not often happen. Usually things were worse than you had been told to expect. My team had been following a company employee around London for about a week, listening to his calls and having a good snoop around anyone he met. He was definitely dodgy. A fat little bloke with greedy eyes, always dapper, surreptitiously meeting people from rival companies and talking on the phone about "packages." On this particular day, it was just coming up to lunchtime, and he had gone from a meeting at his corporate HQ back to his house. He stayed inside in total silence for an hour before he reappeared with two suitcases and hailed a cab. I drove behind it, and soon we were swooping over the Hammersmith flyover. He was definitely on his way to Heathrow. The two guys in a car behind me agreed.

"Client wants me to stick with him?" I asked.

My handler confirmed. Outside their own countries, men of any nationality are easily picked up by a compatriot; behind the bluster they are lonely and nervous, and you have the language in common. I was supposed to get close and scan as many documents as I could. The radio fell silent as we drove on. I kept up an annoyed monologue inside my head. Wonderful timing. This always happened when I had not had time to collect my dry cleaning or grab a camera, and my case in the trunk was half empty. Nothing except summer frocks, and he would probably turn out to be heading for the Arctic Circle. In the past week he had met Danes, Finns and Norwegians.

The cab dropped him at Terminal 2 Departures. I jumped out, leaving the keys in the ignition, and grabbed my bag from the trunk. As I followed the target into the booking hall I saw Richard running across the forecourt ready to park my car for me. Dave was already heading for long term parking. I hoped he could get on the same flight. I tapped his code into my cell phone.

"He's heading for the British Airways check-in at *C*. That's a Copenhagen, Denmark, flight. Can you get somebody to book a rental car at the other end?"

I stood in line behind the little man at the Priority-Gold-Knobs-On-Gee-You're-Important desk. He was flying to Copenhagen all right; I lurked behind him, acting confused, when he picked up his first-class ticket. I wittered. The girl looked at me pityingly.

"Over there for ticket purchase, madam. Boarding starts in half an hour."

I crossed the booking hall to buy a very expensive ticket and Dave, behind me in the line, muttered, "Check this in for me, Jacquie." He put his suitcase on the ground. "I'll pick up the car at the other end."

I smiled at the target in the departure lounge, stood a little too close behind him as we boarded and stretched myself languidly over two seats in business class. I turned, caught his eye and slowly crossed one leg over the other. He sent champagne across. (And they said I'd lost my touch.) I sat next to him the entire time. Was he going to Copenhagen on business? Where would he stay? He had some very dull meetings to go to, and was staying at the Tivoli. And me? Oh, as for me, this was a spur of the moment decision. I had only decided to travel a few hours ago.

"You see, I think what most people have lost is spontaneity," I gushed. "I like to do what feels right for me. I'm writing a romantic novel with a scene set in Denmark, and I've never even been there. So I jumped in my car and came to the airport."

"You're obviously a woman who's in tune with her impulses."

"Never nurse an unsatisfied desire," I agreed, glancing at him Princess Di style from beneath my eyelashes and sipping my champagne. He gulped eagerly at his. I counted three glasses in the first forty minutes. I would have to have a word with Dave soon, before we landed.

The target asked, "Where are you staying?"

"Oh, well, you can imagine, it's typical isn't it," I twittered. "Of course I haven't bothered to make a reservation. I expect I'll find some little place that'll put me up."

"I've got a suite. Two bedrooms."

I mentally punched the air in triumph, but just said sweetly, "How nice!"

"I'm sure you'll be comfortable at the Tivoli. Why don't we see how you like it when we get there? I'm being met. You can come in my car."

I waited for the toilets in business class to be occupied and then made my excuses, squeezed out and stood in line between business and economy. Dave slipped out of an aisle seat in economy and came to stand behind me.

"He's giving me a lift to the Tivoli. That's where he's staying."

"Keep him in the baggage hall as long as you can, I'll rent a car and follow," Dave whispered.

"Where are you going to stay?"

"There must be a Hilton." Dave said.

"If there's a Hilton, I'll try that first. If not I'll phone around the other chains so make sure you get a room at the Sheraton or something."

The occupant was emerging from the toilet. I hissed, "If all else fails, leave a note for me at reception at the Tivoli."

I let Dave's suitcase swing past on the carousel twice before I noticed it. The man was very patient. His meeting was not until four, he said. A limo met us. We swept off to the Tivoli, and I was installed in the suite while he left for his meeting.

Dave and I met at a coffee shop.

"You got them in there?" I asked anxiously.

"Yup."

Dave opened his briefcase and produced a small plastic bottle wrapped in a folded sheet of photocopied paper, secured around it with a rubber band. We unfolded the sheet and stared at it.

"What's fourteen stone in kilos?" I scratched my head. We Brits for some reason use the ancient weight measurement of stones, equaling fourteen pounds, whenever we measure a person's weight. Before I could calculate the conversion to metric kilos, I had to work out what the target weighed in pounds.

"I wouldn't think he weighs that much," Dave ventured.

"You're kidding! More like sixteen."

"It says five hundred milligrams per fifty kilos body weight. Where the hell did you get these?"

"Pakistan," I said. "Gimme a pencil, I've got to work this out."

I selected three of the gelatin capsules and one for luck and wrapped them in a napkin from the café. Then I went shopping for clothes. This was to be my big night.

We went out to dinner in a little restaurant with shaded pink lamps and long white tablecloths that let you rub a man's leg in complete concealment. Two bottles of wine were emptied, mostly into him. Back in his suite at the hotel, he drank another two glasses of champagne before disappearing into the shower. I broke three of the gelatin capsules into another glass of champagne, swizzled them until they dissolved, and took the drink to him in the bathroom. I drank Perrier between his attempts to grope me and would not leave until I had seen him swallow his champagne to the last drop. I returned to the drawing room.

Female Operative Jacquie now had to keep the target occupied for twenty minutes before he passed out. Smoochy music played on the radio. He emerged clad in a thick white toweling robe and we began to waltz around the room. His belly sat solidly against my new black cocktail frock. I should not think he had seen his dick for years. For twelve minutes exactly, we shuffled back and forth with my lipstick reflecting like a peony in the shine off his bald patch. I murmured sweet nothings, bent and nibbled his ear. *Right, you fat bastard, that's your lot.* I began to steer him toward the bedroom. At seventeen minutes we were in a clinch on the bed. His hands everywhere until at last, his enthusiasm waned. He's going, going . . . *Thank you, God.*

With a gargantuan heave I rolled him over, pulled the covers back, and rolled him between them. Then I dropped the rest of my clothes on the floor. He was deeply unconscious. I put the lights out and tiptoed from the room with his briefcase.

Dave was somewhere in Copenhagen doing his bit for England. His job was to gain sight of all the faxes reception took in for the target. Dave's theory being that the easiest way to a woman's fax machine was through her libido, he had invited the hotel receptionist to spend the evening in his company. As I quietly slipped the catch on the briefcase, I hoped Dave would have more joy than me. The material inside the case consisted mainly of bank statements and, without a camera or photocopier, I could not do much with it. I memorized what I could, took a few notes and put it all back. Then I replaced the briefcase and went into my own room for a few hours sleep.

At five, I got up and returned to his muggy bedroom. There he lay, snoring and farting as I climbed between the warm sheets. If Thomas could see me now. . . . It was disgusting. After awhile I quietly called room service, asked them to deliver breakfast at seven, and got up. I was in the shower when the tray arrived and by the time I came out, dressed and perky for the day, he was sitting up drinking his coffee and asking how good it had been. "Oh!" I breathed. "It was wonderful."

In the course of the morning, Dave checked with the man's employers. They were extremely interested to see the faxes Dave's efforts had obtained and confirmed that they needed copies of the bank statements. Dave arranged with the receptionist that he could use the hotel's photocopier in the middle of the night. Again I had dinner with the target, slipped him the knockout drops and took his briefcase. This time I waited until exactly two in the morning and handed it out of the door to Dave. At two-thirty he gave it back, having photocopied everything.

I woke up late on the second morning in the target's bed.

"Morning! Rise and shine." Dave flung the curtains back. A pot of fresh coffee was steaming on the breakfast tray.

"What are you doing here?" The bed beside me was empty. "Where is he?"

"Checked out at a quarter to six. Flew to Zurich, I followed him out to the airport. No worries, we've got what we need."

"Oh." Would you believe it! Walking out on a girl like that.

USING A FLY TO CATCH A SPIDER IS A VERY OLD IDEA. I CANNOT SAY I was crazy about being the fly. People wanted to use me like that too often. Once, in Hamburg, a man stayed wide-eyed and fumbling long after I had given him enough powders to put a horse to sleep. I kept smiling through gritted teeth, expecting him to wilt, yet the more I smiled the harder things became. I ended up banging about downstairs at his home at two in the morning pretending to make coffee. As the machine roared and gurgled, I slipped into his study and stole proof he was buying pharmaceuticals under six company names from his home office. He was certainly taking an antidote to what I had given him. I kept imagining I heard his tread on the stairs. And then there were Arabs, people like the Kuwaiti suspected of passing information to the Iraqis during the Gulf War. I was getting quite expert at dosing lamb kebabs with knockout drops. I told myself it would all look good on my c.v. But if I was going to spend time in bed with a man, I wanted it to be Thomas.

He and I met in Miami for a week and talked about the Circuit and my career. I had not joined the Circuit to become Mata Hari. I wanted to move on, pick and choose the work, and the Circuit needed more women. So, back in London, I began to train a few women, mostly ex-police or former military. I set up by myself and started taking specialist work for female bodyguards. My company joined ASIS, the American Society for Industrial Security. There are members all over the world. The idea is that if a member is in trouble in an unfamiliar country, he can look in the ASIS directory and find a fellow member who will help. It works brilliantly.

It was not long before journalists heard about my all-female agency. They interviewed me and articles appeared. One day I heard a familiar voice when I picked up the phone.

"Hi, Jacquie."

I felt my face freeze.

"Hello, Tim."

"I've been reading about you."

"That's nice. How are you getting on?"

"Very well. I'm in the Diplomatic Protection Group now."

I knew this perfectly well, as I had seen his picture in the paper, guarding the Prime Minister.

"And Janine's just had a baby girl."

"Congratulations, I'm pleased for you."

"So there's still something she's got that you can never have, isn't there?" I put the phone down. What a slimy sense of fun the man had.

Some of the articles about me were syndicated abroad. This led to me being approached by an ex-Circuit guy who knew that I knew journalists. At this time a large civil engineering project was in progress in Britain. It was overburdened with debt and constantly having to run to the banks for re-financing. This man's friend, he told me, had been the official photographer to the construction consortium responsible for the project. He claimed he had been sacked for whistle blowing. The photographer wanted to go to the media with his story. Did I know anybody who could get it in the newspapers?

I met the photographer, a jumpy young man with bad skin and long hair. He talked incoherently about scandal, corruption and bad safety standards, but I thought he was a man with a lot of problems, and an agenda of his own. He was looking for money for his story, which was suspicious in itself, and if safety standards on the job were so bad, why were there so few serious accidents on such a potentially dangerous project? I did not trust him or believe him.

And I had a friend, too. The head of security for the consortium was an ex-Metropolitan Police chief superintendent whom I knew slightly. His department was also a member of ASIS. Given a choice, my loyalty had to go to him.

I went to security at the construction company and laid my cards on the table. I had this photographer . . . he could do some damage. He was mouthing off about how the chairman squandered company funds and how health and safety regulations were routinely overlooked at the site. According to his allegations, men were being injured on the construction site because short cuts were being taken to get the job finished on time.

The head of security went into a huddle with some big cheese at the consortium and came to a rapid decision. The annual general meeting was going to be held in a few weeks' time, and if these stories got out, even if they were unfounded, there would be an uproar at the meeting that the big institutional investors and banks could not ignore. The company would pay whatever it cost to scupper the photographer's plan.

I devised a plan. I told the photographer to hang on while I organized an appointment with a key journalist. As it happened, I knew an investigator from the Circuit who had once worked with the *Daily Mail* and *News of the World.* He regularly sold stories even now. I contacted him and said the photographer must be interviewed but the story must never be used. We agreed on his price.

We hired a conference room in a hotel outside London. I picked up the photographer and drove him there. The person we were going to meet, I told him, was a *Sun* reporter. He happened to be having a big meeting at the hotel today about a story, and he had agreed to give us ten minutes at the end.

When we were shown into the conference room I realized I had hired a real pro. The long table was a mess of empty coffee cups, used water glasses, ripped memo pads and filled ashtrays. The supposed "Man from the *Sun*," tie awry, greeted us in an atmosphere as fuggy as if ten argumentative smokers had been closeted with him all day.

He arranged to do a series of interviews with the photographer. He took him out to dinner to encourage him to talk, not that the photographer needed much prompting; his stories tumbled out. Board members now with paintings in their homes that had earlier quietly disappeared off the office walls; non-executive directors whose wives were somehow able to earn a fortune in consultancy fees; parties with hookers and cocaine at the chairman's home. Explosive stuff, if any of it had actually been true. He had been finally goaded to speak out, he said furiously, when one day he had been at the chairman's London house and some birdseed for the parrot had arrived by special delivery in a Harrod's van. He was determined to disrupt the general meeting brandishing some of his photographs.

My "reporter" shook his head. The story would not be an exclusive then, would it? The photographer saw the point. When the interviews were complete, the reporter had promised that he would approach his editor at the *Sun*. There would be big money in an exclusive on a story like this.

That was probably true, but unfortunately for the photographer, every word he said was being transcribed and sent by courier direct to the head of security at the consortium. On the day of the annual general meeting the shareholders were as satisfied as they could be given the real problems the project faced, and the directors had a nice lunch, while the photographer talked long and hard at one final, all-day meeting with the reporter who he hoped would make his fortune.

A week later, the photographer called. Sorry, the reporter told him, the editor did not think it was a story they could run. The public would not be interested. The photographer accepted this and gave up. The consortium battled through to completion of the project, and I got paid. Personally, I felt it had been a question of loyalty. Mine had been to a fellow member of ASIS.

I had up to five trained female bodyguards working for me at any one time. Not many with about two thousand men available on the Circuit, but it was a 500 percent increase on just little old me. I was pretty happy. Though, often when I thought the ice underfoot was solid it had a nasty habit of turning out to be very thin indeed.

An Italian called my office one morning from Rome. He needed security for his visit to London the following week. I faxed him a routine enquiry form, that he filled in and returned. It gave details of his blood type, the name of his doctor, his height and weight. Was he on a known hit list? Did he have any aliases? Please fax a copy of your passport. All this came back at once. Nothing to declare. I called an FBI friend at Quantico and asked if this man was known or affiliated with any political group. He was not.

There are three categories of clients: high-, medium-, and low-risk. High would be somebody against whom, for instance, a fatwah had been issued, or who represented a country at war. Medium could be a celebrity who had attracted a stalker in the past. Low risk was somebody like this Italian, who could get by with a single bodyguard and driver. I did not ask why he wanted protection. As long as he was not on a hit list, and was far from home, we could assess the risk of some nutter or rejected mistress taking a pot shot as pretty slender.

The form also told me his itinerary and personal details. This was to be largely a business trip, although he had a few errands to run. He wanted to buy a particular breed of dog and export it to Italy, so we had to find out where to get one and how he could take it out of the country. He wanted to go to a restaurant in Notting Hill with paintings on the walls and a piano; he had been there before but could not remember the name. This was the normal sort of research we had to do, and I thought no more about it.

A bodyguard met him off the plane. Our client was a well-dressed middle-aged man about five feet nine with a pleasant manner who spoke good English. He immediately asked if he could come to the office to use the photocopier and fax. That was fine. He produced our fee for the three days in cash and drove away in the back of a limo, with a male chauffeur and a female bodyguard in front. They were headed for Buckinghamshire to buy the dog, a bewildered, expensive puppy, which would one day grow into a bewildered, expensive bullmastiff. Later, we took him to his hotel. He had not asked for overnight security, which would cost more as it would mean taking other rooms for the driver and bodyguard; instead, our people were to pick him up every morning at eight. On the second day we took him shopping. Our girl escorted him the length of Jermyn Street and accompanied him to buy clothes. At night he dined in the restaurant at Notting Hill. The chauffeur stayed outside with the car, to make sure nobody planted a bomb under it, and the bodyguard followed the client into the restaurant and dined at a separate table — omitting a first course, as is usual, as she would have to stay one course ahead.

On the way back to the airport, the Italian stopped off at my office to tell me how pleased he was and how safe he felt. Everything had gone according to plan. We took him to the airport. We said goodbye. That was that. Until the next day, when he sent me a fax.

He hoped I would not mind if he wrote an article about my agency. Under his real name — he had been traveling on a false passport — he was a well-known journalist in Italy and, as it happened, was also a member of the Italian Parliament and on a mob hit list. He had round-the-clock protection in Italy. He had simply wanted to know whether a woman could offer effective protection, he said. He had been impressed.

I was not. I was not impressed at all. I picked up the phone, dialed his number and let rip. I was livid. If he had given us his real name we would have given him a full bodyguard team; he was obviously in a high-risk category. Sounding surprised, he said he would have no hesitation in recommending my agency or using us again. I told him if he went down on bended knee, we would never be available to look after him. I could not understand how he could be so dim.

I specialized in close protection work for celebrities, and won a long-term contract for the popular *Challenge Anneka* television series. Every week the presenter, Anneka Rice, would be shown rising to a challenge to complete a worthwhile charity project: pulling together a team, then charming and cajoling tradesmen and suppliers to provide the expertise and materials to complete the job on time. One Friday afternoon, at the end of a shoot in the West Country, just when we were all winding down and looking forward to the BBC version of a wrap party (a pint in the local pub), my cell phone chirped. A good friend, an ex-policeman with his own security firm in London, had been asked to investigate what a certain woman was up to in the South of France. Her husband suspected that she was spending time with another man. It did not seem necessary to deploy an entire team. Could I fly to Nice tomorrow morning at nine?

I drove back to London. My office in Grosvenor Place overlooked the gardens of Buckingham Palace. There I found that the case file, complete with blurred photographs, had been faxed through. The woman was a bridge player. She had told her husband that she was going to participate in a tournament at Juan-les-Pins. The Cannes Film Festival was on at the same time, and she had said it might be difficult to find a hotel room. My ex-police friend Eddie had booked me, with difficulty, into the Belle Rive at Juan-les-Pins in the expectation that the errant wife, who knew the hotel, was already there.

I arrived at Nice airport at about midday, hired a car and drove happily along the Corniche. The sun sparkled on the Mediterranean;

wind-surfers showed off in the little bays and expensive motor cars crawled past seafront hotels with access to private beaches. The air was a heady mix of thyme and mimosa, petrol fumes and tanning lotion. The roads were invaded by a flotsam of roller bladers, cyclists and tanned posers of both sexes. If my target did not fetch up at the Belle Rive or participate in the tournament, looking for her was going to be a challenge worthy of Anneka.

When I arrived at the hotel, I could hardly believe my luck. I recognized her at once from the faxed picture: a glossy brunette in her thirties wearing a floppy white hat, standing beside me at the reservations desk. There was a man with her — not bad looking, I thought — and they called each other darling. I took a long time filling in forms and messing about losing things in my purse, and heard them being given a room number. She was tired, she said as she took the key, and needed to rest.

I was escorted upstairs. Because there was a shortage of rooms Eddie had had to reserve me a suite. I was not complaining. The bellboy stopped the elevator at the top floor and picked up my bags. I stepped out and saw at least two bodyguard teams guarding different doors.

"Yes?" said one of the men, looming over me. "Do you have any business on this floor, madam?"

"I have a suite," I snarled. "So fuck awf."

I decided that the target couple would probably have a hectic afternoon ahead in the bedroom, so I could afford to putter around a bit. I found the hall where the bridge tournament was to take place and photographed the list of participants on a notice outside. It listed her correct name. By this time it was late afternoon, so I showered and settled in the lobby to wait for them to emerge from their room.

They ate together in the hotel, and I called London to say I had found them. Next morning, I got up at six to sit on the terrace, that they would have to cross to get to the sea. The hotel overlooked a glorious little bay with rocks on the sand and a jetty. It all looked perfect, like a stage set. A scruffy bearded man emerged from the lobby a few minutes later and sat a few tables away from me looking at the menu. He asked the waiter for toast. The waiter clearly did not understand this American who did not have a word of French, and I offered to help. The man invited me to share his table. He was very friendly, wanted to know why I was here and was interested when I told him I was researching a book. I steered him off the subject. We talked about movies. He seemed very knowledgeable.

"Are you here for the film festival then?" I asked.

"Well, yes. You don't know who I am, do you?" He did not say it in an arrogant way; in fact he seemed quite pleased. I peered at him, quickly reviewing all the American films I had seen in the last six months. I did not have a clue.

"Sorry, no. What's your name?"

"Steven Spielberg. What's yours?"

Friendly as he was, he must have thought I was suspiciously anxious to loaf about on that terrace, because when he finished his coffee and left for his first meeting of the day I was still there. I had been at my table for nearly three hours before the target drifted out at nine o'clock to munch croissants. The trouble with being the sole investigator is that you do so much hanging about.

When the man and woman headed for the beach at last I took out my camera and began to take pictures of them with a zoom lens. There was quite a sprinkling of hotel guests on the sands already. The man and woman found a secluded spot under an umbrella near the jetty.

But not for long. Half an hour later, I was lying ten yards away from them, sunbathing topless like most of the other women on the beach. My eyes half shut, I watched the woman's boyfriend dive into the polluted Mediterranean. You would not believe how tough it is, working in the South of France. You smell the ozone and listen to shrieks borne across the water while the sun soaks right through to your bones and if you are not careful, the worst happens, and you are asleep on the job.

I leant up on my elbows and looked out to sea. An American couple scrambled to their feet nearby.

"You mind looking after this stuff for us?"

They left their Nikon and Ray-Bans on their beach towels and headed for the water. When they came back I had just finished taking a few casual shots of the target couple embracing. Now she was heading for the sea. The Americans, returning dripping wet, began talking to me and within ten minutes the boyfriend had somehow fallen into conversation with the three of us as well.

"So what are you doing here?" he asked. He had been watching me curiously.

"I'm researching a romantic novel," I said. I had an inkling that he was not entirely convinced, in fact that he might have noticed me loitering on the terrace, dining across the room the night before, taking his picture or listening as he gave his room number. You need a team for these jobs.

"Who's your publisher?"

"Penguin," I said glibly. The woman came up the beach just then and was introduced. The boyfriend and the American did most of the talking after that. The American woman asked him to take our pictures. I handed my camera to her.

"Will you take a picture of us?"

She took a shot of all of us together: me, the grinning targets, and the American. They asked me a few more questions about my job. Did publishers generally pay so well that I could run off and bask in the sun at Juan-les-Pins whenever I felt like it? The boyfriend thought he must be in the wrong business. I fudged some sort of reply and thought he gave me a searching look.

"My wife did not send you, did she?" he said suddenly.

"I beg your pardon?"

"Oh, sorry." He smiled. "Didn't mean it." He put his arm around the woman. "It's just that we're not married."

"Oh, I see," I said, eyes widening. Gosh. What some people get up to.

I had the pictures developed that afternoon. They were perfect. On Sunday and Monday, before returning to London, I had breakfast with Spielberg again. By Monday he, too, had started to ask questions.

"I give up," I said, in the end. "I can tell you. I'm not really researching a novel at all. I'm an investigator." He seemed fascinated. I did not mind telling him the truth; I would probably never meet him again, and he was such a nice man it seemed petty to deceive him. Besides, he had a close protection team, and I did not want to make anyone suspicious.

Back in London, Eddie asked me to go with him to see the client. We arrived at a huge house in St. John's Wood where we were let in by a butler. A manservant brought tea. The client was a dapper, effeminate, jumpy, fussy little man of at least sixty-five. He wore rings on perfectly manicured fingers. The room was high ceilinged, with pale carpets and slippery, formal Regency sofas. I sat down.

"Oh!" he cried.

I leapt up again. Had I sat on the cat?

He rushed to apologize. "That's where my wife sits, you see. No, no, sit there by all means. Do. Please sit down. Tell me."

I told him. He perched on the edge of a chair opposite twisting his wedding band. It was cruel. I had to tell him how they had arrived together, taken a room together, kissed on the beach. I hated this. I showed him the photographs. He looked very pale and sad.

"What should I do?"

"I can't tell you that. It's up to you. My job was to find out whether or not your wife is having an affair, and I've done that."

"Yes but — as a woman. What do you think I should do?"

He was surprisingly feeble. I suppose I had felt just as vulnerable when Tim hurt me. I had wanted somebody to confide in. I looked around the room. It was full of antique furniture and its high windows overlooked

a beautiful garden. He had enormous wealth, yet he was utterly miserable. My job had not given me the skills of a marriage guidance coun-
selor but at least I had learned to move on. Feeling deep sympathy for the
poor man, I said at last, "Decide whether you want to stay married. And
if you don't, find a good lawyer."

I never knew if he took my advice. You don't. You go on to the
next thing.

Rich men also check up on their mistresses. He was in a clinic in Switzerland, she was going on holiday to Dublin, and while he was about to leave his wife for a newer model, he would not commit himself entirely until he had her spied on for a few days. If I had concerned myself with the moral position in these circumstances, I would have grown dizzy. So I didn't. I hired five men and got on with it.

The client seemed happy to spend any amount of money on this investigation, so I assumed he must have grounds to feel tortured by suspicion. I half expected her to land in Dublin and immediately head off for a passionate affair. We would probably have to hire cars and follow her to the furthest reaches of Galway. The reality was rather tame. We flew to Dublin and checked in, as she did, to the Westbury.

The good thing about working in hotels is that somebody on the team usually knows the head of security. You can get a room on the same floor as your target. Or if you need to dope food, one of you can borrow a uniform and wheel the trolley in pretending to be room service. Even if they do not know you, hotel staff are usually amenable to inducements of one kind or another; it is part of their job to expect them.

I sometimes thought I must have worked or stayed in most of the hotels in Britain by now. Lonhro, the company that owned the Metropole Group, had commissioned me to spend regular weekends at Metropole hotels and write reports on the service. I also had to test drinks to see who was, "on the fiddle." Just about everybody on the staff from Hendon to Harlech seemed to be at it. I would order half a dozen items, sneak off to the loo to scribble a note of what I had had, and submit the note to be checked against the cash register roll. Thanks to me, thieves were getting fired up and down the country. In fact once, when undercover, I had to attend a function in a Metropole banqueting hall that turned out to be a knees-up for the mayor of Barnet and the local Conservative Association. I found myself sitting next to the man I had been engaged to when I was seventeen. He was very nice about it, and told everybody I was a schoolteacher.

One of the Metropole managers had left under a cloud, but quickly found a job nobody else wanted. He took over the notorious Europa in Belfast: the hotel with the dubious distinction of having been blown up more times than the Ho Chi Min Trail. One of the first things he did was ask me to go in and report on the place. I spent an uproarious weekend there with a party of drunken Russian hockey players and an IRA man I picked up in the disco by pretending to be a French tourist. "Great crack," as they say, but the hotel was filthy, with torn carpets and, to my horror, no blast protection behind the plate glass windows in the lobby.

In the Dublin Westbury, we had been asked to record all the mistress's phone calls. The guys bugged her phone, took the room next door and listened on headphones.

She behaved like a model city tourist. On the first day she shopped. Six of us traipsed after her up and down Grafton Street until she took her packages back to the hotel. At teatime I sat in the lobby waiting for her to reappear for afternoon tea. The Westbury is a superb hotel, which manages to make its guests feel cosseted and at peace. Sunk in a deep sofa, awaiting a pot of Earl Grey tea and an arrowroot biscuit, I was enjoying myself. The mistress did not turn up, but the pianist was good, I thought. He was playing *Happy Birthday.* I went over to him and asked him to play *La Mer,* a beautiful old melody and one of my favorites. He was a delightful young man and obliged with a smile. The other guests taking tea seemed amused by my request. I had no idea why. The young man disappeared after that, and it was not even five o'clock yet, so when the waiter brought my tea I asked him why the pianist had left.

"That was not the hotel pianist, madam," he replied, deadpan. "That was Johnny Logan. Yer man's won the Eurovision Song Contest three times for Ireland. He's here with friends for a birthday party."

I blushed, but worse was to follow. On the second morning the woman we were following took herself off to Trinity College library to look at the fabulous mediaeval *Book of Kells.* We shuffled after her into the grounds of Trinity College, up a zigzag path used by members of the public. I have forgotten exactly why all six of us had antiquated radios on this job, but we did. We had the kind that need a stubby plastic receiver in your ear, connected by a cable to the main box at your waist. We were in a conventional pursuit pattern: Dave and Robert ahead, Mike and Ian behind, and me in the middle, when my receiver came loose and Robert's voice boomed out at idling passers-by. Acting instinctively, I hurled myself over a low wall and down a slope, rolling to rest against a thorn bush. I do not know what came over me. Breathless, I opened my eyes. A couple of red faces under woolly hats peered over the wall at me. I was not rational. I must have looked like a rabbit caught in headlights.

"Are you all right, miss?"

I did not answer. I was too busy trying to stuff the receiver back in my ear. The damn thing had probably blown my cover, and my over-reaction had only made things worse. I needed to busk my way out of this, and the two grounds men gave me my cue, bless them.

"Ah, God love 'er, can you not see the poor girl's deaf. Are ye roight?" he bellowed at me, his face concerned.

I nodded and gulped. "Lovely," I shouted back. "Looks like rain later."

I scrambled back on to the path with a hand from Mike. He looked at me as if I had taken leave of my senses. "Felt like some physical jerks, did you?" he muttered. "You want to get in that library," he jabbed his thumb at the magnificent medieval building, crowned by the longest wooden roof in existence and home to one of the finest collections of literature and scholarly works in the world. "We've put our own jerks in there. Robert's found the Winnie-the-Pooh books."

At about seven that night I joined the rest of the team in the room with the phone transmitter. They seemed to be taking turns putting on the headphones and listening to a call the woman was making. I intercepted meaningful looks passing between them. It slowly dawned on me that I was being excluded from some joke.

"What's going on?"

"You don't want to know."

Mike, who was wearing the cans, made a sudden explosive noise, took off the headphones and dashed to the bathroom. He met Robert on his way out. They were muttering something to each other. The door slammed behind Mike. Robert looked dazed.

"What is it?" I insisted.

Dave was a sensible man. The clean-living, vegetarian, non-smoking master of the ironic comment that I usually ended up working with. I knew and liked his wife. She was one of the few wives of men on the Circuit who felt secure enough not to worry about me working with her husband. But now even Dave was pink and spluttering.

"Think you'd better take over."

He flung down the headphones. I listened.

"I'm wearing the black silk. I'm moving my finger just there, and—"

This was an erotic phone call. She was talking to the client. And he had asked for the tapes. The cunning bastard knew all this was being recorded. My team needed a bucket of cold water thrown over them.

On the third day she arranged by telephone to meet a man that evening. At half-past seven she walked the hundred yards from the hotel to the restaurant. We hung about outside. In the center of Dublin, a security-conscious city, this is not as easy as it might sound. A thunderstorm began. Darkness fell. Rain teemed down. Hours passed. We moved, singly and occasionally together, from one shop window to another, keeping the restaurant in sight. Behind its long net curtains we could just see steaks flambéed in butter and bottles of vintage wine being uncorked. We were cold and wet. She did not come out. We were starving. Ten o'clock passed. People began to leave the pubs and pile into taxis and cars. Still the rain splashed on the pavements and the rich man's mistress stayed cozy, dry and well fed in the restaurant. At last, at midnight, she and her friend walked back to the Westbury. He left her at the entrance, the perfect gentleman. The rest of us, damp cloth flapping around our legs and dirty rainwater dripping onto the exquisite carpet hand-woven by leprechauns, tramped into the hotel and gathered in my room. We still had to go over the final report together.

I called for room service. There was no reply. I tried again ten minutes later. Still no reply. I stomped off to the elevator and down to the lobby, where a fat man leaned on the counter talking to the dinner-suited receptionist. I barged up to the desk and let fly.

"I do think that at £180 a night it's not too much to expect 24-hour room service. There are five cold, tired and hungry men in my room—"

"Eeza private party? Or can I come-a too?" interjected the fat man.

I was not in the best of tempers. "It is entirely private."

"I can seeng-a for my supper."

"Well, is that a fact? You can sing. Really."

I gave him an icy look and turned back to the man behind the counter with my sneer still in place. He seemed uneasy.

"Madam, may I introduce Mr. Luciano Pavarotti."

I could have sunk through the floor.

Next day, I found that Mr. Pavarotti had left two tickets for me to the concert he was giving that night. It was extremely generous of him, and I would have loved to go, but I had to fly back to London to do another job.

The Victoria and Albert Museum is a vast edifice not far West of Harrods that contains literally millions of exhibits from all corners of the globe. Prince Albert, the husband of Queen Victoria, made sure it got built with funds from the Great Exhibition of 1851. The V&A, as it is commonly known, is a national treasure house. In the early 1900s visitors could still get in free of charge, as Albert had intended. However, its miles of corridors and cathedral-like rooms, stuffed with displays of everything from priceless statuary and chunks of whole churches to fabrics and jewelry, cost a fortune to maintain. By now, government money and donations barely covered new purchases, never mind repairing the roof. So, amid great controversy, the new director of the museum had dared to instigate a voluntary entrance fee. This was rung up on cash registers as visitors went in. All went well until the management noticed that, although most people paid, the registers never returned much money.

Some of the female operatives I had trained made test purchases. This revealed that even at the august V&A, people are not above being on the fiddle. One man alone pocketed about £120 a day in cash.

Maybe this made the administrative staff wake-up, I cannot be sure, but soon afterward something even more suspicious was reported. A woman in the public relations department took a phone call from a photographer concerning Ham House, an historic building about twelve miles from London that is administered by the V&A. He wanted to hire the place for a location shoot but had not been able to reach the curator there. He had spoken to her previously.

"So, you've been to Ham House before," the PR lady asked.

"Yes."

"Could you give me the date?"

He gave it readily. She checked the records, to make sure no damage had been done and no fees were outstanding, but found no entry. He was adamant that he had the date right.

"It was the curator I spoke to last time. I paid cash."

The correct fee was more than he had been asked for. She smelled a rat and the director called us in.

Next week I called the curator myself, saying I was the personal assistant to a photographer who would like to use Ham House's grounds for a fashion shoot for a day. We fixed a date.

"It'll be twelve hundred pounds."

I hesitated, "Ah. In that case I had better check with him and get back to you."

"Eight hundred for cash."

"That'll be fine."

I turned up on the day with a guy from the Circuit, strung about with cameras, and two of my blonde, six-feet-tall nieces. Ham House seemed appropriate. We hammed it up for all we were worth. They strutted on steps, glared moodily at urns, and clutched trees.

"Give me vital!" yelled the photographer. "Give me wind." I was hair and makeup. The curator, a tiny woman with one of those slightly forced, upper-crust "cut glass" English accents, hobbled out to greet us on four-inch heels. As soon as the "wedge," a bundle of tightly folded banknotes, was placed in her hot little palm she motored gaily off to Kingston to deposit it in her Halifax Building Society account. I knew this because I had someone waiting outside to follow her there.

I put the information in front of the V&A, and they asked me to build the case further. Everything fell into place. Although she lived rent-free in an apartment in Ham House and earned only about twenty grand a year, she had a half-share in a property in Dorset worth a quarter of a million. I call that living beyond your means. She agreed to another photo shoot.

"When you come this time," she instructed me in that awful accent, "Ai won't be available, Ai've got meetings all day. So please give the money to the security man you'll meet near the entrance."

The security guard approached us in a spirit of cooperation, took his eight hundred and nipped off to deposit it in his account. (I was surprised, but at that stage I did not know he was her father-in-law.)

The local CID were ready to move. We agreed that we would turn up at Ham House to make the arrest at eight-thirty on Friday morning.

I rapped the knocker on the imposing front door. I had a detective sergeant and a uniformed police constable with me.

"She's gone to a meeting up town," said the cleaner who answered it.

"We are police officers," said the CID sergeant.

"Well, I can't help you, love. She went out to the museum first thing."

I called the director and asked her to carry on with the scheduled meetings, but to keep the woman in the building on some pretext. We slugged our way back to London through the rush-hour traffic. At the V&A, the curator was alone in an upstairs office. We knocked and entered. She was talking on the phone.

"What do you mean by barging in here?"

"We are police officers." The sergeant asked her to confirm her identity. She put the phone down and stood up. We all towered over her. She was told she was under arrest. She sat down, white as a sheet. Then she stood up again and came around the desk.

"Get out of here. You can't come in. You haven't got an appointment."

She stood there squeaking at us on her high heels, then she glared, puffed herself up, lowered her head, stamped her tiny foot and made a run for the door. We were all ten inches taller and in the way. It is amazing what fools people make of themselves. The detective bundled her flailing form away by one elbow as if she were some weak wild animal.

I was very happy. Christie's, the auctioneers, had asked me to do a job for them; thanks to me snooping around the stallholders in Camden Lock, they had caught a bent truck driver selling their valuable auction catalogs before they went on sale to the general public. And then I had another job for the V&A, and I was asked to run instructional courses on security for the ladies of Christie's auction rooms. Work was flooding in all the time; I could pick and choose. I met Thomas for a few days in the Caribbean.

"You've only got two more years on the Circuit," he said. "If it keeps going on like this you'll be rich when you retire."

"It's downright sinful," I agreed. We were sunbathing. There was plenty of that; we met in all the best places. "Think of it. Retiring at thirty-six with enough money to keep both of us."

"Seriously, I worry about you."

"What, making all this dosh?"

"No. I never know what you're doing. It could be dangerous."

"Not really. I know what I'm doing. Besides, I like it. Stop worrying and start planning where we'll sail on our yacht."

My life as a company director was not entirely trouble-free. I had to deal with some pretty odd people, and not just neurotic clients. Most of the guys on the Circuit had all the resourcefulness and phlegmatic competence you would expect from people who had been in the SAS or the Parachute Regiment or the Secret Service. But there were others, and this type would have you believe they played Frisbee with land-mines for fun. You had to be wary. I was always looking for promising contacts and after years on the Circuit, if I needed an expert in most fields associated with surveillance, protection or investigation, I generally knew where to look.

Although I was running my own agency, I still did work for other people. Paul, whose job it was, knew I spoke some German and asked me to take part in a surveillance operation near Hamburg. On the plane out of Heathrow at 5 AM my companion and I talked. I had never met him before. His name was Rob, he was forty-five, balding and stocky. He had been a major in the army and then in MI6. We made friends over the next few days, in the classic way you do on a surveillance job — sitting for long hours together in the front of a car. He was an open type, straight, and I liked him. He told me he had been married, two kids and a big house in the country, wrought iron gates and a long drive up to the front door, all that — but he was now divorced. He had left his wife for a travel agent called Ruby, and they had a new apartment in Docklands. He did not talk much about the army or MI6, but I did not expect him to. He thought discretion was important and also honesty; he said he would never look at another woman, now he had found Ruby. I thought that was nice. As to expertise, he spoke passable French and could go into houses posing as a telephone engineer and plant bugs, so I expected to use him in the future.

Hanging about in a Hamburg suburb, our conversation ranged over all manner of things, so I was pleasantly surprised when he called me at home before Christmas. He remembered that we had talked about Strauss and the New Year's Eve gala concert in Vienna that Thomas had told me about. Well, there was Strauss at the Albert Hall in London on New Year's Eve and he could get a box, so did I want to come and bring a few friends? I was delighted. Five of us went. Ruby was not quite what I expected. She was very nice, I thought. From Clapham, and worked in a travel agent's office. She told me she had met Rob through the singles column in the *Evening Standard*. He had not told me that part, but still, it was none of my business, and we had a great evening. I waved Rob and Ruby off into the New Year in their Jaguar XJ6.

Rob did not see much of his children, since they were in the big house in the country and he lived in London, but he had started a judo club in Streatham for underprivileged kids and had asked for support from some of us on the Circuit. I was only too glad to help and went along one night. I was surprised when I saw him. For a sixth dan he seemed entirely lacking in skill, speed or grace. He had a class of ten-year-olds, and if he had not been a major and a crack spy and all the rest of it, I would have thought he hadn't a clue as to what he was doing.

However, I needed somebody to bug phones, and he seemed pretty good at that. Another V&A job came up — they suspected a couple of employees were taking kickbacks from construction companies. It would be necessary to investigate and track both the employees and their contacts at home and at work, so I would need several vehicles and a lot of people. Rob would be one of them.

One of the V&A managers was pulling thirty grand a year and yet managed to occupy a two million pound property in Kent, so I was not surprised they had put the finger on him. I started by checking the electoral role, the Land Registry and so on just to see if he or his wife could have come by such a house by inheritance or some such. That drew a blank. Then a couple of my guys sifted through the garbage bins at his home for old bank statements and credit card transaction slips.

We had a surveillance team outside the staff entrance on the east side of the museum in South Kensington. We started by following people home. There was a cab rank opposite, so I put a couple of taxis there, and the rest of the team plotted up around and about. I coordinated the whole thing from my office a mile away in Grosvenor Place. At the end of the first day they were all going to report back to me for a debriefing: two ex-MI5 guys, a couple of ex-army men one of whom was Rob, a woman who had been an army sergeant, and a former policeman in the Met. All professionals I had worked with before.

It was getting on for eight o'clock, everybody had turned up at Grosvenor Place, but I thought there was an odd atmosphere. Rob said he had got to go, couldn't stay — something was on at home. The minute he was out of the door, Charlie, who had been in MI5, said, "Where d'you get that wanker from?"

"Why?"

Dick had been in MI5 as well. "Jacquie, he hasn't got a clue what he's doing," he said with disgust.

It seemed Rob had decided to sit in a café on the far side of the road opposite the staff entrance to the museum. He stayed there much too long and the others could see him, gawping out of the window with his camera equipment out on the table.

I thought it probably was not as bad as they said. After all, they were ex-MI5, he was ex-MI6, and the rivalry between the two departments was notorious. I told them I would have a word with him; give him a few more days.

The next day, the police called and invited themselves around. Two plain-clothes men came in suspiciously.

"What's going on?" they asked.

"I've a surveillance team out there. It's fine, I've informed Special Branch." (Princess Margaret was a patron of the museum and you cannot be too careful.)

"Yeah. Well, we've had a call from this beefeater."

They explained that the man who owned the café had once been a "beefeater," a Yeoman Warder of the Tower of London, and he had called the police because some nutter (stocky, balding, forty-five) had sat in his café for two afternoons running, and when he asked him what he was up to, he had been given the old finger-to-the-lips, hush-hush, nudge-nudge, I'm-Carruthers-from-MI6 treatment. I nipped down to the café myself. The beefeater was gentle but concerned.

"He said he was from MI6. He had this radio crackling on the table; it felt like a taxicab office in here. Well, you have to watch it, haven't you, there's all sorts about—"

I pulled Rob off the job immediately. As it happened, I could do that without a confrontation because somebody had come into the office and asked us to bug his home telephones, which is perfectly legal, so I sent Rob off on this new mission. The others made a great job of the investigation once he had stopped embarrassing them. I had a couple of them concealed in one of the suspect's backyards, and they taped conversations taking place within the house and photographed other goings-on.

When it was all over and I had handed in the report and the evidence, I turned my attention to the Rob conundrum. By this time he had disappeared — and for the second time he had not done the work I had asked him to do, and paid for. I asked Paul about him. I should have asked sooner; but then, that is typical of people in this business, everybody else is pulled apart but once we have decided on the strength of an introduction that we are "one of us," we trust each other completely. It seemed that since I had first worked with him, Rob had turned over a few other people in the industry, taking money to set up work and then not doing it. That was not all. One of the guys on the V&A team now told me that Rob had boasted he could get stun guns and other illegal weapons. He was bringing them in from abroad. This was highly illegal, and I did not like it.

I wanted something done, but I did not necessarily want him to know it was me who had instigated action against him. Karen, who had also worked for me on the V&A job, knew a woman crime reporter on the *Sunday Express*. She told the reporter what I knew and left her to follow it up. She snooped around, traced his family, and came up with a few surprises. His first wife lived in a council house on social security. She was not at all surprised to hear she was supposed to be living in a mansion. Rob had the Walter Mitty syndrome, she said; he had always been the same, just ask his relations, they had given up listening years ago. She had already had the bailiffs visiting about the payments on the Jag. As for his glowing army record, it consisted of six weeks at boot camp before he was kicked out.

It is not unknown for Walter Mitty syndrome to afflict people on the Circuit. It is an extreme form of the mind-set I noticed starting in myself when I first did close protection work in the Intercontinental.

You live the high life; you start thinking you really are part of that world. Only in Rob's case he really did believe he was James Bond.

ROB'S NASTY LITTLE ATTEMPT AT ARMS DEALING WAS SOMEBODY else's problem now, and I hoped he got what was coming to him. I turned my mind to other things.

A world-famous Danish optical manufacturer had been investigating one of its executives. He was involved in a conspiracy to counterfeit their products. To cover all the angles in court they needed proof that he had spent time in New York within the last few weeks. I was asked to gain access to his home and root through his personal effects for any kind of paper trail that would show he had been there.

I flew to Copenhagen with Karen; we hired a car and checked in at a monumentally snooty hotel that fifty years before had been the Nazi HQ in Denmark. For two days we watched the suspect's house. It was a pretty, detached double-fronted place with steep eaves and a long backyard. The house stood close to the road, but its porch and front windows were shaded by tall fir trees. In the evenings, police patrolled the street at regular but infrequent intervals. We could see no visible alarm system.

After dark on the third day we left the hotel, sashaying across the marble entrance hall in cocktail frocks as if we were going out to dinner. Karen drove to a quiet, hidden parking lot. We changed into work gear

— black tracksuits and trainers — and drove past the suspect's house. Tonight was Friday. We had been told there would be nobody there tonight or tomorrow and there was no light in the house, just a faint bulb in the porch. The street was quiet: a few parked cars, other secluded houses with curtains drawn, people presumably indoors having dinner. It was about ten o'clock.

Karen parked away from street lamps in the next side street. I put on gloves and took some plastic garbage bin liners with me. I crept up to the house wall, a shaded flashlight casting a dim circle of illumination on the path ahead. I followed it to the backyard. Three black garbage bins stood beside the garage. I switched off the flashlight and listened. I could hear nobody. I gingerly lifted the lid of a bin and stuck my hand inside. I felt something horribly squidgy, and it stank. I snatched my hand back, realizing I had uncovered a used diaper. These people did not bother to wrap their trash. I quietly tipped the bins on their side and filled the black bags. Listening all the time, I hauled the bags back through the front yard and left them behind the hedge. This took ten minutes, during which time there was not a sound to be heard, except for a faraway lovesick cat serenading his girlfriend and the low grind of traffic on the main road.

We loaded the bags into the trunk, and Karen set off back to the parking lot, complaining bitterly about the smell. We parked in the darkest corner of the lot and began changing back into our finery. I had just pulled my trousers off when a police car glided in and circled around. Then it made a second little tour, and stopped and focused its headlights on us. We were two women, one dark, one blond, blinking guiltily and struggling with our zippers in the front seats of a parked car. Nothing unusual in this liberal country. They drove off.

"Greetings from Denmark," Karen murmured.

Back at the hotel she rolled plastic sheeting over the carpet while I sneaked up the fire escape with the garbage. We put on rubber gloves and set to work. After all my effort, we found nothing. Not so much as a Macy's carrier bag. I took it all downstairs and heaved it into the nearest dumpster. I decided I had to do something I never liked: breaking and entering.

The next night we drove back to the house. I sneaked over the fence. In the darkness all the windows and doors were firmly shut but I had a set of lock picks. I felt thoroughly annoyed about having to do this. Well, I would. In my time I have arrested people for less.

No one could see the dimly lit porch from the road unless they were standing right at the gate, but there was always the chance that I might be spotted and I was glad when the pick worked quickly, and I was able to slip inside. I shone the Mag-lite down the corridor; it was long, wide, dark, and there were several doors leading off it, some of them open. Stairs led to an upper floor.

I had been told his study was the first room on the right. I crept in and shut the door behind me. I knew there was nobody else in the house or garden but there is something unnerving about being where you shouldn't. You are half listening for somebody else's breathing in the room. A computer stood on a huge old-fashioned desk. Also a telephone, a Copenhagen phone directory, a notepad with doodles, something scrawled on it in Danish. I pulled at the drawers one by one; they were not locked. There was no sign of any recent visit to New York. On the shelves, only books. I fumbled about for over ten minutes, and I still had nothing.

As I was about to open an old plan chest in a corner, I took a last look at the very top drawer of the desk. Above it was a slide-out tray for paper clips and business cards. It was locked, but I tried a tiny key I found in the drawer underneath. Gotcha. In one of the compartments, he had stashed the cards from several massage parlors in New York and a two-week-old credit card voucher for earrings bought at a Manhattan jewelry store. I held the Mag-lite on to the front of my camera and photographed all the cards in the tray. I could now, thank God, get out of here.

A peal of laughter rang out. I froze, switched off the flashlight and stood motionless. If I strained very hard I could just hear conversation. Where the hell was it? Outside or inside? I left the room as I had found it and sneaked into the corridor, barely daring to breathe behind the balaclava. The laughter must have come from deep inside the house. I tiptoed along close to the wall. The kitchen door stood open, with the faintest possible light showing from inside. I crept closer; I could smell cooking and hear a murmur of voices. I eased nearer still and peered through the crack between the hinges. Ten feet away, a young man talked to a girl whose face I could not see. They must have been having a candlelit supper.

I tip toed back through the hall and held my breath as I slipped out of the house.

"Go go go!" I hissed as I leapt into the seat beside Karen, my heart pounding. I discovered later that the suspect's stepson and his girlfriend had taken the house for the weekend. Somebody might have told us!

Back in London the following day, I found an odd call on my answering machine. At 01:07 in the morning, *Amazing Grace* had been played through a distant telephone on to the tape. Very weird.

Two days later, I heard what had happened to Rob. At some time not long after one o'clock in the morning, according to a pathologist's report later presented at the coroner's court, he had shot himself.

Earlier that evening he had checked into a hotel near Heathrow Airport. Two women, one blonde and one dark, had arrived from an escort agency. He had ordered dinner for all three of them in his room; the waiter remembered the little party quite well, as Rob must have known he would. The next morning a chambermaid came in to clean the room. She left again, having seen Rob apparently asleep on the bed in an odd position, crouched with his forehead on the bolster. Five hours later she came in again and saw that he had not moved. That was when staff at the hotel realized he was dead.

He had placed a pillow underneath his body and shot himself through the heart. The pillow soaked up all the blood. The more you thought about it, the odder it seemed. Nobody had ever heard of a suicide quite like it. But he died as he wanted to live, the man of mystery.

I began to run training courses. I conducted a seminar for accountants about fraud, and then there were the ladies of Christie's auction house, terribly la-di-dah but terribly "naice," who learned from me how to spot rogues . . . "my deah." Thomas was relieved that I had set off in this new direction. We spent a week near the northern coast of France, looking for a house to buy, and I told him about it. He looked terrific these days, with a permanent tan from months in the Caribbean, and I said, only half joking, that it was getting harder to stay at work for two more years and not retire now and stay in bed. He said, at least while I was teaching people about security, nobody was going to attack me. And I agreed with him . . . for the time being.

I was part of a team invited to instruct the Sri Lankan government's bodyguard squad. I thought I could look forward to r & r on a beach under some coconut palms, but in the end we did not go to Colombo, the Sri Lankan capital; the squad arrived for a residential course at the Hereford training center for eight days.

Eight thin brown policemen in plain clothes, all of them speaking good English, turned up on Monday morning. We four instructors were introduced. Unfortunately, the party had been led through the green lanes of Herefordshire by a sulky individual from their embassy. There was nothing politically correct about this guy. He took one look at me and curled his lip in disgust.

"This is a woman. She cannot teach our security team," he muttered to my colleague.

"Yes I can," I said pleasantly. "I'm fully qualified."

He gave a derisive snort. The policemen sniggered.

"No," he announced, still addressing my colleague, who looked highly uncomfortable. "This is completely unsatisfactory. These men cannot be taught by a woman."

"I can teach them," I repeated. The embassy man turned to me angrily.

"You think so? Sergeant Samaranayeke—" One of the smaller policemen stepped forward.

"Attack this woman."

I knocked Sergeant Samaranayeke on his arse and stood on his windpipe. The man from the embassy looked sick. My foot remained firmly on the sergeant's throat.

"All right," said the embassy man through gritted teeth, lifting his hands in submission.

"Please go away and let us start the course," I said. He took a few paces toward the prone policeman under my boot, but then backed off, furious.

"Enough!" he barked at me. Sergeant Samaranayeke was now a bluish color. I folded my arms, kept my boot where it was and stared into space.

The embassy man had to storm off in his car before I would release his sergeant. He recovered quickly and, although most of the others were equable enough in my company, for the rest of the week I detected strong animosity from him. He did what I told him with a suffering air. He thought I had humiliated him. Stupid, really; it was nothing personal. I had only been making a point. As the week went by I kept telling the whole lot of them not to get into fights with women. Men always hold back out of chivalry, and we fight dirty, I pointed out. Samaranayeke glared.

They were a smart bunch of coppers, fit and quick on the uptake. In fact, by Saturday night we were all delighted that the course had been such a success. We took them down to the pub for a drink and joined in with the locals singing karaoke. One of the Sri Lankans was on stage bawling — "I'm leaving, on a jet plane . . ." — when I nipped out to the Ladies room. When I came back, two of them shyly stopped me in the bar. They had bought me a wooden cross covered in seashells. I was really touched. I thought that was sweet of them and was just saying so when Samaranayeke came over, fortified by a couple of pints of bitter.

"Well done," he said scornfully. "You have turned two men into women."

There's no pleasing some people. I set off on my own back to the camp. It was a fifteen-minute walk down an unlit country lane, and I was very much aware that Samaranayeke was up for Round Two. However, he did not seem to have followed me. I washed my underwear and did some packing and then had to collect something from the supply hut. I knew somebody was in there; I heard a noise as soon as I opened the door. Knowing I must be silhouetted against the light from outside I shut it behind me and stood still in the dark.

"You are a woman and you think you can cause me problems?" said Samaranayeke, up close. He sprayed my face with pepper dust and punched me in the stomach. My face wrinkled like a prune and my eyes flooded with salt tears. I was curled up on the floor getting a good kicking. It was just like old times on the *Britannia*. Only this time I had no radio and I couldn't bloody see. I had no alternative . . . I began to wail. He stopped at once, switched on a light, helped me to my feet and apologized. I was sniveling, genuinely, because of the pepper, but I was getting my eyesight back.

"I'm a woman in a man's world," I sobbed. "I'm sorry. I had to hit you. I have to be like this."

"That's all right." He looked embarrassed. I blew my nose and tucked my hanky into my pocket. Then I decked him.

"You soft bastard," I said, and walked off leaving him groaning on the floor. I had told him. I had been telling him all week. But did he listen?

Three of us were invited to Egypt, where the Ministry of the Interior wanted us to inspect and advise on anti-terrorist measures at the airports and in international hotels. I was the hotel security expert; Bob, an ex-paratrooper who founded an agency I had often worked with, was to advise on dog handling, and Brian, a charming ex-SAS lieutenant colonel, was to lend a bit of gravitas to the proceedings and take the larger view.

We turned up at Cairo Airport in baking heat to be met by a beaming under-secretary and a large official car. Flunkeys took our passports away, muttering about the need for visa stamps. We hung about in the VIP lounge being polite for twenty minutes, and when at last our passports were returned, we were driven to the ministry. They did not ask us in, but the trunk of the official car was opened and half a dozen carrier bags clanking with bottles of Glenfiddich were swiftly transported through a side door. We continued to the hotel. I looked at my passport that now had some odd squiggles around the Egyptian visa stamp. Bob and Brian had the same hieroglyphics in theirs. Eventually it dawned on us that foreign passports had been necessary for the interior ministry staff to buy alcohol from the duty free shop.

The Egyptians were very hospitable and took pride in showing us around. It was rather a shame, really, that we were there to point out shortcomings in their system. There were quite a few. I started to feel downright churlish and carping. Even when we were taken to see the changing of the presidential guard we saw security problems. It was hard to miss them. Anywhere else, overhanging branches next to the perimeter wall of a secure building are cut down. But the Egyptians had a novel solution. They posted sentries in the trees. The changing of the guard meant some sentries climbed down and others climbed up.

We ran a course from eight in the morning until four in the afternoon. I was treated with respect for eight hours. The deference accorded by pupil to teacher meant that all the officers we were training looked me in the eye, spoke carefully to me and tried to impress. After four, when classes ended, it was as if I had turned into a pumpkin. There was no more eye contact, and I was rudely elbowed in the corridors.

As a woman I was treated with the utmost paternalism. The three of us had asked for neighboring rooms so that we could meet easily to discuss course work and solutions to other business related problems, but although the rooms were close together I might as well have been on another floor. No men, including room service waiters or other staff, were allowed to cross the threshold of my room. A male guard observed my door day and night. If such a big strong man had not been there, heaven knows what I would have done. I might have lain awake for hours, worrying and trembling. I should not make fun; it was sweet of them really.

Cairo was hectic, noisy and full of curious locals. Physically, all three of us stood out as we were taller than the general population, but Bob caused a sensation wherever he went, as he was six feet six and blonde. This became a nuisance, and anyway we had work to do, so we tended to spend evenings in the hotel. The Gulf War had not long ended, and one night we were taking coffee after dinner in the poolside restaurant when a party of Kuwaiti princelings sent over a bottle of Johnnie Walker Red Label. "To our allies!" We smiled and nodded and expressed our gratitude. One of the royal party, a skinny prince with an overbite wearing a white dishdash, rose with a meaningful look at me and approached the stage. He whispered something to the band, climbed up on the dais, the music struck up and he performed the sand dance with great passion and verve. His manservant leaned over my shoulder.

"That is for you, madam," he whispered. "Our prince dances for the beautiful lady."

"Gosh," I said. I was jolly impressed. The prince tossed back his head-wrap, flashed me a sultry look over his Bugs Bunny teeth and wiggled his hips. When it was all over he stepped down from the stage to polite applause and I slipped away. Returning five minutes later I came face to face with him.

"I danced for you."

"It was wonderful. Thank you so much."

"You join me now for a drink."

"I'm afraid not. I'm working."

"Ah, you are secretary?"

"No. I am the anti-terrorist expert."

A sort of flicker, like a mild electric shock, affected his mouth. He bowed.

"It has been a pleasure to meet you, madam."

That's got rid of you, sonny.

A few days later we flew to Luxor. The idea was to inspect airport security there, but Luxor was off the scale. It did not actually have radar yet: the army base down the road phoned the control tower to say when a plane was about to land.

Cairo Airport, of course, was different. On our arrival the men from the ministry had boasted about the millions of pounds' worth of German scanning equipment that had recently been installed. Thanks to these high-tech measures there was now no drug or terrorist problem in Egypt. Since the equipment went in there had not been a single arrest.

Impressed, we went to see the system in action. Handlers heaved luggage onto the rolling ramp as we watched from the other side. We remained quiet for a few minutes. At last Brian cleared his throat politely and pointed out that the alleged lack of smuggling or terrorist crime could be — and it was only a suggestion, mind — because the screens were not switched on.

As we peered at the blank screens, passengers had been treading nervously through the metal-detector arches. They need not have worried, as these were not plugged in either. When our hosts confirmed that nobody had been trained to use any of this stuff, we had to design additional course notes in rather a hurry.

I had discovered that there was a circuit over and above the Circuit. It consisted of the international exchange of expertise and information. None of us could do anything to combat international crime unless we collaborated and learned from one another. And of course, expertise could be a valuable export. My company received a government enterprise grant to finance my attendance at COPEX, the Covert Operational Procurement Exhibition, in Baltimore. There I made contacts that would profoundly affect the work I undertook in the next three years.

C OVERT OPERATIONS FAIRS TAKE PLACE IN MIAMI, BALTIMORE AND in England. Women are not well represented at any of them. At COPEX in Baltimore there seemed to be about three thousand men, and me. On the first morning I took a walk away from my exhibition stand, down endless aisles crowded with guys whose lapel badges proclaimed their status. They were officers in the FBI or the CIA, or vice presidents with arms manufacturers or Japanese electronics companies. The few who wore no badges at all, out of arrogance, I supposed, turned out to be from British MI5 or MI6.

Promotional videos boomed and glared unheeded in every corner. Business cards disappeared into a thousand wallets. There were displays of guns, surveillance cameras, communications systems, rigid inflatable boats, CCTV, tanks, tents, telescopes and survival equipment of all kinds. Stuff I wanted, stuff I needed but could not afford, and stuff I could not have found a use for unless I started a small-scale war. All the salesmen ignored me unless I approached them. I was the wrong sex.

After half an hour, what with all this hardware and being treated like the invisible woman, I felt a bit dazed. But then I spotted another alien, just like myself. It was a shock, like Stanley finally meeting Dr. Livingstone. I had given up any expectation of seeing another female and I think she had, too. She was a friendly, dark-haired woman from North Carolina called Ann Walker. She introduced me to her husband, Buddy. We stood talking for five minutes until she was interrupted by insistent enquiries about their firm, ISS, International Security Services.

We were staying at the same hotel, and in the bar that night I met them again. We had been speaking for twenty minutes when I told her I was going on to New York after this. I would be driving there. She asked me where I planned to stay, and when I explained I would find a room when I arrived, she opened her purse and handed me a set of keys to their Fifth Avenue apartment. I could not get over such kindness.

They arranged for me to be shown around New York by guys from the NYPD; I put them up later in London; we became friends, and started helping each other professionally. Ann turned up penniless once at London's Heathrow Airport with a mother and a little girl they had rescued from some horror in Bangladesh, and she stayed with me. That was typical of the sort of thing that happened with ISS. Ann and Buddy had work that kept them overseas a lot.

They had accidentally cornered a market I had barely come across until now: child rescue. When two people from different cultures marry, the children too often end up trapped where one of the parents does not want them to be. ISS helped mothers — it was usually mothers — get their children back. I had read of tug-of-love cases in the newspapers, but I did not know there was anybody who would help a parent to snatch a child back. But after the first few successful rescues, publicity had snowballed.

"We get three hundred letters a week," Ann said grimly. "It's killing me. Most of these women we can't help. We can't afford to. Can you imagine what it costs us?"

"Well," I hazarded. "Fares, accommodation—"

"Bribes, equipment," Buddy said. "You start thinking about how to get kids out, you start getting into real serious stuff. You might need a chopper or a boat." Buddy had been in the crack Delta Force. He was a heavy-set man with a nice smile who did not talk much. I wondered if this was not a bit over the top.

"Choppers and boats? Come on."

"No kidding. There's often no way else. When you start reading some of the info packs we get and hear the case histories, you'll see."

From the first job I did for ISS, I began to see what Buddy had meant. It was really two jobs — one on top of another — both in Saudi Arabia. The first one was typical, because there was literally no way out.

When I was staying in North Carolina, a woman called Ann after seeing her on television. She had recently been to Saudi and had met an American mother called Myra who was being held against her will, with her children. The two women had only managed to talk when they met at a supermarket.

Myra had met her Saudi husband while attending a university in the state of Washington. He was charming, earned a good living after graduation, and over the years they had five children: three boys and two girls. The youngest were nearing school age and the eldest was about ten when he suggested they take the family home for a vacation. He had never taken his wife or the children to the Middle East, but it was part of the children's heritage, he said. They should meet their cousins and grandparents. There would be a large villa in Riyadh, servants to do all the work, a chauffer and trips to the beach when they went to the family's second home in an oil town near the Gulf. It seemed a wonderful prospect.

That had been two years before. Within weeks of their arrival the husband altered. He was permanently ill-tempered and insisted that his wife remain in purdah like an Arab wife. He confiscated her passport, took a permanent job in Riyadh and announced that the children were his property and so was she; none of them were ever going back to

America. He employed servants who reported everything to him. When she tried to reach the U.S. embassy, he found out and broke her ribs. When she attempted to telephone relations in America, he broke her arm.

Ann insisted that Myra herself must ask for this rescue. With the intermediary's help, Ann managed to speak to her. The sad story was true enough. Myra was desperate to leave. There was only one chance to escape. She was to take the children to the Gulf house for the summer while her husband spent six weeks in Indonesia on business.

Money was available, but it was hard to see a way around the practical difficulties. Myra told Ann she was guarded by servants and armed drivers at all times. There were checkpoints on the roads. Women were not allowed to drive and not allowed to be driven unless the man could show proof he was a paid employee, a relative or a cab driver. She could not get to the embassy in Riyadh with her children, and even if she could, the embassy staff would not be entitled to protect them there. Under Saudi law, children became their father's property from the age of seven. Even if she reached the airport she had no passport for herself and certainly no travel documents to cover five children who looked like locals. Not only that, but her husband's job kept him in close contact with airport staff who knew him and might recognize their family name.

Ann, Buddy and I discussed the possibilities. The only scheme we could come up with was to hire a boat in Djibouti, sail along the Yemeni coast and into the Gulf, and effectively snatch the mother and children off the shore. I could sail a boat and felt confident about the Djibouti part, so we dispatched a couple of men to recce the set-up at the vacation home.

It was hopeless. They did their best to get close to the tall American woman robed from head to toe in black, but she was under armed guard all the time and they, as westerners, were too conspicuous to carry out any proper surveillance. They said the boys were driven back and forth to some kind of school, but in separate cars and at different times of day. Roadblocks were everywhere. Women were routinely questioned. Western women in the town, wives of expatriate oil men, stuck together in their compounds so Myra hardly ever came into contact with them. She dressed like a local woman. Her sons were not allowed out with her alone; if she went out with her children, there were male servants around. Myra, speaking on the telephone to Ann, confirmed all this. Ann explained the difficulties. She suggested that in this impossible situation, Myra should take the girls and leave the boys.

"At least you know the boys won't be ill-treated. With girls it's different." (Ann had heard that female circumcision was practiced in Saudi Arabia.)

"I can't do it. I can't leave them here."

It was one of the first child rescue cases I had come across and one of the most harrowing. We could do nothing. The institutions in Saudi Arabia prevent women from having any power over their own lives. If this brute of a husband wanted to keep his wife prisoner, he had chosen the right place. As far as I know, Myra and her children are still in Saudi Arabia.

I had heard Saudi horror stories years ago on the tom squad. Guys on the Circuit would come back from a stint guarding the royals in the Gulf, and they would say to each other, "Remember Tina?" or Nicky or Vicky, or one of the other girls who had hung around the casinos. "Blond girl from Cardiff, married a towel head? Saw her in Dharan last week."

"How's she doing?"

"Desperate. Hanging round the hotels, face wrapped up in a yashmak. Christ, she looked rough."

"What happened?"

"He divorced her, she married a bloke with a Toyota dealership, then he divorced her, she's got two kids and no passport. Kids are Saudi, aren't they? Poor cow, eh?"

That sort of story made me believe the white slave trade still flourished.

While we were looking into Myra's case, a Saudi woman called the ISS office. She was from Riyadh but had got out by marrying a man who took her to live in America. She had been desperate to marry to get away from her father, who used to beat her mother, her sister and herself. After some years the mother had gone to England for medical treatment, and had found a way to stay there. This just left the younger girl. She was now twenty-six and taking the full force of the father's bullying.

The sisters spoke often on the telephone but now Dina, the one from California, was beside herself with anger. Something more terrible than usual had happened in Riyadh. The younger sister had accepted a ride from a neighbor and they had been stopped by the religious police, who enforce the laws of the mullahs. When these people had discovered that she was an unmarried woman traveling with a man she was not related to or married to, they had given on-the-spot notice of punishment. She would have to report to them and receive forty lashes.

The girl was distraught, and Dina had reached a decision. She said her family would spend whatever it cost to get her sister out of the country. She had the germ of an idea that sounded as if it might work. But it would be expensive. We calmed her down and told her we would at least go there and recce the job, to see if we could put the plan into action.

There were times in the next couple of months when I thought we must have been mad to hope we could ever do this, but after poor Myra and her five children, anything looked easy. From North Carolina, that is.

Back in London, I teamed up with one of the guys I knew from the Circuit, along with a friend of a friend who had contacts in Saudi Arabia, and we concocted a visa application. I could not go into Saudi alone as a woman, and if Richard went by himself and tried to speak to the sister he would probably have his vital parts cut off for attempted rape, so for the purposes of this job we were a man and a woman with a mission to sell machine parts. Our contact obtained an invitation for us as the sales representatives of a company making parts for machinery that extruded high-density polypropylene pipes. *That should be a conversation stopper,* I thought.

Our visas came through. They were valid for six weeks; most of the time I was going to be in purdah, swathed from head to toe in robes with my face covered. I visited an optician on Edgware Road, had my eyeballs sized up, and ordered prescription-free brown contact lenses. All I needed for a complete disguise.

There were many stressful aspects to the Saudi job — the heat, the imminent danger of flogging, and so on — but the thing that set us all on edge was the race against time on several fronts at once. We had a six-week entry permit. The punishment lashings had been postponed until the following month, but the date loomed.

The brutal father was in Hanover, Germany, where he usually stayed for several months in the summer. Our contacts kept him under surveillance there. He saw a lot of one woman, so all we could hope for was that she would retain his interest. If he took it into his head to return at any moment we would get advance warning.

At the house in Riyadh a 28-year-old brother remained as chaperone. By all accounts he was a lot like his father, though nobody knew what he did or where he went.

And in America, we had a Saudi supplied with a false passport on standby to arrive at Riyadh airport, collect his "wife" — Amina, the younger sister — and leave. This was the major complication. Because his job and family demanded his attention, there were only three weeks in which he could come from California to do this. He was being paid $25,000 but he was doing it reluctantly, and we knew he meant what he said about the time window. He would arrive on a flight from Los Angeles, plant himself in the departure lounge until the next flight out, and leave with or without her; that was the deal. We would have to co-ordinate flight plans.

Then there was the paperwork. Without the right documents, Amina would never get out alive. To get on a flight, she had to have a passport as a wife. No Saudi woman could leave the country without a passport, if she was unmarried, issued with the permission of a male relative, or if she was married, with the permission of her husband. The back-up story was that she had left legitimately on her unmarried woman's passport, met this guy, married him in America, come home to see the folks on her new-married woman's passport, and here he was to take her back.

We had bought a false marriage certificate. We were waiting for a false passport to be made up in the right name at a cost of $13,000. The passport would be stamped with an exit visa when she left. All this had been organized, and then somebody pointed out that they would smell a rat at the airport because as a US resident she would have had an entry visa when she first came back. That had to be put into the passport as well — an additional $5,000. Everything cost.

On arrival we stayed in an international hotel and wore our usual clothes. Richard and I drove past the family house in a taxi. It was in a district where wealthy people lived, near our hotel. All we could see were whitewashed walls around a courtyard. The street offered a surreal view of parched palms, sand gathering in runnels beneath walls, yellow sky, no noise, no windows, nothing parked, nobody about; Maida Vale it was not. You could not sit around with a Mars bar and the Sun cross-word to keep you company.

After a few days I bought a chador in a market, we changed hotels, and I stayed in my room all the time. I practiced putting on the yashmak, the robe and the contact lenses. I walked up and down the room, eyes downcast, the chador swaddled around me.

I knew what Amina looked like; I knew she spoke English; I knew what she wanted to do. I was now two streets away. But I could not just call her up on the telephone and arrange to meet. The servants reported everything she did and every call she made and received to her father and brother. I also had to assume that my calls from the hotel would be monitored by the internal security services.

I spoke to the older sister, Dina, in Los Angeles, and she told me that "a package" would be waiting for me at the post office on a certain date. So at least I knew where and when I would meet her sister. What I did not know was what progress we were making on the passport. Ann and Buddy had to talk in oblique terms, and I was never quite sure what was holding it all up.

I was powerless. I waited and had to stay out of sight. I could go nowhere for two, three days on end. Meals were deposited on trays outside the hotel room. I wondered what Thomas was doing, but I had told him not to expect a call from me for a couple of months. I watched CNN. I read every magazine on the hotel's rack. I looked out of the window. From high up I could see swimming pools glinting blue in the gardens of rich people's houses. Stuck in my room, I lived from one meal to the next, one telephone call to the next. I remembered the sheikha that I used to bodyguard years ago at the Intercontinental. If this carried on I would be scratching my name on the wallpaper.

When the time came to scuttle down the back stairs and into the street to the post office, I kept my eyes lowered. It was absolutely not permitted for a woman to look a man in the face. Outside, the traffic noise and dust came as a shock. Troops were everywhere. At busier junctions, religious police patrolled in pairs. They were squat bullies with long nightsticks, white uniforms and blue bands on their head-dress. I concentrated on my own feet, moving rapidly under yards of black cotton. I had been told that if they caught sight of your bare legs they sprayed them with yellow paint. If they nicked you masquerading as a devout Saudi woman when you did not even speak Arabic, I guessed they might think up some even jollier wheeze.

I followed the crowds into the main post office. The main room was high, cool, grubby and full of people, like a railroad station and nearly as noisy. I looked for the girl. The little swathed figure was in the right place, and instantly recognizable amid the crowd of identical bundles because she was so tiny; anorexic, with little bones and big eyes like a mouse. I stood next to her and murmured through my yashmak that I was Dina's friend. She nodded. I told her I needed to know when her brother came and went from the house. She promised to write this down and pass me a note, in the same place at the same time a few days later.

That was all the excitement there was. It was enough, since we were both so threatened, but I expect an adrenalin high to build and maintain. This job meant alternating short sharp bursts of danger and concentration with long interludes of tedium. It went on like that for nearly six weeks. We got the information we needed, inch by inch. There was tension on both sides. I never walked the streets in a chador again. Richard found me a cab every time. It was safer.

The brother left the house for three hours in the morning, two hours in the afternoon and three hours late at night. We had to get Amina out of the country before the brother realized she had left. If he alerted the airport, she was a goner. I pored over flight timetables.

At long last we received Amina's passport. It looked perfect. The Saudi "husband" was flying in from LA on a morning plane. He was booked to leave for London, with his "wife," that afternoon.

For several days, Richard had been keeping an eye on the brother's movements as inconspicuously as he could from a taxi. The driver had been well paid and would assist on this last day. We were both pretty sure the brother was out of the way for several hours.

When I left the post office I knew Amina was following me, clasping her two small bags. She got into the back seat of the taxi beside me. Richard sat in front beside the driver. We nudged through heavy traffic, music sawing away on the radio, strips of red and gold fringe wobbling inside the windows and a gold cardboard Hand of Fatima swinging by the rear view mirror. Nobody dared say a word. In the yard behind the hotel, our luggage was loaded into the trunk. I ran indoors to the powder room and changed into western clothes. We were off to the airport.

Richard had warned me that there would be three checkpoints on the way out of the city. At least the guards were not difficult to distract. They waddled, self-important, across to the car and peered inside as they glanced at our documents, and then their eyes bulged. They were riveted. I was wearing a skirt the size of a hand-towel wrapped around my waist, and three-inch heels. I slid out of the car to stretch and strut unconcernedly every time we stopped. Then I wiggled back in, flinging my legs about in case they missed anything. Whatever they were concerned about, it was not Amina's papers.

In the miles between roadblocks we hurriedly filled her in on the details I had never managed to make clear in the post office. We were supposed to be traveling together because, as an acquaintance of her "husband," I had agreed to escort Amina as far as the airport. She would be taken into a cubicle where a female security officer would make her take off her chador to check if she was who she said she was. I was going to distract the male guards again. But she might be questioned.

Dina had always known that suspicious officials might ask her sister about life in America, so she had spent a lot of time on the phone enthusing about Malibu, how warm and sweet-scented it was, how she would be driving this afternoon to the beach, not far from the house, along that lovely street with the palms swaying, to the wide sands and those big houses on the shoreline with decks overlooking the Pacific.

Dina knew the Saudi community in LA was not large. People sent letters home, people gossiped across continents. Any of the security people at the airport could have had relations in LA who would surely have known and spoken of this couple had they been genuine. I did not point this out to Amina. She looked terrified enough as it was.

At the airport, Richard and I checked in her small suitcase with our own. I handed my passport to an elderly official. Amina stood a few feet away. The official peered at me. He flicked a fly from his nose with one end of his white headdress. He looked at the visa stamps. He asked me about the firms I had been visiting.

"You do good business with Saudi, yes?"

"Very good."

He glanced at the tiny bundled figure.

"Why do you travel with that lady?"

"She is meeting her husband. He asked me to bring her here."

Out of the corner of my eye I saw a woman in uniform taking Amina by the elbow. They disappeared into a cubicle with a long green curtain in front, like a changing room. A younger official peered over the old man's shoulder. He picked up my passport, looked at me. He started asking where I had stayed in Riyadh. Inwardly I let out a great sigh of relief. I could spin this along; he was just talking to me out of boredom. Another guard came. They both started flirting. One of them stamped and returned my passport. Then he smacked my bottom. They had not taken a blind bit of notice of Amina. She came back; they barely looked at her documents and waved both of us through with Richard.

In the departure lounge stood the man I had come to recognize from his photographs as the "husband." He was several shades paler than the man I had been expecting, but I knew it had to be him. He shivered convulsively. The air conditioning was not that good; he was just the most scared person I had ever seen. I did not blame him.

He nodded to me and to his "wife" — which if this had been a genuine Saudi marriage would have been absolutely the right thing to do — and shook Richard by the hand. We hung about for the flight to be called in a state of nervous tension. When I saw that British Airways jet on the tarmac it shimmered. It was not just the heat haze. If a yellow brick road had suddenly appeared across the tarmac to that plane, if it had sprouted pepperpot turrets and a rainbow over the cockpit, I would not have been at all surprised. We were two couples now, crossing to the airplane and climbing the steps. I was carrying hand luggage with Amina's jewelry in it. When we reached the top of the steps there stood a flight attendant in her perky hat, looking passengers straight in the eye and smiling like a normal person.

"Good afternoon, sir. Good afternoon madam. Good afternoon, sir. Good afternoon madam."

"Gimme a drink," I said.

We had taken our seats in first class and were taxiing along the runway. None of us were speaking, when the crew curtain began to riffle and move. I stared, fascinated, as a hand appeared, and passed me an uncorked bottle of wine and a glass.

I HAD TWO YEARS TO GO BEFORE I WAS SUPPOSED TO RETIRE AND JOIN
Thomas, and work obsessed me. When I saw Thomas after Saudi,
I was euphoric. But, after a subsequent case involving snatching a
child from an oxcart, I was on a different kind of high. The oxcart incident — looking back on it — could have gone horribly wrong.

I was working with a friend of Buddy's called Dan, who had been
asked to grab a child back from the Middle East. The Arab father was
a violent man, divorced, with no legal custody of his daughter. He had
snatched her from her school in Florida two years earlier. The American
mother seemed both vague and single-minded. She had spent several
weeks with her husband's family in his home country when they were
first married, but now she could not even remember the name of the
village where they lived. All she could give us were photographs of
some ruins taken in 1978 from the balcony of the family home. Dan
sent a couple of guys to the capital on a recce, and they identified the
place from those ruins: a hillside hamlet about thirty miles from the
Turkish border. The house was a two-floored place with the usual black-
clad women puttering about in the courtyard. There were several children. One of them was blonde and looked like the last picture of the
daughter, taken two years ago. Sometime between two and four every

afternoon, the women and children left the house and were transported in the back of an oxcart along a desert track to another village, where they helped to pack dried tobacco leaves.

We had decided to bring the child across an isolated border post and head for Adana, where there are tourist flights. Dan and I and the mother had to organize visas; she must be present when the child was rescued, or we could be accused of kidnapping. Money changed hands behind the scenes. Our documents were in order. We hired a car, and early one morning drove to the flat plain away from the coast.

Journeys are monotonous in this part of the world. We crossed the border out of Turkey without a problem, and the car grumbled over rough road for about ten miles until it met a decent hard-surfaced highway that stretched from north to south. We kept straight on, and Dan's two operatives met us at a small town on the hill road east of the capital. They drove ahead of us past the house. It was early afternoon and the flat-bedded cart stood on the track outside, with no animals between the shafts.

We all wanted to get it over with. We could not park; the way from the house led over dusty tracks, along about a mile of tarmac, and over dust again. There was no reason to stop, so if we did, any other driver would think there was something wrong. On the other hand we could not keep cruising up and down the single road through the town. About ten cars a day passed through this part of the world. We were horribly conspicuous. Despite occasional ruins baking in the sun, it was not a tourist area and we felt that if we loitered for more than an hour or two, the police would come snooping. Dan, the girl's mother and I were in a car with Turkish plates, the two other Americans in the rental car they had been driving for a week. We made a big circle around the district.

We were all tense and three of us carried guns. There was no other way.

At last, far ahead on the empty main road we saw that the ox cart, packed with people, had started moving. The two operatives slowly overtook it. We approached, but hung back a long way. It was an old, sandy cart creaking along on iron-tired wooden wheels, traveling at about five miles per hour. Probably twenty women and children rode on the back, and none of us could see the little girl among them. The car ahead drove cautiously off the main road onto the track to the tobacco village, and disappeared over a hill; the cart lumbered after it. We hung back and then drove after the cart. The guys in front should have pulled across the road at the brow of the hill. Sure enough, the ox cart stopped when it reached the top. We tore up and screeched to a stop right behind it. In a second I leaped out of the car and was running forward with the girl's mother. Ahead of me, one of Dan's mates already had a gun trained on the cart's driver.

Pandemonium erupted on the cart. The driver, a filthy looking old geezer with one tooth and a turban, screamed in Arabic and brandished his fists in the air. Half a dozen huge black-gowned women wobbled to their feet, all shrieking and grabbing at me as I jumped aboard. The mother saw the little girl first, and hauled her from between the obstructive women and out of the back. I held the women off. I saw Dan running around looking for some way to disable the cart, but he gave up. It was a bit low-tech, as transport goes, and they were hardly going to chase us with it. We jumped into our car. The other car rocked around to join us, and we were off, racing back to the junction near the border where we swapped cars and drove in different directions.

Dan drove north. The mother and child were having a tearful reunion in the back seat. He and I said nothing. We were too busy concentrating on what might happen next. We were conscious that we were carrying guns and might have to use them.

The whole operation had taken under two hours. The American investigators had assured us they had paid in advance for us to cross the border no questions asked. When we arrived there, a workers' bus would be waiting; we were to cross in that. We veered off up the grotty road back to Turkey.

The customs post amounted to not much more than a couple of scruffy buildings and some scratching dogs. The bus was the only one there, stationary and baking in the sun. We clambered onto it. And waited.

Dan sat on one side of the gangway, I sat on the other. I gazed through the muzzy fly-spattered windscreen at the barrier, fifty yards away. Behind us the mother and child whispered and murmured. The driver, it seemed, was inside the police post eating his lunch.

Another bus arrived. Wizened men and women, mostly carrying what looked like their week's laundry, climbed out and began to heave their possessions into our bus. We had been sitting in silence for twenty minutes when two armed soldiers ambled out of nowhere, chucked their cigarettes on the ground and climbed in. They stared the length of the bus. I sat near the front.

"Papers."

I handed the soldier my passport. My right hand crept behind my back. I could feel the heavy pistol stuck in my waistband.

He looked at me, shut the passport and handed it back. The two of them moved down the bus, checking documents. The driver returned. The soldiers got off, the bus jerked forward and crawled across the bridge, and half an hour later we were in Turkey, negotiating a taxi fare to Adana.

Thomas and I ended up discussing the oxcart case. I seldom talked to him about work, but there was a bit of a fuss about that rescue. Dan had been informed that the State Department might have to make an apology for the behavior of its nationals in a sensitive part of the world, and it was on my mind. Thomas and I were together in the Caribbean, I was obviously preoccupied, and in the end sketched the event in outline. Not the details, but the fact that guns had been involved inevitably came into it. He looked grim.

"I just want you to give this up," he said. "I admire what you do, but there is no cause worth getting shot for."

I thought of his father, killed trying to escape East Berlin. Thomas knew what he was talking about.

"I won't get shot. It's only a couple more years, Thomas."

"You keep saying that. You're no good to me dead."

By the time Neil Livingstone's book recounting some of ISS's exploits had hit the shops in America, I was discovering that there is more than one way to fall flat on your face in this business. Back in London, we were approached by a woman called Jo Clark, who wanted to get her sons back.

Her story had already been in the news because of an abortive rescue attempt. Twelve years before she had married an Egyptian and had a daughter and two boys by him. Quite recently he had taken the children away to live in Egypt. She hired a bunch of thugs to retrieve them. As operations go it must have been a fiasco, because when she grabbed the little girl, the child's grandfather came roaring at her with a knife and stabbed her eighteen times. Harry Arnold, a journalist from the *Daily Mirror,* became involved. He may have told her about ISS; I am not sure. By now we had a lot of publicity. However it came about, Jo Clark contacted Buddy and he promised to go and see her, with me, when he came to London.

Jo had been in the hospital in Egypt for some time after the stabbing. She must have been an embarrassment to the Foreign Office, but somehow, in the end, she got the little girl out. Now they lived in Coulsdon, Surrey, in a council house. Coulsdon is one of those dull suburbs that function like cross-hatching on the map of a city, filling in the gaps between the landmarks. Jo and little Poppy had nothing; the bare and cheerless front room with its threadbare carpet smelled fusty, and I felt sorry for whoever found themselves in such horrible circumstances.

She was a lot older and thinner than I had expected. I felt almost sure I was looking at an alcoholic. If not now, then at some time in the past, drink must have given her that gray and haggard look. But I was not about to pass judgment on her for that; she must have suffered terribly when her children were taken.

She told us she had been looking for a legal way to gain custody of her two sons still in Cairo, but it seemed hopeless. Buddy advised her to keep the case going through the courts. He told her any kind of covert operation would cost a lot of money. I backed him up. We had already brought an American child out of Tunisia by boat, and although all I had done was sail the ship across the Mediterranean, I knew how much that had cost. Given how jumpy the Egyptian family must be, this was not going to be a straightforward matter of putting Jo and the boys in a cab to Cairo airport.

Jo was not going to let mere financial difficulty put her off, however. She said she was being paid by a newspaper, but because most of that money would go toward the lawsuit, she claimed she had accepted an offer of extra help. The Al Fayed brothers, the Egyptian owners of Harrods, had read about her case and promised to finance any rescue attempt, she said. They did not want to be associated with the case, for obvious reasons, but they would pick up the tab, she assured us.

Buddy was still doubtful. He told her that if she really wanted us to rescue the boys, she must carry on with the lawsuit otherwise suspicions would be aroused. She agreed. She was sure she could get the children from their school; all she wanted was somebody to go with her and help her work out a way to get them out of the country in due course.

We drove back into London. I decided to send Karen. I had trained her, she had been in the army, and she could certainly look after this woman. That is what I thought at the time. The fact is, you can only protect people who are not living out some kind of death wish; and I should have got the message about Jo a lot sooner than I did.

The penny should have dropped when I found she had no friends or relations prepared to take Poppy for a week while Karen went to Cairo with her. Poppy was eleven, a quiet girl and one of my nieces was good with kids and would cheerfully look after her for a week. Poppy would stay up in north London with me. The school gave her four hours of work to do each day. So that was all settled.

Three days after Karen and Jo left, I came home from the office and had just said hello to Poppy when the phone rang.

"Jacquie?"

"Karen, how are you getting on?"

"It's a nightmare. She's been drunk since we got here. She's smoking cannabis. She's fucking the wine waiter—"

"Calm down, Karen, calm down."

Poor Karen was sharing a hotel room with Jo.

"You've only got to tough it out for a week. If she hasn't got her act together by then—"

"No, it'll be next week because the boys are away."

Every couple of days I spoke to Karen and every time she sounded more disgusted. In the end I had to speak to Jo herself.

"How d'you think you're helping your case, behaving like this?"

"What do you mean?"

"Sleeping with waiters—"

"I never slept with a waiter in my life. You want to ask Karen if you think it's me that's putting it about. You should see her. She's all over them. Flashing her tits at anything in trousers."

Since I knew Karen was a lesbian, Jo failed to convince me. I got to the point.

"What about the boys?"

"It's really hard. I'm looking out for them and they're never there."

"What shall I do about Poppy?"

"Don't worry. I've got an idea, I'll be back with Karen in a few days."

Two days later Karen called.

"This is the last straw. I got back and there's a note on my pillow. Listen to this: 'Staying at the Nile Hilton with Achmed. Will call later.' "

"Who the fuck is Achmed?"

"New waiter. She met him last night. Specializes in room service, apparently."

"I think you'd better come back, Karen. And bring her with you, for God's sake."

Jo Clark refused to come back. She had no money, so how she kept herself for the next six weeks I have no idea. She did not bother to call me to say where she was or ask after her daughter. I was giving my niece £20 a day for childcare, and the school was growing anxious. Poppy said her aunts, Jo's sisters, had refused to have her.

Poppy did not cost much to feed, but I drew the line at buying new clothes and the child had only come with enough to wear for a week. A couple of guys from the Circuit went into the house in Coulsdon to collect some fresh stuff for her, and came back looking shocked.

"It's disgusting over there," one of them muttered to me. "The bedrooms are filthy. The sheets are gray, no kidding. Fancy bringing a kid home to that."

Poppy did not like living with her mother. She said she was fed up with having different men around the place all the time. The stories in the newspaper made her embarrassed and her mother was always drunk. She had been in the car once when her mother had crashed it after drinking. I began to feel a lot of sympathy for the Egyptian father. I was sickened by the whole situation. We had misjudged it, and now we were dealing with the consequences. Poor Poppy. I was going away soon, and she could not stay with me forever. She gave me her aunt's phone number.

"Never again," she said. "Sorry she's done this to you, but we've been had before. She's dumped Poppy and gone off for months on end."

"I'd keep her here, but I can't," I said. "I have to go away on business. I won't be here at nights and she can't stay in the house on her own."

"You'll have to sort it out for yourself. I told you, she's a nice kid and we're sorry for her, but we've had it up to here with her bloody mother."

Days were going by with no call from Jo, and I had to be overseas next week. I contacted the welfare department. They said if no family member could help, Poppy would be taken into care.

At the last minute one of the sisters relented, and Poppy went to stay with her. I was overseas for a few weeks working, and when I returned to England I got a call from Jo. She was back in Coulsdon now.

"What's your sodding game, you smart-arsed cow, getting my sister on the phone? Who asked you to call her? Leaving me out there in Cairo on my own. Call yourself child rescue—"

I was so mad I could barely speak. I told her I wanted nothing more to do with her, slammed the phone down, and sent her a bill. Our out-of-pocket expenses alone ran into thousands. She has appeared on television since, flourishing the bill and whining. It was never paid of course. The Al Fayeds made it clear that they had never made any agreement to finance Jo Clark's lawsuits, rescue attempts or anything else.

As for the boys, they now live with Jo and Poppy. She eventually got them back through the courts.

I N ONE YEAR, I HAD TAKEN 175 INTERNATIONAL FLIGHTS. I WORKED ON divorce cases, fraud investigations, surveillances, recces for child rescues and the rescues themselves. I worked for ISS, the Circuit, and independently. Thomas and I did not meet for months. On the telephone, he no longer asked what I was doing because he knew I would always say the same thing: "Working, but I can't talk about it."

"It's dangerous. I don't understand. Why do you feel you have to do this?"

"They need somebody."

The child rescues were the hardest to justify because they were the most dangerous. At worst, I could get shot at, or arrested and charged thousands of miles from home. And to cap it all, we invariably ended up out of pocket. I knew Thomas did not understand how desperate some of these women were. If we did not help them, there were people out there who would offer to commit murder for much less than the cost of a genuine child rescue. And having an ex-husband bumped off was a short cut many of these women would be prepare to take. I could not explain to Thomas how half-crazed and despairing they were. Thomas stopped talking to me about it. He knew that I knew his silence meant he disapproved.

I did not care much what the American State Department thought, or the British Foreign Office, or the newspapers for that matter, but when the one person who really mattered to me began to have reservations, I became defensive. I told myself Thomas would just have to tough it out for two more years until I would keep my promise to retire. Right now I had other men to deal with, men with an entirely different set of problems.

I had already made a reconnaissance in Pakistan for ISS when I drove to Sheffield to meet Anne Lewis. She was a middle-aged woman, introduced to me by mutual friends. We met in the lobby of a hotel and for the next two hours she poured out her story.

"I can't believe Mahmood would do this to her," she kept saying. "I'd never have thought he'd be like that. He's the last person. He was always so kind."

It was another of those cases where a sweetheart turns into a beast the minute he is married. Laura, Anne's daughter, had been whisked off to Islamabad shortly after marrying him in Leeds six months before. And then — silence. Apart from one worried call from a female relative of Mahmood's, saying that Laura was losing a lot of weight, there had been no contact at all until a letter came two days ago. Or rather, a note. Anne handed me a crumpled sheet of lined paper torn from a pad.

> Dear Mum, I really hope you get this. I have got to get out of here. I am locked in the house 24 hours a day. I've got no key and no money and the servants spy on me. M. says I must stop living like a western woman. He hits me every single night. I am twelve weeks pregnant. I stopped eating to get back at him but then he stopped giving me food. I have to get out and he has got my passport. Please come and get me. I'm going crazy. I can't have my baby here. Love Laura.

There was a row of *X*s under the signature and a big blotch, as if she had wept onto the paper.

"I don't know what to do. I can't get her back on my own. I thought maybe the Consul could help or I could write to Benazir Bhutto."

I had to tell her that in my experience, consuls do not intervene in domestic dramas like this one. They are there to promote trade, and if they start criticizing the Muslim way of life, even indirectly, by taking a wife's side against her husband, it's bad for business. So they don't take a lot of notice when English girls are locked away by local men. As for Benazir Bhutto, I had guarded her in the past so her name had come up in conversation with ISS. She had often been approached to help American wives and mothers, without positive results.

"So can you get Laura back?" Anne asked.

"I can try, but it'll be expensive. It'll probably take three or four of us and we may have to hire a boat."

When I had been to Pakistan before, it had been to recce a rescue out of Karachi by sea.

"I'll mortgage my house," she said at once.

By cutting costs to the bone I could barely do the job for the money she could afford. I got visa application forms and started calling around. At the low rates I could afford to pay, and with all the paperwork, it took four weeks to get my team in place. Anne sounded more worried every time I spoke to her. Laura was not getting any less pregnant; time was precious. Also, she would need a passport and she could not hang around in Pakistan waiting for one once we got her away from her husband. I would have to get Laura into India.

There would be three men and myself. Mike and I flew out to Karachi first. As I saw it, I had only two options: either to get her to Srinagar by walking across the border through the low foothills of the Hindu Kush, or to get out by sea.

I rejected the idea of a long trek over rough terrain with an under-nourished woman who was expecting a baby. My idea was to rent a Zodiac, a rigid inflatable boat of the kind used by armed forces all over the world, get Laura out of Karachi in it and land with her on the Indian coast.

Mike and I were in Karachi for three days. We tried hard and got nowhere. I had not exactly taken to the city on my first visit and this second one did not change my view. I found it dusty, noisy and the dirt and the poverty appalled me. You stayed in a hotel, in proper rooms with clean sheets and running hot and cold water, but the chambermaids and the man who cleaned the pool could be living in tarpaulin covered shacks within a hundred yards of you. We could not rent a car without a driver, so we gave up and took taxis everywhere, which played on my nerves but was typical of Pakistan: you were constantly having to interact with helpful people you wished you had never met. Down at the harbor they took us out in fishing boats, they begged off us, they tried to sell us everything from camel rides to dodgy watches, but none of them actually showed us a way out. The harbor was partly blocked by a big concrete chicane that nobody except a local pilot or fisherman could navigate around. The beaches up and down the coast were crowded with vacationers whenever we took a taxi there to have a look. And on the morning when Roger and Dave were supposed to arrive from London, we heard gunfire in the streets. Mike said a man in the elevator had told him it was an uprising. Whatever that meant.

So when Mike went to the airport to meet the others I was pondering other ways around the problem. With half a mind on what I was doing, I pushed my way down a bustling, garish market street and bought shalwar kamiz from a towering display in an open-fronted shop. These are the trousers and knee-length tunics that the local women wear, usually in vivid colors with embroidery, with wide shawls looped gracefully around the face. I chose brown, black and navy cotton. Then I went back to the hotel, with my mind made up.

I had expected the two recent arrivals, and Mike, but when I walked into the lobby they were all sitting there with a new guy.

"This is Trev," said Dave.

"Right," I said. Maybe I looked annoyed. I do not know why, maybe it was irrational on my part, but I thought a six-footer with green eyes and hair the color of carrots was going to be a bit of a liability in Pakistan.

Trev gave me a dismissive nod. *Surly bastard.*

"What's your background?" I asked pleasantly.

"Special Boat Service and French Foreign Legion," he said. "What's yours, darling?"

"That's none of your business," I said. "I'm paying you, so you don't need to know."

He subsided in his chair muttering about the day when he took orders off a woman. The others inspected their shoes.

"Dave, could we have a word?"

Dave followed me across the lobby.

"Where did you get him?"

"You said you wanted somebody that could handle a Zodiac. I've worked with him before. Sorry he's like this."

"What's his excuse, PMS? I'm being very polite, Dave. You never even said you were bringing anybody."

"I couldn't go into it on the phone. I did a deal. He's doing it for two-fifty a day. And he is ex-SBS, I checked with a mate of mine."

We went back to the others. Trevor was reclining with both arms stretched along the sofa back, staring at me as I crossed the lobby.

"Right. You guys must need a rest. We'll meet up at four in my room, okay?

I sat behind the desk. The two easy chairs were taken by Trevor and Mike. Dave and Roger sat on the bed.

"I don't know how much you guys already know, so you can consider this a briefing as well as a planning meeting." Trevor raised his eyes to the ceiling. "This is the deal. The woman we want is called Laura, she's being held against her will by her husband in Islamabad. She hasn't got a passport—"

"No, she wouldn't have," Trevor muttered under his breath.

"But she can get one in India, so that's where we're gonna take her. This is her." I passed around some wedding photographs. "She's a lot thinner since those were taken."

Trevor took an uninterested glance and passed the pictures to Dave. I unfolded a map of Pakistan away from me across the desk and leaned across it to point with a pencil at markings which, from my awkward angle, were upside down.

"Here's Islamabad. There are flights to Karachi every day and we've been talking about getting her out by sea. On the other hand, there is a route across the mountains as far as Srinagar. You can see it there. Just."

"How far's that?" Roger asked.

"About 130 kilometers according to the map, just a little over eighty miles." Trevor made a snorting noise and crossed his arms. "There's no active border post if you go round . . . here," I continued.

"Just fucking snipers," said Trevor.

"Yeah?" I looked at him.

"Yeah," he said, sniggering. "It's not like Hadrian's fucking wall. Pakis vee Injuns, remember?"

"Well, thank you, Trevor. But that's the way we're going. I have decided that getting this girl out by sea is not an option."

"How would you know?"

"Believe it or not, I have been in this country before. Mike and I have just spent three days checking out the harbor here. We—"

"So?" he interrupted. "What about the beaches? Look, darling." He tapped the map. "See those yellow strips near the blue space. Beaches."

"Last time I looked they were full of French tourists."

Trevor leaned back and swung both feet on to the desk. They crushed a corner of the map. "What's the problem? You'll blend in nicely."

"Take your feet off the map, Trevor. Part of the problem is that there is a shooting war going on here in Karachi at the moment. If you'd been watching CNN in the last couple of hours, or even looked out of the window, you'd have noticed armed men in the streets. We are taking Laura over the mountains."

"Brilliant."

"You have a problem with that?"

"You dragged me out here to this shit-hole on a fourteen-hour flight just to walk some daft tart through a war zone?"

I sighed. Mike stared at the ceiling, Roger held his head in his hands and Dave looked at me apologetically.

"What is your room number?"

"Two-ten," Trevor said. "You won't get round me that way."

Nobody laughed. I picked up the telephone.

"Hello. Could you get the bill ready for Room 210, please? He's checking out." I took five £50 notes from my bag and passed them across the desk. "On your bike."

He stood up, kicking the desk. "You know what it is with you, darling? Your head's so far up your arse you can't see daylight."

I waited as he walked across the room.

"Trevor, if you tell anybody about this job, you'll never work on the Circuit again."

He slammed out of the room. I took a deep breath.

"Right, anybody else want out of this? Because if not, we're on a flight to Islamabad in the morning."

And so we were. Dave, Roger, Mike and I fetched up at the Marriott Hotel, one of the tallest buildings in Islamabad. It was a concrete pile with fake Islamic arches on the penthouse floor. I had learned from bitter experience, specifically rampant fleas, to stay only in upmarket hotels whenever I went to Pakistan or India.

Most of this city was four- or five-floors high, built out of mud bricks, with balconies and gaily-painted advertisements in a script that was all dots and curves. Men of all ages ambled about in white kurta, baggy white trousers, and tweedy vests with smart little round hats. Islamabad was slower, cooler and quieter than Karachi and I relaxed.

From the window of my room I could see ten or twenty miles to the foothills of the Himalayas beneath a hazy blue sky.

"Don't get too fond of it," I told myself. "You're working."

I was still inwardly triumphant about the abrupt disappearance of Trevor. I caught up with Mike at the reception desk downstairs.

"We want a Christian cabbie," he said.

"You what?"

"Don't mess me about on this one, Jacquie. I know whereof I speak. I got badly done over by a Muslim taxi driver in Lahore."

"Yeah, right."

Anything for a happy ship. We split up. Dave set off to have a look at the mountain path. Roger went to recce the route to the airport in case the mountains proved impossible, and Mike and I waited for our cab. When it came I saw a cross dangling behind the windscreen. *The guy probably kept a supply in the glove compartment,* I thought. *Buddhas, Stars of David. The customer was always right.*

"Okay, Mike?"

"Right."

We set off for the wealthier suburbs north of the city. The house where Laura was being kept was in a street lined with head-high painted mud walls with trees overhanging from inside. The house had a wide double-sided iron gate. We circled the block and came back very slowly. I looked through the black bars of the gate and saw a skinny creature in blue shalwar kamiz, her head wrapped in a shawl, standing on a path in front of a veranda. As the car passed she looked at us. She was fair-skinned. It was Laura. I thought our eyes met for a moment. Then she was gone.

In the days that followed, we watched the place. The husband, Mahmood, a tall handsome man with a mustache who wore baggy, gray-cotton Pakistani trousers and kurta, left at about nine in the morning and returned mid-afternoon. At eight or nine in the evening he left again, and stayed out for four or five hours. In his absence there was nobody about except Laura, the two servants of whom one was very old, and also a grandfather. The grandfather could have existed only in my mind. We never saw him, but Anne had told me that Mahmood once said there was a grandfather who lived in the house and never left his room. I was taking no chances.

"Any dogs?"

"No dogs."

We were a working team now. Somehow we had all concluded that we were going to get the girl out and take her over the mountains to India. Roger and Dave started to buy water, matches, canned food and Bergens in order to plant supplies along the route. Not as difficult to find as you might think, as this area is a Mecca for serious hikers and climbers attracted by the nearby mountains. They recced the first few miles of the walk. The only obstacle seemed to be an old fort, a relic of the British Empire, now manned by Pakistani soldiers, a few miles out of Islamabad that, they promised, we would be able to hike around.

I just had to get the timing right. Timing was everything. One night, Mike and I quietly left the taxi in the dusk and started walking north. When we reached Laura's house it was dark. Mike gave me a leg up over the wall. I wore my black tunic and trousers, and with a black scarf wrapped around my face I glided silently between the trees in the garden. I approached the house and began to sidle along its walls. Roger thought he had identified Laura's bedroom yesterday, and I hoped he was right, because by moonlight alone I could not see a thing. This was a muggy night and every window aperture with its shutters open looked like a black cave.

At the one supposed to be Laura's I spied a glimmer of light and peered over the sill. She was asleep on a single bunk inside. A tiny rush lamp flickered on the wall. I clambered into the room with inevitable scuffling noises, but she did not wake up. I paused. I could not hear a sound in the house; no television or radio, no snoring. I crept forward.

She lay on her side. I clamped my hand over her mouth and bent down. I saw a glint of white as her eyes jumped open in terror.

"Don't be frightened," I hissed. "Your mum sent me. When I take my hand away don't scream."

I moved my hand and she twisted around to face me.

"Who are you?"

"I'm Jacquie. Your mum sent me. D' you want to leave here?"

"Yes." She sat up suddenly. In the flickering light she looked eerily skeletal. "Of course I do."

"Hold on. You can't go now. Not tonight. Are you all right?"

"I'm covered in bruises. I'm four months gone, does she know?"

"Yes. Can you walk?"

"Of course."

"Can you walk a long way?"

"Yes, I'll get dressed."

"Not yet. Stay there. We've got to get you out without getting caught. I'm going now, but we're going to come back for you this week or next. If an English guy turns up and says Jacquie sent him, do what he tells you, okay?"

"Sssh."

She heard it before I did: a footfall in the corridor. She lay still on her bed. In a flash I was standing behind the door holding my breath. The latch clicked and the door opened inward with a gentle sigh. I pulled the pistol out of my waistband. If whoever it was came in, I would be ready to clobber him with the weight of the gun in both hands. The door slowly shut again. For thirty seconds I held my breath as the person shuffled down the corridor.

"It was only Fayed," she whispered. "He's old, he worries about me. He can't do anything, he's only a servant."

"I'm going," I whispered back. "Be ready to leave day or night."

We had a few days in which to put everything in place. The main thing we did not have was intelligence about the border we had to cross. I wanted to be sure that nobody would try to shoot us in the hills on the way to Srinagar. The following morning we arranged to meet for lunch in the hotel to assemble everything we knew and finalize the time when we would get Laura out.

At a quarter to one the phone rang.

"Is that Jacquie Davis?"

It was a male, English voice I did not know.

"They're on to you. Get out now." The line went dead.

My mind raced. It had to be somebody from the consulate. It would be the only way they could possibly speak to me. If that prat Trevor had said anything, I was going to strangle him with my bare hands.

It had been five minutes since the phone call and I was racing down the back stairs after Mike with maps, washing gear and a change of clothes. Everything else had been abandoned. When we rushed out into the traffic, Roger and Dave set off for the hillside.

Mike waved at me from the cab rank, triumphant.

"Look, I got one."

He slammed in beside the driver and I swung into the back seat. A crucifix swung merrily from the driving mirror. Mike gave him the address.

"What's your name?"

"Aziz."

"Okay, Aziz. Fast."

We roared up to the northern suburbs.

"Slowly past that house. Very slowly. Stop."

It was the same time of day as our first visit and Laura was out in the garden with one of the servants. Mahmood must be out. He had to be. The gates were old, about six-feet high but rusty. I scrutinized the hinges, which were just bolts that slotted in from above but would probably hold. The central clasp on the other hand looked feeble. It would bust open easily. The street was quiet. The yellow cab subsided hopelessly on its suspension.

"Aziz," I said, "here is fifty dollars."

A brown hand shot upward and took the money.

"I want you," I said, "to ram those gates."

Mike said, "He doesn't understand. Aziz, drive very fast into the gates." Mike smacked his right fist into his left palm.

"Those gates? They are shut."

"They will open when you hit them."

"My taxi will also open. Like a big fish." His hands flew apart on the steering wheel and he gulped. "My beautiful taxi. I saved for ten years."

"We will buy you a new taxi."

"More than fifty dollars."

"One hundred dollars."

The hand shot up again. The money disappeared in his shirt pocket. Inside the garden Laura walked slowly past, staring gloomily at the gravel path. Aziz reversed his cab.

"And when we all get back in," I hissed, "reverse like hell."

"He doesn't understand," said Mike. "But don't worry, Aziz is not going to be practicing three-point turns once he clocks what we're up to."

If the gate did not give way the first time, she'd be bundled into the house and the doors bolted before we could try again. I tasted blood on my lip where I bit it with anxiety. Aziz held the jalopy on the clutch for a moment — then roared forward with his foot hard down. I saw Mike duck and I did the same as we hit the gate. It crashed open and we skidded to a stop on the gravel. I leapt out and seized Laura. The servant grabbed her other arm. Mike head-butted him and I pushed Laura into the car. Mike leaped after us and had not shut the door before Aziz shot backward at thirty miles an hour into the street. We banged violently across the fallen gate. Aziz gibbered incoherently as he turned the car and hurtled back toward town.

"Slow the fuck down!" screamed Mike. "You're going the wrong way! We want the tourist vantage point."

It was too late. Aziz, heading away from the hills, had torn right back into the traffic. Turning a corner he braked hard. There in front of us was a classic Islamabad traffic gyratory system. Every kind of light vehicle was trying to get around a cart that had collapsed spilling a load of melons across the road. As they were all trying to get past at once, they were all stuck. The pandemonium was intense, with horns blaring, people yelling and melons a foot in diameter bowling between hundreds of pairs of feet.

"We'll walk. I'll take Laura," I shouted. "Mike, if you can find another cab — I'll see you at the vantage point."

We were out and walking rapidly in the direction of the hills while Mike settled up with Aziz. I heard loud sirens from passing police cars on the main drag. We traced a path through the narrow market streets, our progress impeded by stallholders, small children and goods displayed on crowded sidewalks. We both wore shalwar kamiz but the rucksack I had slung over one shoulder made me conspicuous. I was sure that by now the servant Mike had decked in the garden must have contacted the police. There were no cabs in these back streets and if the misery on Laura's face was a good indicator, she could not go much further without starting to sob. Christ, I hoped she was not going to lumber us. I had finally walked into the main road and was trying to spot a free taxi when Mike and Aziz tore around the corner in search of us.

Aziz dropped us, smiling, at the foot of the tourist walking trail. I gave him another hundred dollars and told him to forget everything. He seemed very happy.

"What kept you?" Dave asked with a grin.

"Oh, this and that."

Dave and Roger set off with us. Mike had already started to walk back down to Islamabad, its buildings and mosques jumbled higgledy-piggledy across the valley floor. He was returning to London by air. Dave and Roger were both ex-SAS. We had maps, compasses, water and food. It was a nice day; the midday heat cooling down now, lots of butterflies. Trudging the first mile up the hill path away from the city we could have been backpackers out for a day trail walking. Only it was four o'clock in the afternoon and we would have to walk all night, while it was cool. We would not sleep until dawn.

"Okay, Laura? Think you can make it?"

Dave was cheery. In fact Dave was a bloody good scoutmaster, at this point.

"I have to," Laura said. She looked determinedly up at the mountain. "I've got to make it for my baby's sake."

"Baby?"

"Laura is four months pregnant, Dave," I muttered. "So, I should have told you before. There's no need to look at me like that."

The first night was by far the worst. We were so tired, so freezing cold and so very aware that the city was still close. At dusk we could see its lights behind us. When darkness fell, and there was only hazy moonlight to illuminate our route, one image kept flickering into my mind: the Exxon tiger. I told myself I was over tired. This was true, as we had been awake for far too long.

It would also be easy to get lost. Most of the time we followed stony tracks across scrubby ground. Sometimes bushes and small trees reached above head height and it was like being on a jungle path. Roger or Dave took turns scouting ahead, navigating by stars and compass, while the other one brought up the rear. Whoever walked in front strode up to a quarter of a mile ahead at times, and had the hardest job. He had to find our way and at the same time stay alert for soldiers.

The fort lay quite near to the start of our route, low in the hills. I had seen a photograph taken in daylight: long mud walls around a barrack square. The place looked neglected but it was patrolled, and we had to make a five or six mile detour uphill to get around it.

We passed it before midnight. The hours were numbing. We rested for five minutes in every hour, drank water, rubbed our feet and slapped our arms about ourselves to keep warm. I heard a sob.

"I don't think I can do this," Laura said.

She did not have much choice.

I expected to sleep soundly during the first day because when we lay down in sleeping bags at dawn I felt exhausted. But concern kept me semi-awake. I dozed for twelve hours, and when we got up for the second night's trekking, I felt as if I had only just lain down. The tiredness persisted. It was not a difficult walk; the higher we went, the cooler we were during the daylight hours and the easier we found it to make progress. Steep hillsides plunged on all sides. Far ahead, the peaks of the Panjal range stretched like a choppy sea to the horizon. Setting off late on the second afternoon we thought we could see the peak of K2 in the distance, snowcapped under an indigo sky. We climbed slowly all the way, on firm ground with no big rivers to cross and no dangerous gradients. The stress came from having to stay silent and watch your feet, because small animals and the roots of trees had made deep impressions in the ground, and if one of us broke or sprained an ankle, we would all be in big trouble. For this reason we moved much faster during what remained of the day than we did at night.

It was about six o'clock, and I had just turned back to check on Laura two yards away, when a bullet hit a tree beside my head. Another gunshot followed at once. Laura's face froze. I grabbed her, hurled her to the ground behind a log and threw myself on top of her.

"Don't move."

Close protection training is a reflex action. Dave, behind us, had hit the deck. Bullets crashed either side of us. We had set off northeast, and now we were traveling southeast. *If these were Indians fighting Kashmiri rebels, then the Kashmiris must be the ones behind us.* These thoughts shot through my mind as I stared at a rotten log a foot in front of my nose. I rolled off Laura.

"Keep still."

Something shot out of the log and between the trees. I do not like snakes. I nearly jumped out of my skin. Another gunshot cracked into a tree. Things rustled in the dead vegetation around me. I would have given anything to get my body off the ground.

"There are snakes," Laura whispered.

"Don't worry about them. Snakes can't blow your head off."

I could see Roger wriggling rapidly on his stomach and elbows downhill toward us. "Are they firing at us?" he gasped.

"Dunno. Think I should go and ask? Lend us a white hanky."

"Very funny."

"It's like that dickhead Trev said. Kashmiri rebels."

Dave crawled uphill toward us. "We've got to head into that firing line."

"We have?" I said.

The firing stopped.

Dave jerked his thumb. "West, Pakistan," he indicated the other way. "East, India."

Silence fell. None of us said anything. There was no wind. Everything, the birds, the beetles on the ground, perhaps even the snakes, seemed to be listening. We moved a short way on our stomachs, then walked at a nervous crouch, then began again to stumble forward through the darkness. We walked all night, silently. Somehow we passed through the firing line unscathed.

For the next two nights we found our way mostly in the dark. There was little time to talk and almost nothing to say, except how cold we were, how badly we wanted a shower, and how our feet hurt. Laura was wearing only sandals and she must have suffered. Sometimes she seemed overcome with despair; she just slowed, like a clock that needs winding, and lost all resistance. The guys tried to jolly her along, but it did not work.

I told her, quietly and in private, that if she succumbed to years of brainwashing and started behaving like a dependant female, we were all screwed. She never complained once after that. She thanked us for all our help and kept moving, mile after mile. Unfortunately, this made me think I had gone too far. I tramped on, worrying that if she got suspicious pains, she might be too stoical to say. If she started to miscarry here in the foothills of the Hindu Kush, the maternity unit would be Dave, Roger and me, a handy first aid kit, a campfire and the five liters of bottled water we had left.

On the fourth day we were slowly waking up in the middle of the afternoon when we heard a single burst of random firing in the distance.

"Brilliant," Dave said, sitting up and scratching his tangled hair. "We're in the right place."

"We are?"

"Yeah. That's shots in the air, you can tell. It's a wedding."

"Oh, Shotgun wedding, I suppose."

"Nah, that's what the locals do up here. It means we're near Srinagar."

The next morning, as light grew, we glimpsed a tarmac road snaking between green terraces only a few miles away. We stumbled wearily up to Roger, sitting on a ridge.

"Made it."

Dawn was rising behind the mountain range. There was a village of flat-roofed houses straggling up the valley. Five hundred feet below us, a bareheaded man strode a deliberate path behind a plough drawn by a bullock. The sound of its bell clanked through clear air.

"I just want to go to sleep." I said.

"Are you sure this is India?"

"Yes, Laura," Roger replied. "We're about three miles from Srinagar. I've just seen two women in saris on that road through there. Don't worry. This is India, you're okay."

In the village we saw a wooden chai house with a veranda around it, where farm workers sat eating bowls of rice with their fingers. They looked surprised at the sight of four dirty westerners striding down from the mountains. The owner flicked the ends of his turban self-importantly down his back and brought out a tray full of glasses of sweet mint tea. We told him we wanted to go to Srinagar.

"My cousin has taxi."

"Good."

"You go to airport at Srinagar?"

"Maybe. Has your cousin got a good taxi?" Silly question really. God I was tired.

"My cousin, his taxi is best in all India. Air conditioned, takes all of you. He takes you to Delhi. You do not need air flight, my cousin very cheap, all four persons. His taxi is very big. You will see." He was on the phone already. It was still before six in the morning but within ten minutes a new Toyota van came bouncing down the rutted street toward us. The driver smiled amiably through the window. Negotiations followed. We settled a price, and we piled in. Raj was the driver's name. We all said hello and settled at once to five or six hours sleep. The air conditioning was a breeze through the window and there were no seats, but I curled up on my sleeping bag on the metal floor and shut my eyes. I was drifting off, as we pulled out on to the main road, when I heard Dave's voice in my ear.

"Have you noticed anything about Raj?" he hissed.

"Nice smile," I said, without opening my eyes.

"One arm."

"What?"

"He's only got one arm."

I was too tired to sit up and look, but now I visualized Raj as he had appeared at the van window, and it was true, he had been wearing the train of his turban draped over the shoulder next to the window and hanging down. I thought about this for a while. Then I drifted in and out of sleep.

"Is it an automatic?"

"No. Shift."

I fell asleep. From time to time I woke up; every time, we were still bowling along. We seemed to be going quite fast. We stopped, ate kebabs and nan bread, climbed back in again and lay dozing. When all the others were asleep I woke and sat up, coughing, amid clouds of smoke. The van reeked of cannabis. Raj was gleefully playing that game so popular everywhere in Asia: chicken. Over height, overloaded trucks with bull bars, their wooden sides painted with flowers and stories, festooned with fairy lights and pictures of grim faced mullahs, would appear on the distant horizon, hurtling toward us in the middle of the road. Raj immediately put his foot down and charged straight at them until they gave way. The outcome of previous chicken games lay rusting on either side of the road.

Raj must have brought a supply of ready-rolled joints for the journey, because he was puffing happily on one of them while shifting gear and steering with his one good hand.

We slowed down and stopped. I lay down again. Either I was dead tired or there had been something unhealthy about that kebab. A policeman leaned through the passenger window. He exchanged a few words with Raj and looked hopefully at me.

"You English? You got cigarettes?"

I fumbled in my Bergen and gave him twenty Bensons. He waved us on. Raj stepped on the gas.

"It's good you give him cigarettes," he said. "Or he stop me. In India, man with one arm is not allowed to drive."

I call that downright unfair.

ANNE FLEW OUT TO NEW DELHI TO BE WITH LAURA WHILE A NEW passport was organized, and I flew back to England exhilarated with sheer relief. Thomas and I spent some time together in London. When he said I seemed calmer than last time, I told him I was pleased because I had been able to rescue somebody. I was, of course; it had been the first big rescue I had done without Ann and Buddy. But I kept thinking how badly it could have gone wrong if I had not kept the team together.

A few weeks later, another middle-aged woman called me. "It's confidential," she said. "Can I come to your office?" She arrived looking flustered, wispy-haired and tearful. She dressed too young for her age and was overweight. "It's been a month now."

She showed me pictures of her second husband. She had done rather well financially out of her first marriage, having received a generous divorce settlement. But now she had fallen in love with this Filipino, they had not been married long, when she woke up one morning to find a note. He had been called away on business, it said; he would be back in a couple of weeks. She had noticed a few things missing. His passport. Silver, jewelry, cash.

"But that's not important. I'm sure he's gone home to Manila. I've got to go and find out what's happened to him. His mother might be ill. He might have had an accident."

"What's keeping you?"

"Oh, I couldn't go all that way on my own."

Some people are so timid. She paid my daily rate, return flight and accommodation in Manila. We were there for two weeks. I did not find the husband. I found his wife and three children, though.

Back from Manila with my sadder-yet-wiser client, I flew to North Carolina to help Ann and Buddy out for a few weeks. Their book, *Rescue My Child,* was selling well and they were overwhelmed by approaches from distraught mothers. They had a heart-breaking case, but they were stuck without money to pay for the rescue. The Bangladesh rescue that Ann carried out had left them thousands of dollars out of pocket, and they were having to harden their hearts, but Sarah Ali's plight was more harrowing than most.

She was an American who had married a Yemenite, had two babies, and separated from him. The girl and boy were four and six years old when he snatched them from their school and took them to the Yemen. The girl had a heart condition and needed medication. Sarah was beside herself, but had no money to go over there, find her children and bring them back. The only way she could earn a living was as a singer and songwriter. She did not make much. We all had faith that one day she would; she was a terrific singer. At the same time, we knew that terrific is not all it takes. Somehow Sarah Ali could never get the right breaks.

She lived in Tacoma, Washington, but came to North Carolina when she could and talked to Ann several times. She was deeply frustrated by the impossibility of making things happen.

And then there was Iceland.

We were hired by two divorced fathers who had children by the same Icelandic woman. They asked us to retrieve their children from Iceland where she had illegally taken them, and it all went pear-shaped.

Buddy spent a year in jail in Reykjavik without trial, and Lawrence and I, the two English participants, found ourselves unable to re-enter the UK in case we were extradited to Iceland as well. I did not mind not going home, but Lawrence had just had a baby daughter. What hurt me most was the *Observer* newspaper. They printed an account of the whole affair that made me out to be a mercenary.

Once we were back in America, for weeks we talked about nothing except how to get Buddy back. Sarah Ali came to see Ann and me at this time but I think she grew secretly disheartened. I could understand that. Buddy was, after all, a grown man and resilient. What Sarah wanted was her defenseless children.

She had one glimmer of hope: somebody else wanted our help in the Yemen, and could afford to get us there. So at least we would be able to recce the country. An Englishwoman called Jan Palmer had called ISS from Birmingham, England. She had read Neil Livingstone's book, she said, and did Ann know about Nadia and Zana, the two English girls whose father had forced them into marriage in the Yemen?

Ann did not. But in England, I had read many articles about Zana and Nadia. They had been ordinary Birmingham teenagers when their father offered to send them on holiday to his homeland. They jumped at the chance. Within weeks they had found themselves trapped in a remote mountain village in the Mokbana mountains and married, against their will, to two local boys. Their father had sold them.

The story had been told in a book by Zana, the older girl, who had finally escaped. Book sales had made enough money for them to approach ISS to try and rescue Nadia. And the children. There were lots of children. Zana had left her baby son back in the Yemen with Nadia, and Nadia had been producing a child every couple of years since she first got to the country. She now wore shabbah, spoke Arabic like a local and spent her days as a good wife should: grinding corn and toting water up from the valley. She seemed, in fact, settled. Zana was adamant that Nadia was desperate to get back to Birmingham but would not leave without her children.

We took down the details. They asked about cost; we estimated $20,000 up front to cover initial meetings and expenses. Jan did not hesitate. Money was not a problem, she said. We met Jan and Miriam, the girl's mother, in New York. Jan was a pleasant-faced woman in her thirties. She said she was a friend of Miriam's from Birmingham and had once been a journalist. Miriam was small, dark and tired-looking. I questioned Miriam, who had been married to a Yemenite for a couple of decades, about the Yemen. She knew hardly anything, other than what Zana had already said in public. (It makes you wonder what married couples talk about.) I sent two guys to North Yemen, where Nadia was living, to come up with some ideas. Meanwhile I flew to Aden, on the south coast, on the pretext of being a travel journalist.

I did not stay long. Staying in Aden, a noisy western-style city, was much like being in Saudi again, so there was hardly anything I could do. When I dressed in western clothes, I got my bottom pinched, and when I wore shabbah, I got fed up with lifting my long skirts over sticky heaps of chewed qat in the dust. Yemeni men seemed to spend half their time squatting in groups gossiping and chewing this stimulant, spitting great gobs of it that looked like spinach.

Foreigners of both sexes faced the familiar problem: the inability to hire a car without a driver. The guys were staying in San´á, a beautiful ancient towering city in the north. They had been driven several hundred miles up toward the Saudi border, and took pictures, until their cameras were confiscated by officious military personnel. The north of the Yemen is mountainous, barren and sparsely populated. The few cultivated patches of vivid green, terraced land make the landscape look like a painting-by-numbers canvas that has been started and suddenly left. The village where Nadia lived perched on top of a crag a few miles off the main road, up a dusty track that only a four-wheel-drive could climb. I do not know what predators live out in those mountains, but the people build their dwellings like fortresses. Most of the mud-built, multi-floor houses were clamped together in a kind of warren against the mountainside around a big dusty yard. There were only about twenty-five families there.

According to the two operatives I sent up there, the men of the village gathered together and prayed, as good Muslims do, every morning at sunrise. This was the only time during daylight hours when the men would be separated from their rifles. So if Nadia and her children were to be taken out of the village, the best time to do it would be first thing in the morning when the husbands and fathers were at prayer.

We could not get her out to the north or east. Thousands of miles of Saudi Arabia lay to the north, and Oman was southeast along the coast. There were checkpoints on the roads from the mountains south to Tai`zz and then to San´á and Aden. The Red Sea coast was not so very far away from her village, to the west of it, but there was no road there, and mountains to cross. There was no airport that Nadia and her children, who all had Yemeni nationality, would be allowed to leave from. Territorial waters were efficiently patrolled. The only possible way out was by rescue helicopter.

Lawrence was now back in England, so I felt pretty sure the Iceland crisis had blown over. I flew to London and drove up the M1 freeway to Birmingham. Zana and Miriam lived in modest circumstances in spite of all the money from the book. It was heartbreakingly obvious that every spare penny they had was going into this last bid to get Nadia back. I had to tell them that the only way ISS, as a professional rescue organization, could return her to them would be to mount a small-scale military operation. Back-of-an-envelope calculations made me think it would cost well over £100,000.

They both wanted to go ahead. Miriam insisted that her French publisher would pay her a hundred grand advance. However, she was nervous about dealing with him. To hear this woman, you would think she could not cross the road by herself. She would have to go to Paris, she said, and she did not know the language and did not like big hotels. She wanted somebody to go with her. In the end I sent a bodyguard and hired an interpreter for the meeting, but it was not necessary as the

Frenchman spoke perfect money. According to Miriam, he said in clear English that he would pay her a £100,000 advance against future sales. If the rescue cost more, he would pay for it out of his own pocket.

The funds were in place, so I went ahead, sat down with the operatives who had been in the Yemen and worked out a detailed plan. We looked at it from every angle and there were two options: flying in under Yemeni air force radar from Djibouti, or flying in from a ship off the Red Sea coast. The Djibouti plan meant a fuel problem, not to mention possible interception by the Yemenis. Djibouti was not a great place for chopper hire anyway. The only way around the problems was to buy a used helicopter, hire a pilot, ship them both up the Red Sea coast and set off on the twenty-minute flight inland from there. Once over the village, our team (including myself) would rappel down a rope, hold the men at gunpoint and take the family back up into the helicopter one by one.

The plan was minute-sensitive. Nothing could be allowed to go wrong, and the only way you can guard against anything going wrong is to plan and prepare. That was exactly what we could not do; there was no way of getting to know the village beforehand and Zana and Miriam had hardly any contact with Nadia. For all we knew, we might shin down our rope at five in the morning only to find her in the throes of childbirth. However, on balance, Ann and I thought the plan looked good and we discussed it with Zana and Miriam. They said we should go ahead. They wired money into the ISS account and we set the whole thing up. We put people on standby, started looking for a helicopter, and checked suitable dates when — Sarah Ali came back into the frame.

Sarah had grown tired of waiting. In Los Angeles she met a man called Logan Clarke, who said he was an ex-US Navy seal. He said if she could come up with $40,000 he would get her children back. She re-mortgaged her home, and he approached a TV production company that made a show called *Hard Copy* and told them what he proposed to do. They lent him a camera. He, some operatives he had hired and Sarah went to the Yemen.

I knew nothing of all this at the time. Sarah was the last person on my mind, busy as I was trying to hire ships, sort out personnel and find a pilot and a boat for Nadia's rescue. But I saw the *Hard Copy* episode later. Logan Clarke left the camera running, fly-on-the-wall style, in his hotel room somewhere in the Yemen while he and the others discussed tactics. They were talking about taking the children off the coast in a Zodiac, and he did not seem to know one end of a Zodiac from the other. The rescue went disastrously wrong.

All the men flew back to California and Sarah was left in Yemen to fend for herself. The first thing I knew about it was a frantic call from her sister. Within days Sarah called ISS from Oman, hundreds of miles to the east. Having been raped by a couple of locals, she had finished up in hospital where the doctors diagnosed bowel cancer. She was now going to have a colostomy before flying back.

At the same time, there was civil unrest in the Yemen, and Miriam called ISS to tell them to do no more for the moment as the situation was too dangerous. Then it all went quiet. Years later I saw a television show in which Nadia insisted that she wanted to stay right where she was.

Logan Clarke began a career in television on the back of that *Hard Copy* show.

As for Sarah, her predicament touched the heart of at least one other person. Apparently a genuinely kind man, he sold his house and used the money to take her to Djibouti. There they hired a boat to sail across the channel between the continents. It is barely twenty-four miles wide at one point, and the sea was calm, and although the waters are patrolled, they were never seen again. According to the State Department, both Sarah and her companion are missing, presumed dead.

CALL ME PREDICTABLE IF YOU LIKE, BUT I COULD NOT THINK OF Iceland without a shudder. It had not been a good year. Now, when I was supposed to quit the Circuit the following summer, I knew I had not achieved all I wanted.

I needed time off to rest and think. My sisters went to Hawaii every year and I sometimes joined them; I loved the place. There was a strong Spiritualist tradition in the island, and I visited a medium there. He told me that I had been pretending to be other people for much too long. I should learn to look into myself. I should find out about the real Jacquie.

I did not have a clue where to start. You look back, you see what happened, what you have learned, but there is no particular pattern to it. However, I decided to stay in Hawaii for a while. I could keep in touch with North Carolina by email and fax.

I rented a house in Kailua, on the Oahu coast not far from Honolulu. It was a big low place, high on a hill, with a lawn surrounded by mango trees and banana palms. I swam, went scuba diving and woke up every morning to a view across the red roofs of neighboring houses to the Pacific; it was the kind of place where you can make big decisions. Or, in my case, avoid them.

When Thomas came to Hawaii early in the year, he did not point out that this would be the year of my retirement. We both knew I was not ready to discuss it. I was flying back and forth to the East Coast regularly, running ISS courses in close protection and evasive-driving techniques. Child rescues came in all the time, and I still had a lot of plans. We had not even talked about where we would live, if I quit. For his part, Thomas still loved the Caribbean and he was not ready to retire. My five-year-old promise to stop work hung between us, not quite confronted.

I had a neighbor named Tammy, a cheerful tanned woman married to a marine sergeant, with two small blond children. The US Marine Corps air base was just up the road, and I knew her husband, Dale, and many other marines from the diving club. Tammy and I occasionally stopped to pass the time of day in the supermarket or on the beach. Whenever we talked, she seemed to be about to spend an evening at something called a CODA course. All her friends, who were other marine wives, went to this CODA course as well. I asked what it was about, and she said Dale was on Level Three, it was a support group. I was more bemused than ever but too busy to get involved. It was like my spiritualism or Ann's born-again Christianity — one of those private things. And as usual, I had a plane to catch.

It was a beautifully landscaped development of ranch-style houses in Florida. As I walked across the lawn to a big two-story house in the trees, I got that sinking feeling. I had been handling meetings with bereaved relatives since I was eighteen years old and in uniform, but it is never easy. The man had sounded calm enough on the telephone, but the controlled ones are sometimes the quickest to break down.

"Our daughter was killed in a car accident three months ago," he said. "But our grandkids are still down there in Columbia."

The door was opened by a composed, fair-haired matron in her sixties. She took me to meet her husband. We sat out of doors in the late afternoon watching sprinklers sway twinkling fountains of water onto the grass. The man was stooped, silent, as if defeated by the tragedy.

"The boy's eight and the girl's five," his wife told me. "They're all we've got of Carrie now."

"But how come they're in Columbia?"

"They've been raised by Carrie's ex-husband's family. They're wealthy people. The little girl was born down there."

"So, shouldn't they stay there with them?"

"Carrie left him when the girl was one year old. She went back to him last year, and then she came away to us again. She said there was a bad business goin' on, with those kids."

"What exactly?"

The woman laid her left hand on her knee and began picking at the fingernails with her right. She looked hesitantly at her husband. He leaned forward and said to me, as if the neighbors several hundred yards away might hear, "Their grandpa was interfering with both of 'em. And their father's got a brother, who's a pest. Carrie had trouble with him."

"You think they're molesting them?"

"I'm certain of it. I wanna get them back," the old man said.

"Have you got photographs of the children?"

"That's the crazy thing. That family never sent Carrie one picture. She didn't have one with her when she—"

"Among her effects," finished the woman quickly. "There wasn't a picture." She took her husband's hand. "The kids are all we've got left of Carrie."

They spelled out their daughter's married name, Da Souza, and the family's address in Medellin. Buddy had it checked out and called me.

"First the good news," he said. "These guys have got nothing on them for pedophile stuff."

"Not that we know of," I said.

"Not that we know of, right. But we know a lot. Already, we practically know what shoe size they take. The Da Souza's are one of the families in the Medellin cartel."

"Ah . . . "

"And Ann and I think it'd be cool for you to go in under cover, Jacquie."

And these were my friends. However, Bud was right about the shoe size. Short of DNA mapping and old school reports, there was not much more that we needed to know about the kids' father. His name was Lambaro, he was five feet eleven and thirty-nine years old, and he lived in an extended family with his parents and brothers and their children. The head honcho was his father, the one the Florida grandfather thought was a child abuser. Old Da Souza had an excellent relationship with other members of the cocaine cartel, with certain senior military men in government, with one or two judges, and undoubtedly with influential members of the police force. So, if I fell flat on my face I would not expect help from Victim Support.

We would figure out how to get the children out later. My first task was to get inside the house, report back on the general situation and take photographs of the children. As there were more than just two children living in the house, without some means of identifying the right ones we could hardly start planning to get them out of the country. The grandparents were convinced that they would be able to name them from the pictures I took.

"This is the most exciting thing," the woman told me on the telephone. "I'm so thrilled I'm going to see pictures of my grandchildren. You'll get them out of there, I know you will."

"One step at a time," I said.

I flew to Columbia from Heathrow, just in case anybody checked up on me. Medellin is a hilly city high up in the mountains with a wild, frontier feel to it in spite of all the factories belching smoke into the sky. Young men roamed the streets looking sultry, and the women wore tight, short-skirted Californian power suits and their black hair long. There was a good life here. In the afternoons people sat about at pavement cafés under shady trees, eating ices and gossiping to the constant racket of overheating traffic. All the men drove like maniacs, roaring up to corners in top gear, holding a fist on the horn if the lights were slow to change and yelling ribald comments out of car windows at the girls.

I took a taxi straight to the Hilton. It was one of the few Western hotels in town and a DEA intelligence report said the Hilton bar was where Lambaro hung out. I had studied photographs of him and knew exactly when he should turn up and who was likely to be with him. On the night after my arrival I entered the bar and immediately caught sight of him drinking at a table in the corner with his cronies. I sat on a high stool at the bar and skimmed the pages of a magazine. Lambaro and his party were ordering trays of drinks from the waiter. Soon, most of the tables were occupied, largely by locals rather than hotel guests. I bought an aperitif and chatted quietly to the barman, asking him questions about the city.

At last Lambaro approached the bar and ordered a drink.

"You are English?" he asked me.

"Yes."

"What is it you are looking for?"

"A church, a swimming pool, a public park, a restaurant . . ." I smiled at him. "You look confused. I am writing a book. I need to find these places to make my story authentic."

"Oh, I see! You are writing a book. What kind of a book?"

"It's a love story."

"A love story! A love story that takes place in Medellin? I hope the hero is tall, dark and handsome."

"He is."

"You must let me show you these places. I know the town very well. I was born here."

He was so kind, so close. "You speak English very well," I breathed. "What do you do?"

"Ah, that is a secret."

"No, really, tell me." I smiled and put my hand on his arm.

He laughed. "Why is Columbia famous?"

"Mmm . . . coffee?"

"Coffee. Of course. Anything else?"

"I can't think of anything."

I had overplayed it. Nobody could be this dumb. I saw a flicker of suspicion, but he said, "You are nice. You will come in my car tomorrow, and I will show you everything you want to see."

At eleven the following morning I was summoned to the lobby. Lambaro stood beaming in casual clothes.

"Come, we will go for a drive."

Outside, two limousines had pulled up. Bodyguards had assembled around a heavy armor-plated Mercedes. One of them held the rear door open for me. I stepped in, the bodyguard climbed in after me and Lambaro was ushered in at the other side. Two men sat in front, and we pulled away with two more bodyguards in the following limo. I was feeling the tiniest bit crowded. A message was being delivered, none too subtly. I chose to ignore it. I told myself that women who wrote romantic novels set in Latin America probably get this treatment all the time.

Lambaro was very friendly. He showed me some lovely old churches and parks and took me for lunch at a pavement café. There was no mention of any wife, ex-wife or dead wife. As far as Lambaro was concerned, he had never been married; which rather put the mockers on asking him about his offspring. Would I have dinner with him tonight? he asked. I accepted. We were getting on rather well, I thought, given the pack of lies being peddled on both sides.

I was lying on my bed figuring out some literary excuse to get invited to his house when he called at six o'clock.

"Tonight I would like to invite you to have dinner with my family," he announced. "I shall send the car in one hour."

He certainly had lovely manners. And to be invited to meet the family, so soon! Perhaps I should entertain expectations. It was quite enough to turn a girl's head. In the shower I tried to imagine myself telling Thomas that I was giving him up in favor of marriage to the heir of one of the world's major cocaine suppliers. At least he would see the funny side. That, I decided, was the main thing wrong with Lambaro, apart from the conceit, lies and drug trafficking. No sense of humor.

The bulletproof Merc swished out of town and up to the mountains. Everything was green and lush. The car wound upward for twenty minutes along progressively narrower roads. We passed a high wall and turned through curlicued iron gates to the courtyard of a villa. Armed guards patrolled the boundary wall and waved the car through the gate.

Fountains played in the courtyards. Lambaro appeared, smiling, at the top of the steps that led to the front door.

"Jacquie, my dear. It is so kind of you to come."

A short fat glowering bandito in expensive threads had appeared behind him.

"You must meet my father."

Da Souza was over sixty, one of those guys with rough edges who is always going to be a short fat bandito even if you dress him in a Savile Row suit. But he got a lot of respect. Everyone, especially the crowd of small dark children who now tumbled out to meet me, deferred to him, and the armed guards were practically peeing themselves. His wife was a handsome woman of about sixty, very elegant, with a high-bridged Spanish nose and perfectly plucked eyebrows. She wore her hair in a tight bun and smiled a lot. She spoke no English; none of the older women did, I was to discover.

On a terrace overlooking the swimming pool high on the mountainside, cousins and brothers and sisters had gathered for drinks. The children ran about between grown-ups, happy in their own world. I wished I spoke Spanish, because I would have liked to have found out whose kids these were and work out the right ones by a process of elimination, but it could wait. I was kept busy answering questions. It was mostly the men who asked me about the book I was writing. By the time we went in to dinner, I was starving, but I had pretty much formulated the plot of a saleable trashy romantic novel.

The children were dispatched to some other part of the house before dinner. The rest of us ate a delicious meal at a long table in a paneled dining room. Afterward, in classic macho style, the men stayed to smoke cigars and the women repaired to the terrace where some of them actually picked up tapestry. A senior army officer arrived at about eleven o'clock, emerging from the house with his peaked cap in hand to pay his respects to Madame, Lambaro's mother.

It was a lovely place. I could look across the pool to the jungley edges of the property and the lights of Medellin on the hillsides below, and I could smile and nod, but that was about it. Without Spanish, I could not contribute a great deal to this gathering. At eleven-thirty I returned to the city. Lambaro, ushering me into the bulletproof motor with gentlemanly courtesy and a tender kiss on my hand, assured me that he would call the next day.

The following morning he called me at the Hilton. He was devastated, today he was entirely occupied with business. But I must spend the weekend at the house, he insisted. The pool would be at my disposal. The car would arrive after lunch tomorrow.

When Saturday afternoon came I was shown to a bedroom overlooking the entrance. I put a swimming costume on under my wrap, and went out to the terrace with a little camera in my pocket. All the children were splashing about in the blue water below or running on the surrounding grass. There were seven or eight of them, and the eldest was about ten. Behind them, beneath the blue sky, the city lay steaming in a heat haze. I saw the guards watching me and suspected they might think this was no place for a Kodak moment.

I swam for half an hour and exchanged smiles and nods with the charming ladies at the pool. I learned the names of the children; none of them were the names I had been given in America, but that did not necessarily signify anything. The guards seemed to have lost interest so I risked a few photographs while their backs were turned. There was a small boy and girl nearer the house, so I moved behind them as if to get the scenery in the background. Out of the corner of my eye I saw a servant scuttle indoors.

"Jacquie, how are you?" Lambaro appeared smoothly at my side. "I hope you are enjoying yourself. I should be spending more time with you."

"Oh, but you're so busy."

"Unfortunately, yes. So much work." I tried to envisage what international drug supremos did all day and came up with something out of a Second World War movie involving maps and deployment of resources. He gazed at me with rapt attention and pushed my hair away from my face. "But I promise you that this evening you shall have the whole time with me. After dinner tonight, we will spend a little time together, I think." He kissed my shoulder. Then he kissed my other shoulder. "Until this evening, Jacquie."

I should coco. Half an hour later I made my exit to the bedroom. I stashed the film in my purse, took my make-up off with lots of grease, and lay down with a magazine. Time for dinner. I did not move.

At last there was a knock on the door.

"Senorita?"

An elderly servant poked her concerned face around the door. I groaned. I turned over. I pointed at my stomach.

Five minutes later up he came.

"Jacquie, my dear, do you need a doctor?"

"Ooooh," I groaned.

I closed my eyes. An hour passed. A doctor arrived. He prodded my stomach.

"Oh. Oh."

"Did you drink water?"

"Yes. In a café this morning."

"Gastroenteritis."

Soup arrived. I left it to get cold, swilled it around my mouth, stuck my fingers down my throat and threw up in the lavatory. I did not bother to pull the chain.

Lambaro returned.

"Lambaro, I am sick. I must go back to the hotel."

He insisted that I stay overnight. He ran a finger tenderly along the nape of my neck. He bent over me in concern. I groaned, turned toward him and breathed a soupy gust in his direction. He drew back sharply.

I left in the morning for the hotel and was on the first flight out on Monday.

I developed the photographs in Miami. They were pretty definitive pictures, given the stress I had been under when I took them; if there were any resemblance to Carrie, it would show up. I spent a whole afternoon with the grandparents and those photographs, but it was no good. They could not be sure which of the children were hers. I left two very sad old people behind at that house.

"Colombia?" Thomas's voice crackled on the phone. "Are you crazy?"

"It was fine. I was only there for a few days."

"Jacquie, your luck can't last forever. Remember what you said? The time has come."

"Yes."

"So?"

"You mean the five years are over. I know, Thomas. I'm thinking about it. I'm tying up loose ends."

"And you are staying in Hawaii while you tie them up."

"Just for a few months."

"You said that before. And now I turn my back for two minutes and you're in Columbia. You have to learn to say no. You can't keep going off on these mad jobs just because people ask you. One day you will be in trouble."

He was working toward his own retirement with no faith that I would ever give up the Circuit. At first, I had not trusted him. Now, he did not trust me.

"What's Level Three?"

I was in Kailua, ambling up the beach road with Tammy.

"It's like, when you've had an alcohol problem or drugs, it's like the marines say — this is your last chance. If this doesn't work, pal, you're out of the service. It's a residential course for six weeks. First they do detox, then they go on a twelve-step AA program. You know the big pink hospital on the hill?

"Uh-huh."

"Dale was up there."

I was not surprised her husband had a problem. One of the younger marines had hinted at it.

"So he drinks?"

"He's got a coke habit."

I was shocked. I had always been told that cocaine addiction was nature's way of telling you that you had too much money. I had seen a hell of a lot of drug abuse when I worked as part of a security team that clamped down on "Heaven," a club in the West End of London. We were talking about a marine sergeant here, for God's sake, married with children, who lived on the beach and went scuba diving.

"How can he afford it?"

"He can't. We can't, Jacquie. In any sense."

One of the marines had invited me to a party that night, as it happened. I do not know what I expected. Maybe it was not going to be the policeman's ball. Maybe people would get legless and fall over.

Make fools of themselves. Fight, even, though I hoped not.

You could say I was totally unprepared.

I walked into a riotous crowd and within minutes I had been offered a line of cocaine. People smoked marijuana wherever I looked. I grabbed a drink, talked to a few people and hated what I saw. Most of the marines here had wives, young women they had already introduced me to at the beach, and nearly all of them were slobbering over a flashy girl or another man.

The marine who had invited me was giggling in a corner with a friend of his. I pushed a path through the room and grabbed his arm. He was a good-looking corporal in his twenties.

"What's going on here?"

"What?"

He saw the disgust on my face and took me out to the veranda. His friend followed.

"What's the matter?" he asked.

"How can you guys behave like this?"

"Am I getting the right message here? Jacquie, you have a problem with this party?"

"Too bloody right I do! You're all fucking yourselves up. All these drugs."

"We're adults. We can handle it."

"Well, that's what most people say, right before they become addicts," I said.

His friend put his arm round my waist. "None of us are addicts, honey." He grinned at me. "We've been medically discharged from addiction. That's official."

I was bewildered. The Marine Corps did everything it could to help its people, but if people won't help themselves. . . .

The corporal looked uneasy. "Maybe this isn't the right place for you, Jacquie. Some of us are just, letting go. We've come outta Level Three. If you know what that is. Can I take you home?"

"No, thanks. I'll make my own way."

I strode back inside the house. I wanted the loo and struggled across a couple of rooms full of people and up some stairs. The door at the top usually led into the bathroom. I opened it. On a bed, Tammy's husband, Dale, shut his eyes and moaned. He was getting sucked off by a young marine I knew.

I turned and left.

"They treat us as well," Tammy said.

"They do?"

"Sure. Women keep making the same mistakes, you know. Some of us have been married to abusers before. So on the CODA course we find out what makes us keep going back for more, and change it. CODA stands for co-dependency."

"What's that?"

"Come to a meeting and find out."

I had nothing better to do and frankly I was fascinated. Did Tammy or her friends have the first idea what sleazebags their husbands really were? As I locked the door to my house that evening, it crossed my mind that maybe I should stay indoors with a good book. I was humiliating these women, going to their therapy group to spectate. It was hard not to feel superior. While my marriage to Tim had been awful, at least I had not repeated my mistake.

They met at a big house about three miles away. When I arrived, eight women were about to sit down on chairs in a semicircle in the garden. I knew most of them already; they all had kids and I had met them at barbecues or the beach or with their husbands, diving. The facilitator of the group asked them all, in turn, how the week had gone.

"Joe was, like, he's going to take the boy up to his buddy's for an hour before we go down to the beach."

"So, what would have happened before?"

"Little Joe and me would have been stuck at home all day while he stayed up there drinking. He'd'a come home, we'd'a had a fight. You know . . ."

"So, what happened this time?"

"I was, like, this is what happens when we go down this road, and how it made me real hurt inside just thinking about it. And little Joe wanted to do something else. And I came up with alternatives. A whole other plan for the day. I kept on like that."

"And?"

"He was kinda surprised that I was talking. Like, before I'd react to him. It was, like, because we both knew I was gonna get hurt, he could get to play wife-beater. This time I was laying it on the line. I was saying, we both know I could get hurt, the kid could get hurt, and we, none of us, want that. The road starts here. So let's go in a different direction."

"But he still wanted a drink with his buddies?"

"Sure he did. But he's working on that, too. Like, before he felt, like 'I'm Joe, I'm a drinker.' Now I'm treating him different, I'm helping him to get a different identity."

I was surprised, the way they picked out small incidents to illuminate something. They were much more self-aware than it had ever occurred to me to be. They were people trying to gain control in out-of-control situations.

One of them was at the group for the first time, and had a lot to complain about. Her husband was always out or asleep, he spent all their money on heroin, she had to do everything because without her the family would fall apart. Her reactions and concerns sounded pretty reasonable to me.

"It doesn't matter how hard I try, I can't do the right thing." She started to cry. "He just, like, blames me for everything." She was right. What else could she do?

The facilitator and the others in the group started asking her about her marriage. He had been a smack head since his earliest days in the marines. Why had she married him?

"I thought he'd change."

"Why?"

"I guess I thought I could show a shining example." She gave a timid laugh. Nobody had been interested in her for years, nobody had listened, and now here were eight people who wanted to know exactly what was going on. "I thought, if I was good, like, if I cleaned the house and cooked like his mom and looked nice and never slipped up, he would appreciate me."

"You mean, he'd feel sorry for being bad to you?"

"Yeah, I guess."

"He'd see you as a martyr and be real contrite. 'I bin so bad, I got a saint here and I owe her.' That stuff?"

"Yeah. In the back of my mind that was what I thought."

"Your daddy expect all that from you?"

"Sure, my dad's got real high expectations. He used to beat us if we didn't do what he wanted. It never did us any harm."

The others laughed, and she looked surprised for a minute. I did not understand either, at first. Then I fell in. She was repeating the same situation. The beatings had done her a lot of harm.

"What do you think, Jacquie?"

"Erm . . . I . . . "

"What about you?"

It was perfect timing. It was what I had been looking for: some kind of explanation. Why did I need to work so hard? Why was I so desperate to be strong and independent? Why did I always see help as condescension? Why did I always see myself as a rescuer? Why could I not play any other part than knight in shining armor? Over the weeks that followed I went to every co-dependency meeting. I listened to the others and found in their accounts much that was in common with my own patterns of behavior. I began to understand why I had been trying so hard to please.

I finally realized I did not have to try to impress other people. I did not have to risk my life at the drop of a hat. "You're no good to me dead," Thomas had said. He was right. What I had to do was find out what Jacquie wanted.

I COULD NOT STOP WORK STRAIGHT AWAY. I WENT BACK TO ENGLAND and began to wind my business up. My reputation was shot to pieces since the *Observer* article, so I did not exactly expect people off the Circuit to be beating a path to my door. At Christmas, I told Thomas I would definitely come to him in the spring. Yet somehow by the end of February I still had too much on to drop everything.

"Jacquie, you said this before. I'm ready. I'm just waiting for you to say you are ready, too."

Thomas was on the line from the Caribbean. In my mind's eye I saw the serious way he looked when we discussed this issue.

"But not just yet. I've gotta—"

"You know, I am beginning to think you have a problem. You sound like an addict."

"How can you say that?"

"It's true. You get a high from being on the Circuit. That's what you are going to miss."

"Oh, for God's sake. I don't need this."

I was furious. I thought I knew myself pretty damn well since my psychological co-dependency had become crystal clear. The last thing I needed was amateur psychoanalysis from my boyfriend. The arrogance of it.

I happened to be away working for six weeks after our phone call, and we did not speak during that time. At Easter, just as I was desperate to break the silence between us, he wrote me a sweet letter of invitation to an annual gala dinner in Hamburg.

We made up. He was wonderfully kind; he was romantic; he gave me a lovely wristwatch, and I knew then that we cared about each other so much that we had to be together for good. It was time for me to make more of an effort. Only, by now, I had taken on so many little bits of work that things were starting to snowball again. If I stopped now, I would be letting people down.

We talked often through the weekend in Hamburg. I told him everything that had become clear to me since the co-dependency course, and how I was seriously trying to extricate myself from commitments. We came to an agreement. I set myself a serious deadline. By the end of September, I would quit. I promised him that, after September, I would never take another job on the Circuit, and I meant it.

It was July and this would be one of my last assignments. I needed some sunshine, so I was pleased when I had to follow my target to the Spanish coast near Marbella. He was my client's husband, and I had been watching him for weeks.

Madeleine was an elegant woman in her fifties. Her husband had an interesting job and traveled all over Europe, while she shopped and lunched and had her hair done. They owned a big house in Hampstead, one of the most expensive areas in London, and an apartment in Spain. They were, by all conventional standards, very successful.

"He's having an affair, I just know it," she said. "He's been different ever since we went to Spain after Christmas. I think he met somebody down there. He hardly ever came back to the apartment, he was always out. And it's the same story now. He's got appointments in the evenings, he has to spend all these weeks away. I just want to know who it is, that's all."

"Have you asked him?"

"Yes. He said what you'd expect a man to say. That I was being neurotic and it must be the change of life. We've been together for thirty years."

I began to follow him around London. He was gray-haired, red-faced, chubby, short, and looked anxious. You would not notice him in a crowd. I was sure he must have wonderful qualities but, sadly, I could not see anyone falling in love with him. He might have been a regular little dynamo at work, but apart from one or two descents into a dubious basement bar near his office, where he had a quiet drink and left, he led a social life of extreme timidity. I never saw him talk to any women. He was predictable. When he said he was going abroad, he drove out to Heathrow airport.

Once there, though, he did not fly to Milan for a week, as he had told Madeleine; he got on a plane to Malaga. So maybe she had been right. Perhaps he did have a girlfriend in Spain.

"He's going away again in a fortnight," Madeleine told me. "He says it's Frankfurt, but wherever it is, I want you to follow him."

I checked up. He had bought another flight to Malaga, and was going to stay there a week. She gave me the phone number of the English people who owned the apartment next door to them in Malaga. I called them and arranged to rent their property for the week the husband was there. Now all I needed was a companion. I would feel a lot less conspicuous if two of us went, and Emma, a friend of mine, had just been through a divorce. She felt low and jumped at the chance of a week in the sun to cheer herself up.

Malaga is a pretty little town on a headland, with a gritty beach and rocks to sunbathe on, and a friendly promenade of bars and shops. The apartment building looked like a spreading Spanish house, festooned with ivies and pelargonia with balconies all around. You could lie out on the balcony in dark glasses and a sunhat and pretend not to listen to what was going on next door. I spent the entire first morning out there. The couple on the other side were at it like bunny rabbits before breakfast, which was fascinating but unimportant. From the errant husband's flat, not a sound. If he had a woman in there, she was either asleep, dumb or she'd gotten a headache. But, perhaps he was waiting for her to arrive.

All that day, which was a Friday, I watched him. He ambled off to the shops at about ten and bought some groceries; then he ambled back. Emma, who was enjoying herself and, I suspected, working through some of her own issues concerning unfaithful husbands, watched him at the mini-market and said she could not tell whether he was buying enough groceries for two people for two days, or one person for four. I was none the wiser. I heard him coming into the apartment and nobody greeted him.

By the end of the morning I was pretty sure he was on his own. *Maybe he was having some sort of business crisis,* I thought. *Maybe he wanted to get away from creditors or sell the business and follow the Path to Enlightenment advocated by some guru or something, and did not want to share his troubles with his wife. This was probably a wild goose chase with no woman in the story at all.*

He sat on the beach most of the afternoon, with a book. At six o'clock he was back in the apartment, and I heard the shower running. At seven-thirty he left, with me and Emma a hundred yards behind him. He walked purposefully down to the seafront, past the tourists drinking at tables in the dusk, and into one of the bars. This was more like it. I was sure he was going to meet somebody; he was not smartly dressed or leaving a pungent trail of aftershave, it was just the way he seemed to know exactly where he was going.

When we walked into the place five minutes later, he was sitting at a table with his book and a drink. On his own. A paunchy English vacationer of fifty in a pale yellow polo shirt and gray slacks, minding his own business on the Costa del Sol. He could have robbed a bank in the next five minutes, and if you had put that description out there would have been dozens like him pulled in straight away.

"Hello, girls, what can I do you for?"

I was sure I had seen the barman somewhere before. He was conspicuously tall, about forty, with receding hair worn long at the back like a seventies soccer star, and dressed in a black embroidered vest and a white shirt with full, bloused sleeves. We sat at the bar, so that I could keep an eye on the front door, and looked around. It was quiet so early in the evening; just me and Emma, the target, and a few other tourists starting to drift into the one big dimly lit room with a stage at one end a dais for a band over to one side.

We asked for two glasses of sangria.

"Down for the week, are you?"

"Yes, it's nice here, isn't it? D' you live here all year round?"

"I do, indeed. You nurses, are you?"

"Yes, how did you know?"

"We get a lot of nurses."

It was the vest that rang the bell at last. Its silver embroidery looked just like the coat of arms on the board outside Her Majesty's Prison, Brixton. Years ago, one of my policemen friends in Marbella had pointed this barman out as the driver of a getaway vehicle in a famous robbery. Well, at least he had put his ill-gotten gains to good use. He was very friendly, the life and soul of the party, and in the next hour the bar began to fill up nicely. I could no longer see the target, but he had not left and nobody had joined him in the last five minutes. I got up to go to the loo.

When I returned, I saw that his chair was empty, though the rest of his table was occupied by a noisy group from the north of England, and I decided he must have gone to the Gents. I went back to the bar.

"Can you see him?" I murmured to Emma. "Did he go out?"

"No, I've been watching the door."

The barman looked across at our long faces.

"The cabaret's coming up now," he said encouragingly. "You'll die, honest. Can I get you another?"

I was considering a Campari and soda when a sudden *Twang!* boomed from a speaker above my head. I nearly fell off my stool. I swiveled around open-mouthed. Lights had gone up on stage, illuminating a false marble column and a black backdrop. As I watched, fascinated, an immensely tall, glamorous transvestite, robed from head to toe in a lemon satin flamenco frock, all diving décolletage and a black polka dot frou-frou on the fishtail skirt, swayed on to the stage, seized the mike and began to belt out a loud and passionate song. I tore my eyes away and scanned the crowd.

"D' you think we've lost him?"

"I can't see him anywhere."

Emma had been struggling through the audience, trying not to look as if she was looking for him. I decided to finish my drink before I went walkabout to see if I could find the target further along the promenade outside. I could not leave now; the singer was terrific. He wore a curly black wig like Joan Collins and looked half blind from the sheer weight of mascara. Stomping his heels and clacking his maracas, he swanned off stage blowing kisses and tossing paper roses into the crowd. Beneath the applause and catcalls the music changed.

Out of the wings bounded a second figure: a shorter and altogether tubbier performer, in a black halter-neck swimsuit with white straps and fringes and an outsized conical brassiere clamped firmly on top. As this ersatz Madonna teetered on her stilettos, tossed back her wild blond hair and pouted her scarlet lips, I recognized the two chins.

"Like a VIRGIN—" she bellowed.

Speech almost deserted me. I nearly fell off my stool. I dug Emma in the ribs. "Em, it's 'im."

"What? Where?"

She peered at the front door.

"It's HIM!"

"On the very FIRST DATE—"

Emma dissolved in giggles and spluttered sangria down her nose.

A lady from Scarborough was laughing so much she looked in need of medical attention. My target was the sensation of the evening.

"Who are they?" I gasped at the barman. "Do they work together?"

He flicked a limp wrist. "Well, love. They are good friends."

I went back the following night and took pictures of the whole act. My target bawled a lovely version of Una Paloma Balanca in a bursting crimson flamenco frock with three tiers of frills and matching crimson lipstick. His upper arms were mottled with fake bronze and the things that man could not do with an ostrich feather fan were not worth doing. Oh, I did enjoy myself.

Breaking the news to the client was going to be a delicate task. I would have to keep a straight face, for a start. She called me the night I arrived back.

"Did you see her?"

"Yes, I saw 'her.' I think we'd better meet. I've got some photographs."

"Wonderful. Shall we have tea? I'll be in Piccadilly tomorrow. Let's go to the Ritz."

"Er . . . let's not. Perhaps somewhere a little less public?"

We met at Brown's Hotel. It is quiet, discreet and well upholstered, so if she burst into tears the sound of her sobs would be absorbed by wall-to-wall soft furnishings.

"Did you bring the pictures?"

"I did," I said, reaching for my bag.

"What's she like?"

"Very tall. Dark. Spanish."

I took the Kodak pack from my bag and pulled out the shot of the slender flamenco singer in the yellow satin dress.

"Oh my God," she said. She looked dumbfounded. "I never thought it would be anybody like this. I can't compete."

"It gets worse," I said. I laid the shot of "Madonna" on the table.

She froze. She leaned forward, and I could not see her face, but she did not move a muscle for about twenty seconds. Then she burst into hysterical giggles.

"I'm so sorry," I said, poker-faced. It did not seem entirely the appropriate comment to make. Her shoulders heaved, and her eyes streamed as she lay back in her chair.

"It's such a relief," she said, and exploded with laughter again. Women from the Shires were looking at us very oddly. I had to keep passing her tissues with which to wipe her eyes.

"Why is it a relief?"

"I was thinking of sacking the maid," she gasped. "My underwear keeps disappearing."

I often wonder what she did about it. I rather think they are still married. Anyway, I went home with a smile on my face.

Later that evening I took a phone call from Aruba in the Dutch Antilles, one of the Caribbean groups of islands. It was the chief officer of Thomas's ship, the second in command. I knew something was wrong.

"Now, sit down. Stay calm, Jacquie."

Thomas had had a heart attack.

"Is he all right? I'm coming. Tell him I'm coming."

"No, stop. There's no need for that. It is a mild attack only. He will be taken back to Europe before you have arranged a flight. You would have to fly to Caracas — just stay where you are."

I spoke to the chief officer several times the next day and the day after. Thomas was in hospital, Thomas was fine. He would be med-evac'd home probably tomorrow. In the middle of a phone call to a friend I heard myself saying, "This is the beginning of the end. If they take his ship away, he'll be lost."

The chief officer kept saying Thomas was about to be flown back to Hamburg. It would take me a day to get there, as there was no airport on Aruba. But this was going on too long. I could not sleep; I was helpless. I found the telephone number of the hospital and called. I had to speak in Dutch to the ward sister.

"How is he?"

"Comfortable."

"Please tell him I love him."

"I can't tell him anything. He's unconscious. He can't hear."

"But that's not a mild heart attack!" I said in English. And then, "I'm flying out to see him."

"No. He will arrive in Hamburg tomorrow." She went away and came back with the flight number. At last I had something to do. I booked a flight to Hamburg that would arrive an hour before his.

I watched the arrivals board. He had landed, thank goodness. I would see him. I needed to see him, he needed me, we had to be together through this. I willed him to be strong. I strode up and down.

I was being paged. I heard my name on the public address system. Something was wrong. Two men from the shipping line waited at the information desk.

"We are very sorry—"

Thomas had had a second heart attack, literally on the tarmac. They had not been able to save him.

Some things you cannot change, no matter how much psychological insight you think you have. Like the way you deal with death. I switch into organizational mode. I deal with the funeral arrangements and the will, and the grieving relations and the flowers, the wake and the memories, and I have to tell myself I will carry on for the sake of other people.

At first, this was no different. His children and his first wife came to Hamburg. We grieved together. I brought his mother from

Düsseldorf for the funeral. Not long afterward, I took her back to live in East Berlin. She had lost her husband years ago, and now her only son; she had never been to the West until after the wall came down, and there was nothing for her here now.

The second wife wanted Thomas's cabin cruiser. She had no right to it, as they had divorced with a full and final settlement, but she insisted. She announced that she intended to contest the will. Thomas's daughter was upset.

"Don't let her have it, Jacquie. Dad wouldn't want her to."

I thought about this. I thought about the ugliness of a court case and the cruel behavior of this woman and I said, "We'll sink it."

I drove to Vlissingen with Thomas's daughter and we pulled the plug. When we drove away we knew that over the next few hours the vessel would slowly subside to rest on the bottom of the marina.

Thomas was never coming back. He would not be there in September, we would never share the house in France, we would never sail the blue Caribbean together. Alone, a few weeks later, I took his ashes out into the Baltic Sea and scattered them to the music of *The Carnival is Over.* That was when I realized that Thomas's death was different, after all.

In him, I had found what I wanted at last; and I had been too slow to see it. I had been too selfish: I had wanted to stay on the Circuit.

Everybody I had ever loved had died. Without Thomas, there was no point in carrying on. If only I had understood that sooner.

Perhaps somebody was trying to tell me something: You can't have it all.

AFTER THOMAS DIED I KNEW I NEEDED TO RE-EVALUATE MY LIFE. Life does go on, and dad did not bring me up to be a quitter. I moved back to England and found a small terraced house in Elstree, Hertfordshire. Elstree felt comfortable. It is a quiet town on the fringe of London, not far from where I grew up in Barnet. The streets of the old working class part of town are lined with solid Victorian red-brick terraced homes, while the wealthy live in detached seclusion on the edge of the borough where London finally filters out in the woods and fields of rural Hertfordshire. But Elstree does have a discreetly racy side. It is the nearest thing we have to Hollywood. The Elstree studios are famous for film production and spectacular special effects. Steven Spielberg made the *Superman* movies there, and the history of the studios goes back to the black-and-white film days. It even has a small, secluded airport where local legend tells of mysterious comings and goings involving celebrities with a need for secrecy.

I shared the house with a shy, young chap named Peter. We shared the cooking, hired a cleaner and became friends. Life in the house became settled. I did not want to start running all over the world again. I had had enough and craved a normal everyday existence. Fortunately

I found work as a chef at the local BBC studios and worked on the set of a British soap called *Eastenders*. The plot revolved around a square in the east end of London with characters from Pauline the local busy-body, with three kids and a gardener husband, to hard cases, Phil and Grant Mitchell, the local heavies. Part of the set had a café forever serving English fried breakfast, and the local pub, the Queen Vic, always hosting parties to celebrate the locals births, marriages and deaths. I prepared the food the viewers saw on the set: from wedding cakes to egg and bacon. I learned that mashed potatoes with pink dye becomes ice cream, as the real stuff melts under the lights. English style sausages are raw, with gravy browning brushed over them so they do not dry up. For one Christmas episode we had sixteen turkeys in various stages of cooking, from just popped in the oven to one forgotten and burnt to a crisp.

Apart from the job at the film set, I also worked at a senior citizens home cooking for fifty elderly, all with Alzheimer's. While cooking at the home, I met Barbra. Barbra is short in height but big of heart, a local girl who came from a large family of six children. She met and married Simon and they had two girls, Rebecca and Elizabeth. Barbra would always tell you the truth; if you asked her if a new dress looked nice she would either say it looks great or, no it's horrible and doesn't suit you.

I lived ten houses away from Barbra and her family. We car-pooled to work and spent time at each other's houses drinking tea or watching Elvis Presley re-runs on television. It was a new and different life for me, staying in one place and working in a conventional job. But it was what I needed at the time, and I was fortunate to find a great friendship with Barbra. I became fairy godmother to the girls, who at four and six were complete opposites of each other: Elizabeth, dark-haired and very petite, the image of her father, with Rebecca bigger built with blonde hair and a cheeky grin, just like her mother's sisters. I made the girl's birthday cakes, brought them candy and showed them pictures of the countries where I had traveled.

Eventually, I left work as a chef and became personal assistant to the managing director of Douwe Egberts Coffee, a Dutch subsidiary of Sara Lee. I spent about three days a week flying between London and Amsterdam. Luckily I spoke Dutch, and this proved useful when the president came over for meetings at the London office. I enjoyed my time at Douwe Egberts; more so because it is the only brand of coffee I ever drink. I felt I had landed in catering heaven, free coffee and cheap products from the Sara Lee range. I ate so much chocolate fudge cake I put on pounds.

One hot, humid August night as I slept with my bedroom window wide open, naked as the day I was born, with just a sheet over me, I woke up to the sound of someone moving by my bed. I rolled over and still half-asleep saw a man dressed in black with a balaclava on his head. He held his fingers up to his lips and said, "Shhh, it's the police."

In my dozy state I thought, *Oh! I wonder if they have followed some enemy of mine, maybe a Muslim fundamentalist, to my house.* I turned over to go back to sleep.

The next thing I remember is the sheet sliding off me. I sat up, fully awake. The intruder loomed over me.

"It's the police. Where's your old man?"

What old man? My father? He was dead. Thomas? He was dead.

I let out an ear-shattering scream and lunged off the bed, he tried to pin me down; I could only see his left hand in the dark and was not sure if he had a weapon in the other. The instant he raised his right hand to strike me I knew it was just him against me: he had no weapon. My training kicked in — I hit him with a flurry of blows knocking him off balance, then bundled him out of my bedroom and slammed the door. I groped for the phone.

Peter, who was in the next room with his girlfriend, shouted, "Who are you? What do you want?"

I could hear more feet pounding up the stairs, and wondered if there were accomplices. I found the phone and punched in 999, screaming, "Help, I'm naked and there's a man in my room!" After providing my name, address and telephone number I fumbled around for some clothes, while my next-door neighbor shouted in the street. I soon heard police sirens, so I rushed out the door to see if Peter was okay.

I later had the opportunity to hear the tape recording of my call to the emergency operator and realized that no matter how well trained you are, it all goes out the window when you are roused from a deep sleep and the element of surprise is on the attacker's side.

My neighbor's dogs had heard the front door being kicked in, which is more than I did. They barked, then my scream apparently woke half the road. As my neighbor rushed down his stairs and out his front door with baseball bat in hand, the attacker ran out of my door and into a waiting car that sped off into the night. It was all over in seconds, but the knowledge that I had not held onto my attacker haunted me.

"How could this happen?" I asked the police sergeant, who I happened to know from the old days.

"Jacquie, it happens. Now, did he touch you at all?"

"No." I repeated, "No."

I could see the look in his eyes, I knew he did not believe me; he thought I had been raped but would not admit it. My best friend for the past twenty years, James, arrived on my doorstep. He is also a police officer and was on duty at Heathrow when the sergeant called and asked him to come over. James took me into the kitchen and sat me down.

"Jacquie, tell me what he did to you."

"Nothing, I promise, nothing, he just grabbed at me. Who was he James? What did he want?"

Out of the corner of my eye, I saw Peter and his girlfriend come into the kitchen. She was crying and Peter was visibly shaken. Trevor, my next-door neighbor, gave a statement to the police. He described the car and the driver; there had been only two of them. Now I felt even worse, I could have saved Peter from the beating he took. I heard James and the sergeant discussing me in the next room.

"I think he raped her," the sergeant said.

"Maybe," said James. "But you know Jacquie, she'll never admit it."

The police left, and Peter and I sat up and watched the dawn break. Trevor made tea and several other neighbors woken by the commotion came and joined us sitting in the front garden.

"I expected you to come charging through the door and beat the shit out of him," Peter said.

"Yep, me too," I admitted. I felt I had let him down.

The next morning the forensics team dusted for fingerprints. The CID arrived and took more statements.

"Have you got any enemies?" they asked.

"Where shall I start? Let's see: there's the Colombian drug baron, the Muslim fundamentalists, the IRA. Shall I go on?"

"No, that's fine," the detective sergeant sighed. "Let's make this easier — any ideas?"

I telephoned Douwe Egberts and told them what had happened. The finance director, Mark, told me to book myself and my friends into a local hotel and they would pay for it. I was so grateful; the thought of staying in that house was too much. I now know how the many people who had been burglarized, from whom I had taken reports felt: the violation of your own space, the fact that someone had come into your house and rummaged through your personal belongings. Many weeks later I discovered that a house in the same road, No. 23, had been fire-bombed over a bad drug deal a couple of weeks before my break in. I lived at No. 123! It was a case of wrong house.

I decided to go to America for Christmas. I needed a break and I wanted to treat Barbra and her family to a vacation. Barbra had never been to the U.S. Also, she had just been diagnosed with lupus and Simon was dealing with a bowel disease. How could so much bad luck hit one family? Elizabeth and Rebecca were so excited; I had planned to fly into New York then rent a minivan and drive down the east coast to Florida, stopping off at Baltimore, Washington, Virginia and Fayetteville, North Carolina along the way. We would then drive back up again but stay on the beach in North Carolina for a couple of weeks before taking our time to return to New York and the flight home.

We landed at JFK and went through the usual immigration and customs formalities before I marched off to pick up the van.

"Now stay here with the luggage," I told them all, "and I shall return with our chariot." Fayetteville, North Carolina, home of Fort Bragg, American special forces and the elite Delta Force, was our first stop. I had arranged to stay with Anne and Buddy for a couple of days before we headed on down to Florida. I showed Rebecca and Elizabeth around Fayetteville and took them to Fort Bragg; they had a great time meeting American soldiers who, "Just loved their accents."

Two days later and we were back on the road. Next stop, Orlando and that famous mouse's home, Walt Disney World. For a week we whooped it up in the Magic Kingdom, rode the biggest rides, watched the parades and waved at Mickey, Goofy and Pluto. I finally had to admit to being "Disneyed out," though we had had a great time. A day later we were sitting on the beach in North Carolina. We had decorated the rented house with tiny lights and pictures of Santa Claus; Christmas would be English-style.

After two weeks in North Carolina we drove up the east coast, chased by a bitter ice storm. I took the girls to the White House, and used my contacts in the Secret Service to get a VIP tour.

"This is the home of the American president," I announced proudly as we stood in the famous rose garden.

"Hey look at the squirrels!" Rebecca shouted, as she watched a couple of them race across the lawn. I laughed so much; it taught me one thing: Kids, no matter where you take them, will always be more fascinated by animals than history. We rode the last flight out of JFK airport before all flights were grounded due to bad weather. We had a great time, and I was surprised to find my spirits lifted. Yes, life does go on.

I KEPT TELLING MYSELF I WOULD KEEP MY PROMISE TO THOMAS AND stay off the Circuit. As bored as I was working in what I considered to be mundane office jobs, or cooking, I tried to stay true to my word. It was not long before I broke my promise, and after saying a silent prayer and asking Thomas to forgive me, I replied to a letter via a journalist from a woman who was looking for her child who had been taken to Pakistan. The woman knew I had been there and her letter pulled at my heart strings. I went to see her. Although I could not help her directly, I put her onto some colleagues who could, then they asked me to help them plan the escape route as I knew the area so well. Having finished the escape plan for them, one of the guys asked if I could cover a bodyguard job for him as a personal favor, as he would now be away on the rescue. I agreed, and after spending several weeks looking after a foreign royal princess I realized how much I missed the job I was trained to do. I took several more assignments. Slowly but surely I came back onto the Circuit.

At the same time I found my past catching up with me in a way I had not expected. As one of very few female bodyguards working in the world, and inevitably moving in media circles in the course of protecting high profile celebrities, I attracted interest from journalists and television and film producers. I received requests for magazine interviews and was asked to participate in documentaries and talk shows. This was a mixed blessing as discretion and anonymity are part of my job, but experience has taught me that you only draw attention to yourself if you want to. I could appear on prime time TV in the evening, and the following morning nobody would recognize me. It's part of being a professional.

Early 1999 found me in southern Spain chasing a woman who had sold topless pictures of the future wife of Prince Edward. Kara Noble was an ex-DJ who had known Sophie Rees Jones when she worked in public relations for a radio station. While on a road trip, Kara had taken a picture of Sophie lifting up her top. As soon as Buckingham Palace announced that Miss Rees Jones was to become Prince Edward's wife, Kara sold the picture to an English newspaper. They printed the picture, a great scandal broke and Kara disappeared. Another newspaper asked me to find her so they could have the first interview as to why she did it. The answer to me was obvious — she did it for the money, some $200,000. When I found out from sources that Kara had a place in Marbella, Spain, I took a photographer from the newspaper with me to Spain to try to find her. Hiring a car at the airport we set off to find our hotel and get our bearings.

I know Marbella well. It is the home of what we in the UK call the "Costa Del Crime." The area is full of English ex-pats on the run from the police. Spain had no extradition treaty with the United Kingdom so criminals found it a safe haven. Next to Marbella is Puerto Banus, a lively marina crammed with multi-million dollar yachts and expensive bars and restaurants. The light is hard: hurled back in your eyes by the glittering water and the chrome fittings on the yachts. The air is pungent with the smell of suntan oil and money. A paradise where criminals love to hang out.

We found many famous English soccer stars surrounded by almost-dressed blondes. We played a game of, "spot the bimbo." Which one would we see in next week's Sunday papers selling her kiss-and-tell story?

One famous English soccer player seemed to be having the time of his life. I watched, fascinated, as he took one girl out of the bar, walked her down a side alley, had sex with her in the shadows, and then walked her back to the bar. Then he had a quick drink and proceeded to do the same thing with another girl, and then another. My photographer friend's finger itched on the shutter button of his camera. I put my hand on his arm and shook my head. We had a specific job to do. But for all the well known famous faces we did see, there was no sign of Kara.

The next day, we set off along the Carrera, Spain's famous freeway. After just three miles we ground to a halt at the tail of a long line of stationary traffic. As we sat there, sweating, with traffic fumes stinging our eyes, I glanced in the rearview mirror and froze as an eighteen-wheeler thundered toward the rear of our car. I had nowhere to go. The impact as the truck hit, smashed us into the car ahead and knocked us senseless for a few seconds.

After a horrible silence I realized my head hurt and I felt a twinge of pain in my hip. I squirmed out of the car window and checked myself over. *Nothing broken,* I thought, *so I'm okay.* We helped the elderly couple in the car ahead of us climb out of their car and waited for ambulances and the police to arrive. A doctor at the local hospital checked me over. He smiled reassuringly.

"You've just some pulled muscles in your leg," he said.

"Great!" I offered up a silent prayer of thanks to my guardian angel.

We collected another rental car and the search for Kara continued. Seven days later, we had exhausted all possibilities. She was not there, so we returned to the UK.

The nagging pain in my hip did not seem to be easing when I walked, so I visited my local doctor for a check up. He came back into the examination room and held up the x-rays. He turned to me, his face incredulous.

"It's broken Jacquie. You've been walking around with a broken hip."

No wonder it hurt like hell. I had to stay home for a few weeks to let it heal. But I could still play a hunch. We found Kara hiding on the Spanish island of Majorca. The newspapers got their photos; I got to stay home and rest.

It seemed as if the Royal Family were never far away. Lindka Cierach, who became famous when she created Sarah Ferguson's wedding dress for her marriage to Prince Andrew, called me. I had borrowed several outfits from Lindka over the past year for appearances on talk shows or for photo shoots. She was going to a fashion show in America and would be taking Fergie's wedding dress with her for the show. "Can you come to protect the dress, Jacquie?"

"Delighted!" I told her.

We flew to Boston for the first show and booked into the Ritz Carlton hotel. At four o'clock in the morning the fire alarms snatched us from sleep. I grabbed the dress and evacuated the hotel from our room on the fifteenth floor via the stairs, ushering Lindka in front of me.

On reaching the ground floor the firemen showed us the way out, spilling out on the Boston sidewalk in the chilly October night air in just our dressing gowns, but with the wedding dress safe in its specially-made cover. "Come on, "I told Lindka, "I'm not standing here looking like the ultimate upmarket bag lady."

I nudged Lindka toward the lights of a coffee shop next to the hotel, shining like a beacon of warmth. A fireman saw the trouble I was having with the dress and helped me inside. To my relief the place was spotlessly clean. I turned to the fireman who had rescued me.

"Could I bum a fag off you?"

His jaw dropped, every head in the place turned toward me and Lindka collapsed in hysterical giggles. In the excitement I had forgotten we were not in London where my simple request would have raised no comment. I blushed furiously.

"I'm sorry, I meant to say: Can I cadge a cigarette?"

He grinned and offered me a Marlboro. I had just proven once again that while we speak the same language, certain phrases can have a completely different meaning!

As is so often the case the evacuation was for a false alarm.

The show went well in Boston and we continued on to New York, where Lindka hosted a cocktail party and show for Fergie. We arrived at the Waldorf Astoria to be met by one of the directors, Patrick Anderson, a lovely man. He showed me around the various suites and rooms until I was satisfied that, security-wise, all was well. Fergie only turned up for an hour, but the rich and the good of New York packed the place. The show was a success; I had made a friend in Patrick, which later would stand me in good stead.

Two weeks after arriving back in the UK, I slipped on some spilt diesel fuel while walking past a gas station. I heard a crack as I crashed to the ground. A wave of nausea swept over me, and I knew I had broken something. I crawled to Lindka's office, luckily, just around the corner; she rushed me to hospital where they confirmed I had a broken elbow and a broken knee. So, thirty stitches later, after an operation to replace my knee joint, my arm in plaster and a couple of weeks in hospital, I left the UK for a Christmas holiday in Malaysia.

It was the millennium year and I wanted to celebrate. Boarding the plane was tricky, but as soon as I was seated a very handsome blonde male steward came to see me. He massaged my feet and cut up my dinner as I only had the use of one arm. They let me leave my seat in the bed position for take off and landing, so my legs were elevated all the time. Emirates Air was just great.

Whilst on the Malaysian Island of Langkawi, I went to a private clinic to have my stitches removed, I took my credit card with me as I thought it would probably cost me a couple of hundred dollars. After waiting for a female doctor to be found (the island is mainly made up of Muslims so I was not allowed to let a male doctor see me half undressed), she removed my stitches very gently.

"Ah, Miss Davis, you have a beautiful scar." She stood back to admire the work. "That will be twenty-five cents, please. I am sorry that is twice the usual price."

I stared at her. "Only twenty five cents?"

"I am so sorry, but that is the rule, we have to charge foreigners double." She looked embarrassed. She must have misunderstood me.

I shook my head in amazement and gave her a dollar. I walked out smiling.

For the next few weeks I had to trawl the Internet in a hunt for pedophiles. A job had come my way through an agent who represented a family whose child had been missing for several years. They had been told by an anonymous email that a picture of their missing child could be found on a pedophile web site. The agent asked me to find the picture and identify who ran the site. It took several weeks just to find a computer expert with the skills necessary to crack the codes that the evil perverts who run these sites use. The owners of the site demand money from the would-be user, who is then given a password to enter the site. Most of the really offensive sites are hidden behind others. It is a very complicated way of trading. Police experts have caught up with the technology now, but the dealers in kiddie-porn pictures could trade without much interference at that time.

I found myself haunted by pictures of children, including infants, being abused by men. I would happily string these perverts up personally if I ever had the opportunity. For weeks I looked at pictures of children with dead eyes and pained expressions.

278 • Jacquieline Davis

We never found the child for whom we were looking. I just hope he was never subjected to this kind of cruelty.

While walking around Barnet High Street one day, I heard a very familiar voice calling my name. I turned around and there stood Helen Cliffe, an old colleague and friend of mine. I had not seen her for about six years. Helen had served in the British Army and on leaving had approached me for a job. She then worked with me for a couple of years on surveillance and close protection. Helen had a very similar outlook on life to me as far as children were concerned. We both claimed to dislike children immensely, and often laughed at people whom we knew that had got themselves tied down with the little rug rats. Helen joined the police service just as I left to do a hostage rescue in Iceland back in 1993; I had not seen her since.

"Hey, guess what? I've had a baby boy," Helen announced.

I nearly fell over with shock, surely this could not be the same Helen that I once knew, but here she was proudly showing me her son, Michael. Helen was in the midst of leaving the police force to move to the Isle of Man, a small island between England and Ireland known mainly for its annual long distance motorcycle races run over the public roads, the famous Tourist Trophy. The bikes touch nearly two hundred miles per hour in places — some tourists! Helen's mother came from the island, so she decided after leaving the force it would be a great place to raise a child.

I went to Helen's going away party which was held in a Greek restaurant. Now this was the Helen I remembered: too much drink and making an arse of herself with the Greek waiters. I said my goodbyes, and promised I would visit her on the island as soon as I could.

I needed to spend some time with my goddaughters, Elizabeth and Rebecca. I decided to take them camping to Devon, a pretty coastal county in the southwest of England. As we sat outside our Winnebago one morning, watching endless waves rolling up to break on the wide sandy beaches, while seagulls soared on the gentle winds above the cliffs under a clear blue sky, my cell phone rang. I mentally cursed the intrusion on our idyll, but I sat up when I heard Christopher Little, the literary agent, on the other end of the line.

"Jacquie, could you handle security on a book tour for a woman called Jo Rowling?" Christopher asked. I thought about it long and hard — for about two seconds.

"Certainly," I said. "Who is she? I've never heard of her." I love reading, and thought I knew all the contemporary authors.

"She's written a book about a boy wizard, called Harry Potter."

Saturday morning the eighth of July, 2000, found me at the head-quarters of the publishing company in London, where I was introduced to J. K. Rowling, a small, blond, pretty woman.

"The name's Jo," she said with a smile, shaking my hand.

We prepared to embark on a book tour that would use a train called the Hogwart's Express to travel from Kings Cross railroad station to Scotland, I had asked Helen to assist on the tour, and she had gone ahead to Kings Cross with our suitcases.

I opened the office door to check out the position of the limo. Photographers swarmed outside but I could see no sign of a big Merc or Cadillac, there was just a funny-looking little blue car that I recognized as a British Ford Anglia, built in the 1960s, parked outside. Typical of British cars of the period, it was so small it looked as if it would fit in the trunk of a modern compact. I turned to the publicity manager.

"Where's the limo?"

"There's our transport." She grinned and pointed to the little blue Ford. I stared at her and she must have read my mind. "No, really, that's it. I haven't gone mad," she reassured me.

I smiled and shrugged. A quote from a Lord Tennyson poem sprang to mind. Ours not to reason why, ours but to do and die. We piled into the little two-door car. Jo and the publicity manager somehow squeezing into the back while I sat next to the driver. Photographers crowded the windows, the shift crunched, and we roared off as quickly as the driver could manage, which — believe me — is not very fast in a Ford Anglia.

At King's Cross Railroad Station, the publicity lady jumped out and I drove onto the platform with Jo Rowling. About ten thousand people, including media from across the world, pressed against barriers as we drove onto Platform 9¾. A magnificent steam locomotive, with a painted board proclaiming, "Hogwarts Express" fixed over the boiler, simmered gently opposite the barriers. A huge cheer went up as Jo got out of the car.

The train was actually the "Queen of Scots," famous for having The Haig Treaty signed on board in 1919. It took us back into another more stylish era of travel. Gleaming brass was beautifully set off by the dark oak paneling in all the cars. White jacketed stewards served tea from silver pots while the English countryside rolled past the windows. However, we were not there to enjoy ourselves. I did not think the Wicked Witch of the North had a contract out on Jo; our main job was to ensure the safety of all the children involved. In the event the tour went superbly well. Jo Rowling is one of the most kind, caring people it has been my pleasure to meet and it was a delight to see smiling, happy children at every railroad station and bookstore, all eager to meet the woman who had brought the magic of reading into their lives. I finished this part of the tour with my faith in human nature restored after the recent investigations I had been involved in.

I had a week off before I rejoined the Harry Potter tour. This time it was London bookstores and a signing event in the southern coastal town of Brighton. I spent two days doing recces of the bookstores, some of them were in central London and getting Jo in and out of the front doors would be difficult. I rang various police stations to ask for help on the day and most of them readily agreed to provide crash barriers and police officers. The Hogwarts tour had been on the news every day for the last two weeks; the cameras had shown the thousands of people queuing outside bookstores and at train platforms up and down the country, so at least the London police had advance warning of what to expect. I asked Helen to come back over to the mainland to help again. This time I wanted her as the advance party; she would drive ahead to every location and radio me to let me know the state of play. In the event, this part of the tour went without a hitch.

I HAD EARNED ENOUGH MONEY FROM THE HOGWARTS TOUR TO TAKE MY
friends on holiday, so Elizabeth, Rebecca, Barbra, Simon and I flew
to North Carolina where I had rented a house on the beach for four
weeks. I love North Carolina; it is one of the states where you have both
mountains in one direction and the sea in another. Helen and her little
boy Michael had also decided to join us at the beach along with her
then-boyfriend Fred and two of his friends.

I had promised Barbra a surprise, both of us being Elvis Presley
fans. I had booked a trip to Memphis so we could visit Graceland. We
locked up the beach house and flew to Memphis for four days, staying
at the Ramada Hotel near Beale Street, the center of town. We found it
easy to walk around and visit the various bars, shops and cafes. Our day
trip to Graceland was fabulous. As it was just two days after the
anniversary of his death when we toured the house, we found that fans
had laid flowers and wreaths around his gravesite. I was very touched
by all this and the kindness the staff at Graceland showed to the children. In the evening we went to Beale Street where at every other bar
or café an Elvis impersonator belted out his hits. Simon and the girls
looked bored as yet another rendition of *Love Me Tender,* was crooned
over a microphone, but Barbra and I loved it. It was wonderful to see

her happy, and although I know she spent a lot of the time in pain, not once did she mention how her bones and joints really hurt.

We flew back to North Carolina so we could spend the last two weeks of our holiday relaxing on the beach and visiting friends whom I had not seen for a couple of years. I was having a great time when the telephone rang and again it was Christopher Little.

"Are you and Helen available to tour with Jo to America and Canada in October?"

"You bet!" I said, and hung up. I called Helen,

"Hi mate! Can you do two weeks in October?" I asked her.

"I can if someone can look after Michael."

Organizing the security of a foreign tour takes a lot of time well in advance of the actual tour dates. I called Ann Walker in North Carolina and asked her if she wanted to work with us on the tour as SAP team leader. Ann was thrilled to be asked, so we set about doing advanced recce work. The tour was to take place for one week in New York City and one week in Canada — Ontario for four days then on to Vancouver for another four days before we would fly home to the UK.

I had worked in New York many, many times so did not feel it necessary to do any recces of that area. But I had asked Ann to go to New York two days before we arrived so she could check out the hotel as it was one I did not know. Ann also flew to Canada and carried out the reconnaissance there. Every day she called or emailed me from locations to ask what I wanted to change. On a sunny fall day Helen and I met Jo at Heathrow Airport. We boarded the American Airlines flight to New York and sat back in our first class seats for the seven hour journey and another highly successful tour.

A few weeks later found the three of us back in New York with different clients, staying at the marvelous Waldorf Astoria Hotel. Patrick Anderson was the complete professional as always. Nothing is too much trouble, he is always helpful and his security arrangements are top notch.

Helen, Ann and I shared a two-bedroom suite. We had a lounge and a kitchen, and I love the Waldorf Astoria beds — comfortable or what!?

The hotel crawled with Secret Service agents as a large dinner was arranged the next day in the ballroom for all past presidents and Hollywood *A*-list persons. We were even invited but turned the invitation down, as we were too busy. At one point I went down to the lobby to buy some magazines and found Billy Crystal, the comedian, in the elevator when I got back in.

"Hi!" he said. "Going to the ball?"

"No, too busy at the moment, how about you?"

"Maybe later. I'm off to a party in Hilary's suite first."

"Have a nice time," I said, as we reached the eighteenth floor and he got out.

Ann and Helen came into the suite laughing some ten minutes later. They had stepped into an elevator with Hilary and Bill Clinton and when it stopped on the eighteenth floor they got out with them. Nobody challenged them, even though Secret Service swarmed everywhere. After looking around they got back in the elevator and came up to our floor.

The next morning we were due at NBC television studios and were driving down Fifth Avenue when the radio crackled into life. It was Helen with the advance party.

"Al Gore has decided at the last minute to go on television at the same studios."

"Okaaay . . . try and meet us at the back entrance and I'll call if we have a problem."

Two blocks from the studios we found the road closed with Secret Service guys standing everywhere. I jumped out of the car and spoke to a guy with a radio.

" We need to get to the studios."

"No can do, ma'am," he drawled, "The vice president is in there."

"Look, we have to get into the studios, our clients are due in front of the cameras." He was unimpressed. I kept my professional cool, but fixed him with a glare that penetrated straight through those shades.

"Find me a supervisor."

A Secret Service supervisor in regulation dark glasses and a bulge in his jacket came over, apologized for the delay and waved us through. Sometimes you just have to get to the rank that can get things done.

One evening we were headed to the theatre on Broadway to see the musical *Aida*. Ann had gone ahead to sort out the parking, and Helen was already in the theatre. As we pulled up outside the theatre Ann told Lou, our driver, that this was his parking spot for the night.

"I can't stay here, I'll get a ticket," he said.

"No, you won't, trust me," Ann replied.

I took our clients into the theatre and left them with Helen. Lou sat in his limousine outside, incredulous that he could stay parked there, not knowing that Ann had paid the hotel doorman next to the theatre fifty dollars for the parking space.

"Told you we can smooth the way," I said to Lou.

"Hey! I like you girls," he smiled.

The next morning I took Lou down some muffins that we had ordered for breakfast. I forgot that in America everything is bigger than in the UK so an order of muffins for three became twelve of them in a basket with Danish pastries and croissants. I hate eating when I get up so I took them with me and shared them with Lou as we drove along. We visited the Empire State Building and the World Trade Center. Our clients had always wanted to go there, so we arranged with WTC security to pass the lines and go straight to the top of the building. Little was I to know as I had my photograph taken with them that this would be the very last time I would ever stand here.

Our week in New York was a long one, we seemed to be going all day and half the night. The secret of being a good bodyguard is mostly diplomacy and seeing that your client gets what they want, without them knowing all the trouble you had to go through to get it. I played a trick on Lou on our last night. We had arrived back at the Waldorf at about nine o' clock and our clients had retired to their suite saying they wanted an early night. I had let Lou go with the limousine then about an hour later I called him.

"Hi, Lou where are you?"

"Brooklyn."

"Yeah? Well how long to get back here? They want to go out."

"Are you kidding me? Okay . . . it will take me an hour in this traffic."

"Just kidding," I said. "See you in the morning."

"You just wait, I'll get you." I could hear him laughing down the phone.

The next morning my telephone rang at five thirty waking me from a deep sleep.

"Your car's here, madam," Lou said in a lousy British accent.

"Oh my God! What's the time?" I thought I had overslept.

"Just kidding," said Lou. "Bye! See you in a couple of hours."

CHRISTMAS HOLIDAYS WERE COMING UP, AND I PLANNED ON taking Barbra, Simon, and my goddaughters to the U.S. We started out in Las Vegas, the gambling capital of the world; I had been here for *Soldier of Fortune* conventions several times but had never been here with children. From the plane windows as you swoop toward the airport you see the whole of the famous Nevada strip lit up, thousands of neon lights in the night darkness.

We came out of the airport and into a waiting stretch limousine for the ride to our hotel, the kids' faces a picture. They watched the TV in the back of the car as Barbra and Simon drank champagne. I knew they would remember this for a long time. Barbra's illness was steadily getting worse, sometimes she could not get out of bed for two days at a time. The hospital had put her on steroids for the lupus, and they made her really sick. Her attitude to her illness was marvelous, she would make the effort to get up and see the girls off to school even if it meant crawling down the stairs on her backside.

"I've got a family to look after," she would say.

We were staying at one of the few hotels that allows children to stay. I love to play blackjack, after being taught by Delta Force guys one year at the SOF convention, and had set myself a limit of one hundred dollars a day for the four days we were staying there. If I won, great! If not, I would get up and walk away from the tables once my hundred dollars was gone. I showed Barbra how to play and sat next to her while she won seventy dollars. She bought the next round of drinks, which was pretty cheap as I no longer drink alcohol and she could not because of all the medicine she was taking.

On Christmas morning at about five o'clock I dressed up in a Santa suit complete with white beard and crept from my room. I passed a group of happy drunks in the corridor.

"Merry Christmas! Ho Ho Ho."

I let myself into the girls' bedroom and put their presents at the bottom of the bed. Then, after opening the balcony door, I lightly brushed Rebecca on the face then fled onto the balcony, jumped across onto my balcony and disappeared through the door. I stripped off my Santa costume and jumped back into bed. Fifteen minutes later I heard a knock on my door. I opened it pretending to have been woken from a deep sleep.

"What's the matter?" I asked.

"Santa just came into my room and then flew out the window," Rebecca said, standing there with Barbra.

"What?" I said. "You are kidding! In all my forty years I have never seen Santa. Wow, you're lucky."

I went to the girls' room and watched them open their presents. Later in the day we were queuing for the restaurant when behind us four men started saying how much they must have drunk the night before as they were sure they had seen Santa Claus in the corridor at five in the morning.

"You did," said Rebecca interrupting them. "I saw him, too."

The last morning in Las Vegas, I went downstairs to buy some coffee for us all and fresh muffins. My hands were full with the tray of drinks when a group of young men came toward me as I crossed the casino floor. I had tucked my purse under my arm. As they drew level with me, one of them made a grab for my purse. I threw the tray of hot coffee at him and followed it up with a swift knee to his groin. He lay on the floor moaning as hotel security came running. The rest of his friends just stood there looking at me.

"Jeez, ma'am, he was only joking," one of them said.

"Yeah? Well not to me he wasn't; he tried to grab my purse. That's what happens when you do that. People get hurt. Maybe he won't do it again."

The police and paramedics arrived and after a brief conversation with the cops, I left the man being tended with an ice pack to his nether region. The police officer watched a tape of the incident from the hotel security cameras and agreed with me. I made a statement and left.

We drove from Vegas to Los Angeles through Death Valley via Calico, an original mining town in the Nevada dessert. The road stretched long and dusty and the sun blazed down. Jagged mountains on the horizon glowed through a kaleidoscope of colors as the afternoon shadows lengthened. Arriving in LA we stopped at a hotel I knew right off Hollywood Boulevard.

New Year's Eve we visited Disneyland in Anaheim, California. The girls and I made a rush for the Small World train, my favorite part of the Disney park. Sad that a grown woman should want to ride around on a train that goes through tunnels with puppet dolls singing songs from around the world — but hey! I guess all of us are kids at heart.

We sang *Auld Lang Syne* at midnight, then left to get back to our hotel, for on New Year's Day we were flying to Hawaii. I had promised this to Barbra when I first met her and now here she was, going to the place she dreamed of. We flew from LAX to Maui, then boarded a small plane that should have been taking us to the island of Kauai. Once in the air, the captain announced the plane was now going to Honolulu instead. "Don't panic," I said to Barbra, "This is Hawaiian Air, the islanders use planes like we use buses." We alighted in Honolulu and went to the Hawaiian Air desk.

"Just hop on the next one to Maui," they said.

"But I don't have any boarding cards left."

"No problem. The next flight is due in twenty minutes."

We boarded the next flight and finally landed in Kauai at about six in the evening. A guy stepped forward and greeted us all with Leis and said Aloha. Unfortunately our luggage did not arrive with us. The typical Hawaiian saying of, "no problem, hang loose," greeted us at passenger services. We picked up our rental car and drove to our resort on the far side of the island. On booking in I explained we had no luggage, but the airline had said they would have it delivered to us when they found it. We went to our apartment on the ground floor and threw the sliding doors open; right outside our patio was a hot tub. I stripped off my trousers and T-shirt.

"Welcome to Hawaii," I said, and slipped into the bubbling hot water. The others soon joined me.

"I can't believe I'm here, Jacquie," Barbra said.

"Well, believe it, mate."

I was so glad I could make her dreams come true. I also believed I was showing the kids how other cultures lived. I hoped that by showing them the world, they would be more understanding of other races. I also wanted them to have happy memories of their parents; we did not know how long Barbra had to live and like my parents had done with me as a child, I wanted them to be able to come back and visit these places when they were adults and remember their mother with affection. I often revisit places in Europe my parents took me — Italy or Germany — just to remember them as they were.

While on the island we visited Guava fields and waterfalls. The children met Hawaiian people who made arts and crafts from natural products like shells and stone. We did the hula hula on a boat sailing down the river and sat through a loua, the Hawaiian version of a pig roast, while the locals wore grass skirts and danced in their traditional way.

I tried hard not to cry as memories of Thomas flooded back. I remembered how we used to sit and watch the sunset from the beach.

In January, Georgina Bruni, an author, asked if I would go with her to do some research for a book she was writing about an event that happened in a forest outside a United States Air Force base in Southern England. Rendelsham Forest surrounds RAF Bentwaters and RAF Woodbridge in the county of Suffolk, England. There are three American Air Force bases within a short ride of each other. All on Royal Air Force fields, hence the "RAF" in the address. In 1980, a strange light appeared in the forest and several American soldiers were sent to investigate; some of them swear it was a UFO.

"Georgina, what do you want me to do if I see an alien? Throw myself in front of you and say, 'Take me not her—'?"

"No, no," said Georgina. "I need you to come into Rendlesham Forest with me at midnight so I can get a feel for the place. I want to go on the bases that are now closed down."

We drove to RAF Woodbridge and met the head of the Ministry of Defence security team, who walked us around the now-empty base. He took us into an underground bunker and showed us the nuclear-bomb-proof operations room. It was like something out of a sci-fi film: banks of computer terminals and wall maps covering entire areas of wall, showers to walk through and airtight doors. I was fascinated.

In other buildings, we found beautiful drawings of planes swooping from the sky, obviously left by Air Force pilots. We went out to the old control tower, and I climbed to the top. The view was magnificent. While there a helicopter hovered overhead, and I saw men in black rappelling down ropes. The MOD guy explained that Special Forces now used the area as a training ground since it had closed to normal use. We spent the evening with the old deputy commander of the base, Charles Holt, who was without a doubt a fascinating man. At midnight we entered the forest and walked the path from the east gate of the base to where the lights in the sky had been seen on Christmas Night 1980. People from all over England had phoned RAF West Drayton to report the sightings of these lights, but they had come to rest in Rendelsham Forest. There was an eeriness about the forest, but the sky was bright and the ground crisp underfoot. I walked along wondering about aliens and other intelligent life forms. I am very open-minded and never say never to anything.

Once Georgina was happy with what she had seen we walked back to our parked car, and went off to spend the night at Charles Holt's house. He had retired from the United States Air Force and married an English woman, and they had settled very near to the bases. After reading many statements from American Air Force personnel, I have to admit I believe they did encounter something in those woods, and I also believe the American government tried to cover it up. Georgina eventually wrote her book called, *You Can't Tell the People,* a direct quote from Margaret Thatcher after Georgina met her and told her about the Rendelsham Forest incident. It became a best seller.

March is a cold month in England; we still wear coats and sweaters and often have the heating on at home, so I was happy to receive a phone call from a theatrical agent in Los Angeles asking if I could help one of his actresses. Charlene Chandon was a blond, thirty-year-old living on the West Coast. She had attended acting classes from an early age and for the past couple of years had appeared in various daytime television soaps and comedy shows. Helen and I flew to LA to meet her and find out what was needed. We knew it would involve some form of investigation, but had no idea it would involve yet more pedophilia.

Charlene, or Charlie to her friends, told me she had been abused from the age of four by her uncle who was a chauffeur to a well-known Hollywood producer. He had sexually abused her, and when she reached her teenage years had involved her in drugs. He eventually made her dependent on him for heroin. For her to get her daily fix she had to perform a sex act on him. About four years earlier, when Charlie was twenty-six, she decided to clean up her act and went into rehab. She told us she had now been clean for three years and had not seen her uncle since. Now, she wanted to file charges against her uncle for the abuse she had suffered at his hands. The police department was supportive, but had told her she needed evidence or statements from other victims.

Charlie knew that her uncle had also abused his stepdaughter, Joanna, from an early age and she had run away from home at the age of sixteen. Nobody had seen her for thirty years, although it was widely rumored in the family that she had fled to England. Charlie's aunt had divorced her uncle and moved away with another child she had, who was now in his early twenties. She was not sure where the aunt lived but thought it was in California. The uncle had since remarried and had a daughter of his own, who was now twenty years old. This daughter, Alicia Jane, now studied at university in San Francisco. Nobody knew the whereabouts of the uncle.

I was shocked at what Charlie told me. Although I had dealt with pedophilia over the years, never had it been on such a large scale in one family.

"So, what do you want us to do then, Charlie?" I asked as she sat there nervously playing with her hair.

"Please find my uncle and also Joanna if you can."

This was a tall order. We had no idea of Joanna's surname, or where in the UK she had gone to, if in fact she had gone there at all.

"We'll do our best, but the only guarantee is, there is no guarantee."

Helen and I left the meeting and returned to our hotel.

"Well, I guess we need to find the uncle first, then try for Joanna in the UK," I said.

Helen looked angry. She had been abused as a child. Not by a family member, but she still felt Charlie's pain.

"Do you want out of this investigation?" I asked. I did not want her to have to drag up old memories if it was too painful.

"Are you kidding?" Helen replied. "Let's find this dirty bastard and him put away."

"Okay. That sounds like a plan to me."

We started looking for the uncle. We knew his name was John Sharple and the last address Charlie had for him was in Beverly Hills. We started with public records and found that Sharple had moved to his mother-in-law's house in West Hollywood. We drove to the address and found a house that had obviously seen better days. It stood on three floors with a small front yard cluttered with rubbish.

We parked our rental car and watched the house from a side road opposite. After about three hours a well dressed black woman emerged from the front door. She walked to a nearby convenience store. We took several pictures of her as she certainly fitted the description of Sharple's second wife Rosemarie. Helen looked back at the house.

"Hey! Look there."

She had seen a man looking out of a second floor window who could be John Sharple. He was about sixty years old with greasy gray hair swept back from his face. He was wearing just a T-shirt and you could see the fat oozing from his body. We took more pictures and felt quite hopeful that this was our man. For three days and nights we sat opposite the house in West Hollywood. Rosemarie kept up the same routine. Every afternoon she left the house all dressed up, walked to the 7 Eleven, purchased cigarettes and beer, then walked back to the house. We also saw the same three boys, each aged about eighteen years, coming and going to the house on bicycles. This, along with the cars that pulled up at night where the driver got out, went to the door, then left and drove off again, convinced us that Sharple was dealing drugs. We had something on him.

On the fourth day, at nine o'clock in the morning, the front door opened and John Sharple came out holding Rosemarie's hand. He stood six-feet tall and weighed a good two hundred and fifty pounds. He dressed impeccably, in a linen suit with co-coordinating shirt and tie.

They hailed a cab from the street, and we set off following it to a doctor's office about ten blocks away. I drove and Helen snapped away with the camera. We parked our car in sight of the doctor's office and waited about an hour before they emerged. They hailed another cab that we had to follow through very unfamiliar streets — I must have driven through about six red lights in an effort to stay with the taxicab, these drivers had no respect for lane discipline or pedestrians. We eventually pulled into the parking lot of a large hospital. Helen jumped out and followed the couple inside. I parked the car and waited. Helen came back fifteen minutes later.

"I followed them to the cancer care unit, but I couldn't get any further without running the gauntlet of the receptionist."

We had the film developed in a shop on Hollywood Boulevard, hoping that no one would recognize any of the people in the pictures, and then arranged a meeting with Charlie.

Her eyes turned dark as she viewed the pictures laid out on the coffee table in our hotel room.

"That's him and his second wife," she said. "That's definitely him."

"Well, he appears not to be working anymore," I said. "He has no car and we followed him to the cancer care unit at the hospital. He may even be seriously ill. You have to consider that."

"Couldn't happen to a nicer guy," Charlie snarled. Helen nodded in agreement.

"Okay, so now we need to find the other possible victims. My suggestion is we start looking in San Francisco, then return to the UK to look for Joanna." I looked at Charlie carefully. "Charlie, I have to warn you that although you say you have healed, some of the information we find out may set you back a bit. Are you prepared for that?"

"Yes, I am," Charlie said. "I'm fine. Just get him for me, please."

Helen and I packed the next day and drove up the Pacific Highway to San Francisco. I had been here before so I knew the basic layout of the town. We pulled into the Holiday Inn at Fisherman's Wharf and asked for a room for three nights. After the long drive we could relax for a couple of hours before we started looking for Alicia Jane.

We checked the university, we checked public records, but we could not find her. We knew we would have to wait for a few days for a check with the Department of Motor Vehicles, so thought it better to return to the UK and find Joanna.

We knew nothing about Joanna except that she was now forty-seven years old and was of mixed race. Her mother had moved in with Sharple when Joanna was about twelve years old. She complained to her mother on her fifteenth birthday about how Sharple would touch her and come into her room. Her mother, another heroin addict, told Joanna she should leave the house and get as far away as possible from him. Joanna did just that. She kept in touch with Charlie's mother for a couple of years, but by the time she was seventeen no one knew where she was. Charlie's mum had a postcard from her thirty years ago sent from Blackpool, a seaside vacation resort on the northwest coast of England. Nothing since.

We tracked down Joanna's mother and brother in Las Vegas. We asked a friend of ours, an investigator who worked out of Nevada, if he could go and interview her on a pretext of some sort. He reported back that Joanna had married about twenty years ago and was called Joanna Crawley; the mother had not seen or heard from Joanna for over twenty years. We started the investigation in Lancashire, the English county that Blackpool is in. It only took us a matter of days to find a woman matching her date of birth on the electoral register. We drove to Blackpool and watched the house, situated on a low-rent housing estate on the edge of town. We had started out early as we had no idea of the movements of this woman, and were sitting on a main road trying to blend in with other parked cars. Helen suddenly looked pained.

"I need the loo," she said.

"Where's the ice cream bucket?" I asked her.

This was something we always carried for just this sort of emergency. Getting caught short on surveillance is very common, especially when you can sit there for sixteen hours at a stretch, drinking coffee from your flask.

"I forgot it. Help! I'm busting for a wee."

I went to the back of the car and found an old red fluffy handbag one of my goddaughters had left in the car. The inside of the bag was red plastic. It was the best I could do. So with a blanket on her lap Helen peed into the kids handbag; when she had finished she zipped it up.

"What shall I do with it now?"

Just as I was going to reply a taxi pulled up to the front of the house and honked its horn. Out came a very attractive mixed-race woman who looked about thirty-five years old, not forty-seven. Helen quickly put the bag out of the window into the gutter. I prayed some kid would not find it and take it home to mum.

We followed the taxi through the streets until we reached the main shopping area. The traffic was quite heavy so it was not hard to keep up with the taxi. It stopped outside a pharmacy and she jumped out, paid the driver, and entered the store. Helen lay in the back seat of the car snapping away with her camera. I parked the car fifty yards away, ever aware of traffic wardens waiting to pounce and dish out a parking ticket. I stayed in the car while Helen went to the shop. She came back within minutes.

"I'm sure that's her. She works there anyway. She's got an overall on now and is drinking tea at the checkout."

Further checks on the house where Joanna lived revealed she had two children: a boy and a girl both now in their twenties; she appeared to live in the house alone.

We spent the rest of the day watching who we believed to be Joanna before driving the several hundred miles south back to London and home. I telephoned Charlie in Los Angeles and found her to be in very high spirits.

"Well, it seems we have found two of them, now we have to find Alicia Jane. Charlie, you have to know that the police will want to interview Joanna. And as it's been a long time, she has obviously got on with her life. Are you sure you want to do this?"

Charlie giggled down the phone, "Yep, I'm sure."

"Have you been drinking?"

"Yep, just call me Champagne Charlie," she said.

I realized this was getting us nowhere, so told her I would call her again when I had some more news, hopefully in a couple of days. I then telephoned her agent.

"Have you spoken to Charlie recently?"

"No, not for a couple of days. Why, is there a problem?"

"I think she's drinking again, and, I'm guessing, but possibly back on the white stuff."

Three days later I called Charlie to tell her I had the photos and had also found Alicia Jane in Boston. There was no answer so I left a message on her answering service. I called every day for a week. Nothing but silence and the click of the machine coming on. "Hi, this is Charlie, leave a message and I'll be right back as soon as. . ."

Another four days went by and while at a meeting in London I took a telephone call from her agent.

"Charlie's dead," he said, his voice tired and flat.

Charlie had returned to drugs and alcohol. The cleaning lady had found her. She had been dead for two days. I do not know if it was my information that pushed her back on the drugs, but I did warn her. Not wanting Sharple to get away with what he had done, we flew out to California and met with the local police drug squad. We told them everything we knew, handed over pictures of the people we had seen coming and going to Sharple's front door, and car registration numbers. As I stood at Charlie's graveside I couldn't help feeling what a waste of a life, but, to me, Sharple was responsible for her death. I promised her as a cool breeze swept across the cemetery that I would do everything I could to have him put away. Sharple died from cancer before he went to trial.

SEPTEMBER 11, 2001: AT FIVE O'CLOCK IN THE MORNING I STOOD AT the American Airlines desk at Heathrow airport waiting to board a flight to Raleigh Durham, North Carolina. With me were Helen and my friend James. We were going to Wilmington to make a video called *Stay Safe, Be Aware*. Earlier in the year, Helen and I had made a documentary with the Travel Channel about staying safe in London. I planned to make a video to show women how to look after themselves and their families. James, my friend from the police force, agreed to come with us as we needed him to play the assailant in the film. Also, James and I had decided several months earlier that we were no longer just friends but also in love with each other.

The check-in girl apologized to us for the delay but said the flight to Raleigh via Chicago had been cancelled; would we mind going via New York? We did not mind at all. We boarded the flight, which I had taken on many occasions. I did my usual thing on a plane: put a blanket over my head and slept. I woke about half an hour from landing at New York's JFK airport. I saw a member of the cabin crew running through the galley crying. I turned to Helen.

"What the hell is up with her?"

A few minutes later the captain announced there had been an incident on the ground, and we were awaiting further instructions. A woman in the next row pulled out her cell phone and started dialing as the captain came back on air. He sounded shaken.

"Ladies and gentlemen, I regret to tell you an American Airlines plane has flown into the World Trade Center."

The people in the row in front of me started crying,

"Our dad works there," they said.

More people started using cell phones to find out what was happening. The first woman with the phone gave the whole cabin a running commentary, as it was told to her by her husband in New York. Two planes had now crashed into the World Trade Center. One had been hijacked from Boston and was an American Airlines flight. There could be other hijacked flights still in the air. The captain came back on and announced we were being diverted to Boston's Logan airport. Helen, James and I all looked at each other.

"Why are they taking us to the crime scene?" I asked.

We landed at Logan and waited for our luggage. Another flight had come in at the same time so now we had about three hundred people milling around the conveyor belt.

"Once you have your luggage, go to the American Airlines desk, and you will be allocated hotel rooms." A member of ground staff shouted across the luggage hall.

We made our way to the check in desk on the first floor. A woman in an American Airlines uniform stood at the desk crying.

"What do you want us to do?" I asked her. She tried to get her words out through her tears. The place fell silent as we strained to hear what she was saying.

"There are no hotel rooms and no rental cars available," she said.

"Please go and wait in the bar until we know more." The three of us went to the bar and took up residence on three bar stools. We stacked our luggage under the counter and ordered drinks, within seconds we were surrounded by reporters and television crews.

"What do you think?" demanded a reporter.

"I think you had a wake-up call in 1993 when the WTC was bombed the first time — then you went back to sleep. Your airport security is awful compared to ours in the UK," I was in full swing and wanted the American people to know just how bad their security was.

"In the UK we have to show ID to get on a plane. In the U.S., you just stroll through to the gate. You have no metal detectors. I am not surprised that this has happened. And why," I finished off, "are we all being allowed to traipse across this airport? It's a crime scene and should be sealed off."

After repeating the same thing to several different reporters, a woman from a Boston radio station approached me. Her name was Toni Randolph; once I had finished my now many-times-said piece she offered me the use of her email.

"How bloody ironic. I'm here to make a video called *Stay Safe,*" I said to her, "and I have to let the people who are expecting us in North Carolina know we are okay." Toni took down the email address and promised to send it as soon as she returned to her office. In the meantime the state troopers turned up and walked into the bar.

"Sorry folks, everybody has to leave."

"Where shall we go?" I asked a trooper.

"Outside ma'am," he said.

"Yes, but where outside?"

"Just outside, ma'am."

We stood up and walked down the escalator. People just started following us. Now there were about three hundred people standing outside the glass doors of the airport that were locked behind us. There was nothing outside: not a taxi, not a bus, nothing. All three of us were thinking the same. If the hijacker took off from here there is a good chance there is a car bomb in the car park. At the time we had no idea the mad bastards that had done this wanted the world to know who they were. We were just presuming they would have parked a car in the parking lot and placed a bomb in it to destroy any evidence. It was time to get out of Boston. As I looked further up the road I spied an Avis car hopper just sitting there. I ran to the door and asked the driver to take me to the Avis car rental office that I knew to be off airport. I also knew that once on an Avis bus they were obliged to find you a car if the bus took you to their depot. I waved over Helen and James and we literally ordered the driver to go. He took us to the off-airport depot that was full of cars but no people.

"Hi, can we have a car please?" I asked the woman who looked bewildered behind the desk.

"They are all reserved for incoming flights," she said.

"But there aren't any incoming flights," I pointed out, "and your bus brought us here for a car."

"Well, in that case then, I have to find you one."

James pulled out his credit card and asked her for all the insurance they had. It seemed the penny had dropped. She had found us a bigger car.

"You will bring this car back here when you are finished, won't you ma'am?"

"Look, luv, I'll dance naked on this counter with a rose in my teeth if that's what it takes to get a car and get out of Dodge," I assured her.

We drove from the parking lot stopping to ask a state trooper the best way to go. By now the plane had smashed into the Pentagon building in Washington, so I knew that the usual route down I-95 would be impossible. The trooper told us to go west then south.

We purchased a map and took off. Getting out of Boston took us over an hour, but eventually we found the freeway we wanted and headed west. We stopped at telephones along the way, but always heard the same response, a recorded voice saying due to an emergency all overseas calls are banned. We tried several ATM machines, but they were also all out of commission. We drove for a couple of hours then stopped at a roadside diner — between us we had about thirty dollars. The assistant at the counter would not hear of us paying for our coffee and another customer we spoke to told us her son was an American Airlines flight attendant working out of Boston. She had no idea if he was alive or dead. We told her the roads to avoid and wished her a safe journey before setting off again. Several hours later, low on gas, we pulled into a gas station and told the attendant where we had come from, we had no idea if our credit cards would work, but could he help us out with some gas? He filled the tank, ignored our credit cards and wished us luck. The radio was playing *I'm Proud to be an American,* by Lee Greenwood. The news just gave us lumps in our throats. James turned and said, "Well, if I was going to be in a disaster with anyone, I'm glad it was with you two."

Tears steamed down my face and I had no idea why. To me the world had stopped. Fanatics had bombed the USA and the three of us were on a road journey not knowing if we would ever reach our destination. I felt as if I drove for hours. We took it in turns not wanting to stop for the night, in case we never had another one, at least if we were awake and on the road we would know what was happening in the world. I woke up about 6 AM from the back seat. We were pulling up outside a Waffle House.

"I need food," James said.

"Mmm, me, too," said Helen.

We walked inside and sat down. It was eerie. The TV showed the planes crashing into the WTC and talked of the fourth plane that they said had gone down in a field in Pennsylvania.

After we had eaten we left the diner and headed on to Richmond, North Carolina where we crossed over onto I-95 then down onto I-40. We eventually arrived in Wilmington after a twelve-hundred-mile, twenty-two-hour drive. I stopped at David, the producer's, house. He was making the video with us. He had received the email from Toni Randolph in Boston, and had also called Barbra and Simon in the UK. They were happy just to know we were alive. They were looking after Helen's son, Michael.

After a cup of coffee we drove to Carolina Beach where we had booked an apartment for the week. I knew the girls in the rental office and apologized to them for being two days late.

"No problem," they said. "No charge for the two days and let us know if you need to stay any longer." We had no idea how or when we would ever get home again.

The next day, after a great sleep, David and his cameraman Scott came over to the apartment to talk me through the scripts. We decided to take the rest of the day slowly and start filming the next day. The TV was permanently tuned to CNN and we just sat and watched it over and over again. We could now make telephone calls back to the UK. I had no one to phone, the two people I would normally call in an emergency were my two best friends and they were both with me. James called his family and assured them he was okay, as did Helen. She called Barbra and spoke to her son.

"Of course Mummy's okay," I heard her say. "I'm a bodyguard, remember? I protect people. I'm one of the good guys."

The very same thing I say to my goddaughters on the odd occasions they asked me if I am going to be okay when I leave for a job.

"The good guys always win . . . don't they?"

I called Ann in Fayetteville. I knew she would have the intelligence information on what was going on, being in the heart of Special Forces land.

"Buddy has gone," she told me. "He and all his ex-Delta Force buddies all took calls the very day it happened. They had left by night fall."

I promised her we would drive up and see her, it was only about an hour and a half away, nothing after the marathon we had driven.

We started the filming next morning on the beach, I had to run along wearing my jogging gear, then stop and say something spectacular to the camera. After two false starts, I got the words right. Then a siren went off, and Scott's cell phone rang; it was his wife.

"Scott! Get everybody off the beach. A tornado warning has just gone out and it's headed for the beach!" We watched it rush toward us and then it was gone.

"What's going on God?" I yelled at the stormy sky. "You couldn't blow me up, so now you want to sweep me away?"

The filming carried on for two days. We had local actors come and play the parts of a pedophile trying to lure a little girl away from her school. The little girl is a real blond cutie. Her dad, she told me, was in the army so he had to go and catch a bad man who stole a plane . . . such innocence.

We had put a Union Jack flag and a Stars and Stripes in the rear of our car with the words "United We Stand," written across the top. Wherever we parked, Americans came over and hugged us and said thanks. I was proud of our prime minister, and the queen for playing the *Star Spangled Banner* at the changing of the guard outside Buckingham Palace. If we were at war then at least we could show solidarity with the American people. In the UK, we had been bombed many times by the IRA. Their bombs have killed many innocent people in London and the surrounding towns. We know what it is like to lose people to terrorism; it hurts so much because it is such a pointless waste of life. The American people woke up to terrorism in their own country by a foreign fanatic on September the eleventh, and what an awful awakening it was.

I telephoned American Airlines.

"No rush, but when can you get us home?" I apologized to the girl on the telephone for bothering her. I felt she must be feeling the pain of losing her colleagues and getting me home seemed so minor to her feelings. The flight ban had been lifted, but of course there were many backlogged passengers.

"You can fly out of Raleigh-Durham, straight to Gatwick Airport in England in three days," she told me.

"We have an Avis rental car, and I really have no wish to return it to Boston, can you speak to the Avis people there?

"Hang on the line," she said. Within minutes she came back on and told me Avis had said because of the exceptional circumstances we could leave it at Raleigh-Durham Airport with no extra charges. When something goes wrong in the U.S., it's marvelous how everybody pulls together.

We arrived at Raleigh Durham three hours early expecting there to be strict security checks to go through. We had seen on the news the various measures that airports said they were putting in for security. Well, nobody told Raleigh. At check in, the woman told us they were only screening every tenth bag. This happened to be Helen's. We waited while they x-rayed it and then watched it disappear down the conveyor belt. Next we walked to the security checkpoint, a woman stood there twiddling her hair and two men stood around looking bored. I placed my handbag on the security table and saw it go through the x-ray machine. It was a pity the person looking at the screen did not really look, they were too busy eating a sandwich. Another security officer asked to see my passport. This was an improvement! Then I realized he had never seen a foreign passport before and had no idea that in the UK the picture and information is on the last page. I took pity on him and showed it to him.

Since my last time at the airport it had become a no-smoking area. As all three of us are addicted to nicotine we turned around and walked back through security to the outside of the airport where we could fill our lungs with the dreaded tobacco smoke before we had to go without for the seven-hour flight back.

About half an hour before boarding, we walked back to the security area. I went to put my bag on the x-ray table.

"Oh, that's okay," said the lady hair twirler. "You've been through once."

We stared at her in disbelief, shrugged, then walked through to the boarding gate. We could have picked up a rocket launcher outside the airport and brought it back in with us, nobody would have noticed; security was terrible. We boarded the plane, that only had about thirty passengers on board, and noticed three middle-eastern looking men, all seated separately. We took one each. Keeping an eye on the men who we knew could also have slipped through with a bomb.

We sat in our seats ready for take off. The captain's voice crackled on the PA.

"Good evening ladies and gentlemen. For your safety today we have two male flight attendants on board, as well as myself and the First Officer. If there are any passengers with special skills on board please make your selves known to the cabin crew."

We sat there in silence. First, I looked at the male flight attendants, mincing cheerfully through the cabin. They weighed about one hundred and twenty pounds soaking wet. We were not about to let any would-be attackers know who we were, we wanted the element of surprise, not to be the first ones to have our throats cut. The flight went without a hitch; we landed safely at Gatwick. Now all we had to do was find a way to get to our car at Heathrow airport some fifty miles away.

May is the month of National Law Enforcement Memorial Week, which is held in Washington, DC. I had been several times before, but in 2002 I was going with thirty other retired or serving British police officers; we wanted to show our solidarity with our colleagues across the water. Helen and I arrived at Heathrow airport and met up with the others who were flying out for Memorial Week. This group had been arranged by Jim McNulty, an ex-Scottish police superintendent who was also trying to start a police memorial in the UK.

Some of us only knew each other via email. We all belonged to a group called the UK Police List, this was again founded by Jim and brought together about one hundred and fifty ex-officers and serving officers from around the world, we emailed each other with Police related subjects, and those of us in the UK met up every couple of months for our now famous curry nights.

This involved about twenty of us taking over an Indian restaurant for the night and having a good drink and a gossip. The officers came from all over the UK, but luckily they considered London a good place for a curry night, so it was very near where I lived. One of the officers had designed and had printed T-shirts for us to wear. The logo said, "British Bobbies at Police Week," and a bar across the circle read, "United We Stand." It was easy to pick people out as being part of our group at the airport; they all looked like police officers. Helen and I said our helloes and we headed for the boarding gate. I carried a British police helmet in my hand luggage. These are highly prized in the U.S., and we wanted this one for the raffle, so some poor police constable at Heathrow Police Station would at some point go to his locker and find himself without a helmet. Shocking really, crime reaches everywhere, but all in a good cause in this case.

On arrival in Washington, our flight was met by Jim and another ex-inspector, Dick Coleman. We went straight through immigration and customs, to find standing outside the terminal a coach with a huge banner on the side with our bobbies logo on it. In front of the coach, sixteen motorcycle riders sat revving their engines. This was unbelievable. We boarded the coach and took off for what should have been a two-hour drive to Bethesda on the outskirts of Washington. The outriders went ahead and cleared the way. I felt like the president. Traffic stopped and we swept along the cleared road. Forty-five minutes later we pulled up outside our Bethesda hotel.

We thanked our hosts and various police officers for the amazing ride and greeting, and settled into our rooms, Helen and I shared a room. On Sunday we gathered at the memorial area, so those who had not been before could familiarize themselves. Helen and I sat outside a café near the memorial and watched as over two thousand motorbikes roared past. These were the Blue Knights, another police group from across the world that gathered once a year to ride into town and honor their fallen colleagues. In the evening, we attended a candlelight vigil where the families of fallen officers gather to remember the heroes who have died in the line of duty. More poignant in this year than any other. The NYPD lost over seventy officers in the World Trade Center disaster, but we had to remember we were also there for all the officers who had fallen in the line of duty around the country.

Just up from the actual memorial itself is the memorial shop and museum. In a glass case are a pair of kid's leather cowboy boots. Next to the case the inscription read, "Dad I grew too big for my boots so now you can have them." I saw these and the tears rolled down my face. I purchased some memorabilia and had to leave the shop.

The day of the memorial service saw us all gathered in the VIP area by the Lincoln Memorial near the Capitol building in the center of DC. Several of the British bobbies had put on full uniform, we had many American cops coming over and thanking us for coming. A little boy of five years old wearing a state trooper's uniform came over and hugged one of our guys. We all lost it when five-year-old Rocky Eales saluted our colleagues and said, "My dad is a hero, he died."

Rocky's father had been killed on duty, and every year Rocky came in his old uniform cut down to size to pay a tribute to his dad. I passed out handkerchiefs to the men now weeping openly. President Bush gave a speech thanking us all for coming and saying what heroes cops are. Mark Anthony sang a song, then a uniformed American cop got up and sang *I'm Proud to be an American.* There was not a dry eye in the house.

In the evening, we went to the biggest street party you have ever seen, thousands of cops gathered outside the Fraternal Order of Police building, a beer truck parked at either end and a beer tent in the middle. A stage had been erected and music blared from large speakers. Helen and I met some guys from the New York Organized Crime Unit; they were built like brick houses — I was so glad they were on our side. I explained that some of the British cops would be going to New York the next day and asked if they could help us get them into One Police Plaza. Two cell phone calls later found me speaking to a deputy commissioner of the NYPD.

"No problem," he said. "Come to my office when you get to New York, and I'll arrange it."

The party went on for three days. We hugged, kissed and danced the nights away. Police officers have to come to terms with grief, and they do it in many ways. Some members of the public may frown on it, but drinking and swapping jokes is the best way we know to cope with the aftermath of the horrendous crimes we have to deal with. The street party is just a cop's way of forgetting the bad times for a while, and showing the world we are truly one thin, but continuous, blue line.

Afterword

The events of September 11, 2001 brought home the message that we all need to be more aware of the dangers posed by international terrorism. On recent trips to the USA I have been pleased to see how much security has improved in nearly every location, and particularly at airports. American Airlines, my personal favorite carrier for transatlantic and domestic travel, has made great improvements in security and crew training, adding a feeling of safety to an already excellent standard of service.

I regard myself as fortunate to be able to still travel the world, and for all its problems it is still a beautiful place. But it is also a dangerous place. Headlines scream news of murder, burglary, mugging, rape and child molestation at us. Many people wring their hands and talk about how terrible it all is. My question to them is: "What are you going to do about it?" We can all make a difference. Caring for our communities is a great start. Looking out for our neighbors, working with local law enforcement to make our streets and homes safer and caring about all children, as well as our own, will all make for a better world.

But what about when we leave home? Outside our familiar environment we are more vulnerable, especially if we leave our sense of awareness behind. Many women who have to travel in the course of their work, ask me what precautions they should take and if a self-defense class would help. I looked at the classes on offer and found that most are run at a gym with the students wearing a jogging suit and sneakers. This does not address the problem of the real world for women where skirts and high heels are often required dress for work or

314 • Jacquieline Davis

social events. I devised a course that I teach on behalf of large corporations and other organizations to help their staff avoid dangerous situations and how to react if they are the victims of an assault.

But I continued to worry about all the vulnerable people out there who fall victim to predators every day: the women raped and murdered on the way home from work, the children snatched from schoolyards. My pals told me I could not protect everybody, much as I want to, but an old friend and comrade made the point that knowledge is strength. I could help many more people than just the corporate personnel if I shared the knowledge and experience I had earned the hard way. We devised and produced the *Stay Safe, Be Aware* video, a hard-hitting lesson in how to protect yourself, your family and your home against the criminal and accidents. At the same time I found myself increasingly in demand to speak on personal and security issues.

I still provide executive protection services for select clients, but my time is increasingly devoted to teaching and lecturing in awareness and self-protection.